THE BALD TRUTH

THE
BALD TRUTH

Secrets of Success from
the Locker Room to the Boardroom

David Falk

POCKET BOOKS
New York London Toronto Sydney

Pocket Books
A Division of Simon & Schuster, Inc.
1230 Avenue of the Americas
New York, NY 10020

First Pocket Books hardcover edition February 2009

For information about special discounts for bulk purchases,
please contact Simon & Schuster Special Sales at
1-800-456-6798 or business@simonandschuster.com

Manufactured in the United States of America

10 9 8 7 6 5 4 3 2 1

Library of Congress Cataloging-in-Publication Data

Falk, David
   The bald truth : secrets of success from the locker room to the boardroom / David Falk.
     p.   cm.
   1. Success in business.   2. Falk, David. Sports—Economic aspects—United
States.   I. Title.
   HF5386.F234   2009
   650.1—dc22   2008025725

ISBN-13: 978-1-4165-8438-4
ISBN-10:   1-4165-8438-2

To Pearl W. Falk,
a loving mother, an inspirational educator,
and my lifelong mentor, whose words
remain in my heart and in my mind:

"Always shoot for the stars and never settle for second best."

Acknowledgments

I have spent my entire professional career in the male-dominated world of professional sports. All of my clients have been male professional athletes, primarily in basketball and football, but my support system has been almost entirely female.

My wife, Rhonda, has shared my entire career with me. Ironically, we married on June 2, 1974, just one week after I began my unpaid internship at ProServ. She has urged me to write this book for the past fifteen years. There is not enough space on these pages to thank her for her unwavering love and support of me and the sacrifices of time and presence I have had to make for my immediate family in order to take care of my extended family of clients.

My eldest daughter, Daina, is my partner in Pokeware, an Internet advertising venture I helped launch. She has a preternatural confidence and maturity, and has undoubtedly inherited her grandmother's facility for foreign languages. If my mother and I were "Elma and Selma," my daughter Daina must surely be Thelma. Due to some unfortunate changes in the sports industry, I dissuaded Daina from starting her career at FAME. I know that she will be highly successful at whatever she does and I expect that one day the *DF* in *FAME* will refer to Daina Falk.

My youngest daughter, Jocelyn, followed her mom and dad to Syracuse University, where she is majoring in TV, radio, and film.

Her wonderful sense of humor and caring personality warm my heart. After the decades I spent managing athletes, Jocelyn became the first Falk to win an event in sports, capturing the Montgomery County, Maryland, Tennis Championships in doubles in 2006.

Growing up, my brother Mitch had an uncanny ability to root for teams that were the archrivals of my favorite teams. Our competitions as fans were mirrored by our games of one-on-one at our playground court. I knew early on that my success would not be a function of my ball-handling abilities or on-court moves.

My "domestic sorority" at home is mirrored by my "office sorority." My long-term executive assistant, Mary Ellen Nunes, has literally managed my life for the past twelve years. I have often joked that Rhonda should get the Nobel Peace Prize for the past thirty-four years; Mary Ellen would come in a close second.

Danielle Cantor started at FAME as a marketing intern and has become an invaluable member of the team. Although I hesitate to recommend that she become certified as a negotiating agent in the boutique relaunch of FAME, she has far transcended the boundaries of client marketing. I have no doubt she would be an outstanding agent.

I first met Mark Vancil in 1985 when he was the Chicago Bulls' beat writer. He has enjoyed tremendous success coauthoring a series of Michael Jordan books. His insights, dedication, and talents have had a major impact on this book.

Finally, I would like to thank my roster of clients, from the first class in 1976 of John Lucas, Wally Walker, and Adrian Dantley to the current class of Roy Hibbert and Patrick Ewing, Jr. It is a special treat for me to manage the careers of John Lucas III and Patrick Ewing, Jr. Perhaps one day Jeffrey or Marcus Jordan will grace the list.

Contents

Foreword

by Michael Jordan

I was drafted by the Chicago Bulls in June 1984 at the age of twenty-one. I had known that I would receive an NBA contract and probably an endorsement deal to wear Adidas shoes—my favorite at the time—but I didn't really have a good sense of what else I could expect as an NBA player. Well, except that I was about to work harder than I had ever worked before in my life.

Over the next twenty years, David Falk taught me the business of sports. From my very first contract with Nike to wear Air Jordan basketball shoes, through a myriad of corporate endorsements, licensing contracts, restaurants, books, and movies, David prepared me to become a successful businessman every bit as much as Dean Smith and Phil Jackson prepared me to be a successful basketball player.

I've often teased David that after he conceived the idea for "Air Jordan," he never had another good idea. But seriously, he knows how much I value his creativity, his guidance, and his passion to be the best. I was very proud to call David my lawyer, and prouder still to call him my friend. He has guided a whole generation of players not only skillfully but also with great care and integrity.

There are moments in everyone's lives when you have to trust that your advisor will look you in the eye and tell you the truth, even when it's not what you want to hear. I always knew that David would tell me what he truly felt even when it wasn't popular or politically correct. As much as I always valued his skill for negotiation and his creativity in marketing, I especially admired his courage to express his convictions when it mattered most.

David and I share a special connection because of our very competitive personalities. And make no mistake: David is as competitive in business as any athlete I've played against on the basketball court. I know for sure we also possess another special bond. From the very first day I met him in Chapel Hill in May 1984 and selected him to be my lawyer, I've always felt a kinship with David because, along with my father, we ended up bald. So, when he tells you that the account that follows is the Bald Truth, you can take it from me, it is.

Introduction

If I have seen further [than other men] it is
by standing on the shoulders of giants.

—Sir Isaac Newton

For the past thirty-five years, I have been privileged to manage the careers of some of the greatest athletes and coaches in history. I've often thought that men like Michael Jordan and Patrick Ewing, John Thompson and Mike Krzyzewski were genetically programmed to compete without quarter. Clearly they wanted to win, but there was no singular force driving them toward their goals—not simply pride, nor money, nor fame—except a relentless pursuit of perfection. Although my role was to manage their careers and to inculcate in them an ability to make prudent business decisions, in many ways they were all amazing teachers to me.

My greatest teacher, however, was my mother, Pearl Falk. For as long as I can remember she would instill in me her philosophy, "Always shoot for the stars and never settle for second best." As the daughter of immigrant parents, my mother found it hard to ever satisfy her very demanding father. Undoubtedly she passed this personality trait on to me. I find it amusing that critics of

mine have labeled me arrogant, greedy, insensitive, and used a
host of other less than complimentary descriptions to explain my
success in the very cutthroat business of athlete representation.
What they have failed to grasp is that I was simply trying to fulfill
my mother's credo and likely also trying to prove that I was worthy to be her son.

Whether from nature or nurture, I would describe myself as a
compulsive perfectionist. And in a poignant way my own drive to
achieve dovetailed with the genetically predisposed competitive
drive of my clients. I've always believed that this common drive,
more than the success we have enjoyed together, has enabled me
to relate well to my clients.

Over time, I came to view my role as a bridge between young,
predominantly African American superstar athletes and older,
predominantly white corporate executives and team owners. And
in dealing with the superstars in both of those worlds, I received
an education in business and human psychology that I could not
have obtained in the doctoral program of any university in the
world. In the last ten years, the landscape of the sports industry
has changed dramatically—regretfully, not for the better. Rookie
wage scales, maximum limitations on player contracts, and the
widespread use of illegal inducements to recruit clients have
largely taken the creativity out of the deal making and the integrity out of the recruitment of new players. So, why have I stayed
in the business? That's a question I've asked myself many times in
the ten years since I sold my company, FAME, to SFX. It's an issue
I've discussed at great length with Michael, whose advice and insight I truly value. And the answer is that all of the restrictions

and all of the infractions, which otherwise have made this profession far less enjoyable, cannot take away the tremendous personal satisfaction I derive from performing the most important job in our society today: teaching.

And so, after thirty-five years in the business, from the trench warfare of recruiting to the highest pinnacles of corporate marketing, I want to share the unique education I've received from the "best and the brightest." Because education necessarily involves learning from your mistakes, I did not have enough room on these pages to share all the mistakes I've made from the tender age of twenty-three in trying to perfect the interwoven skills of negotiating, marketing, and managing. But rest assured, there were many painful lessons I learned along the way.

When I was in the fifth grade, my mother wrote to me, "A little knowledge is a dangerous thing; drink deep, my son." And so I offer to you *The Bald Truth*: my education in business, my amateur primer on human psychology, and my personal philosophy of attaining and managing success. I hope you find the experience of reading this book as enjoyable as I found the experience of writing it. It brought back some amazing memories and a renewed realization of how fortunate I have been to view the world on the strong shoulders of giants.

I'd Rather Have a Good Enemy than a Neutral Friend, and Other Lessons from Chairman John

In many ways, my career started when I met John Thompson, Jr. Having grown up in a very modest background, I could never have imagined that I would meet and deal with high-profile individuals as diverse as senators and congressmen, even a president or two, not to mention superstar athletes, entertainers, and chairmen of many of the most influential corporations in America. But without question, the most influential person in my life— other than my mother, who passed away when I was twenty-seven—has been John Thompson.

The fact that John played such an influential role proves that hard work and commitment to excellence can be matched, if not trumped, by circumstance and good fortune. The twists and turns that brought us together were certainly not in the game plans either of us had crafted for our careers. That John became my first and, for many years, only coaching client is ironic, given the wisdom and guidance he has provided me over the years.

I had aspired to be an attorney since the age of ten. In fifth grade, a friend named Greg Mallow wrote in my autograph book that I should become a lawyer because I was "a good arguer." Joseph Weber, my maternal grandfather, was an immigrant who frequently served on grand juries in New York. Pearl Weber, my mother, dreamed that I would one day become a Supreme Court justice. Despite these strong influences, my only role model for being a lawyer was Owen Marshall of the eponymous television series in the 1970s. I had absolutely no idea what being a lawyer was all about when I graduated from Syracuse University in 1972 and not much clearer of an idea when I graduated from George Washington University Law School in 1975.

During my first two years of law school, I worked part-time for the Bureau of Land Management at the Department of the Interior and at the Washington, D.C., office of Sidley & Austin, a prestigious Chicago-based law firm. In Washington, the joke is that one out of every twenty-five males over the age of twenty-five is a lawyer. It seemed to me that most of them had an Ivy League background that I clearly lacked. At Sidley I was determined to overcome my lack of pedigree by sheer determination. Initially it seemed to be working as many of the younger partners entrusted me with legal research projects. But when the summer came, I was relegated to being a messenger when two "summer clerks" who were recruited from the University of Virginia and the University of Pennsylvania arrived. If I had a chip on my shoulder about my lack of Ivy League pedigree when I interviewed for clerkships in law school, after the snub at Sidley it grew into a block. When Donald Dell finally allowed me to work—for free— at Dell, Craighill, Fentress & Benton, which was the law firm part of the sports agency ProServ, in the summer of 1974, I was committed to overcoming my lack of nurture with my compulsive nature.

At the end of that summer, Donald hired me as a part-time clerk. As a full-time law student, I was permitted to work twenty hours a week. My lack of personal pedigree and ProServ's surroundings better informed my approach. Donald Dell was a Yale man with a University of Virginia law degree; Lee Fentress went to Tulane and Virginia Law; Frank Craighill attended North Carolina and Virginia Law; and Michael Cardozo, the associate, was the grand-nephew of Supreme Court justice Benjamin Cardozo and a Dartmouth and Virginia Law School grad. I probably worked an average of sixty hours a week and went to school just enough to graduate. Later on, when I attained some success, I probably developed a reverse exclusionary discrimination against Ivy League types. Obviously it takes all types, but one of the questions you might ask about a player who grew up wealthy is whether that player is hungry enough to do what it takes. The need to achieve doesn't always come from pure economics. With the background I had, I knew I never wanted to make a living with my hands.

After I graduated, Donald finally hired me as a full-time associate for the princely sum of thirteen thousand dollars a year to work eighty to one hundred hours a week. I eventually became

Donald's assistant, or chief of staff. I read his mail, attended many of his meetings, and received great exposure to the various parts of the business, from marketing to legal. But we were very different people. Donald operated by seat-of-the-pants instinct and intuition. I am extremely logical. I wanted to have a well thought out argument when I presented my position. Donald preferred to leverage his power. He would read and think for five minutes on the plane flight to a negotiation. From my perspective, he would wing it while I was always a nut about preparation. I loved the intellectual stimulation that came from trying to change an existing model, or making an impact on that model by analyzing the research and applying a measure of creativity to the results. That approach eventually defined groundbreaking deals for Michael Jordan, Patrick Ewing, Juwan Howard, Danny Ferry, Alonzo Mourning, and dozens of others in the 1980s and 1990s.

John Thompson had been an all-American at Providence College in 1964. He ended up playing two seasons for the Boston Celtics, backing up Bill Russell in one of the more racially divided cities in America at the time. When John became Georgetown's coach in 1972, I was finishing my first year of law school.

Because salaries were so modest, even for the world champion Celtics, John lived in the home of a Boston couple named Harold and Mary Furash. They had no children and John became the closest thing they had to a son. I had met Harold a few times through Leon Frank, my future father-in-law, and Harold had told John about me.

John and I met for the first time in 1980 when John Duren was going to be his first player selected in the NBA draft. We made a presentation for ProServ to represent Duren and his teammate Craig Shelton. Both of them selected us, and we got the next big Hoya star, Sleepy Floyd, who became the No. 13 pick in the 1982 draft.

The Georgetown connection became a cornerstone of our basketball practice. Donald Dell and Frank Craighill had a long-standing relationship with Dean Smith at North Carolina, but I was never going to have a power position in that dynamic. Smith wanted to talk "CEO to CEO" and he insisted on Donald doing the deals for North Carolina's rookie players. For me, Georgetown represented an opportunity. Not only had John turned the program into a major college power, but the connection allowed me to move away from tennis. While I liked working with tennis players like Arthur Ashe and Stan Smith, I loved basketball. It also felt more comfortable because I grew up in an environment much closer socially and economically to basketball players than to tennis stars.

John boosted my career at ProServ by viewing me and promoting me, even to my boss Donald Dell, as an asset and talent independent of the company. But he also challenged my assumptions about people, race, success, and just about every other aspect of life. You always know exactly where you stand with John. He is wont to say "I'd rather have a good enemy than a neutral friend." This is one of the many lessons I have taken from our friendship. Only the depth of compassion and loyalty he extends to friends matches John's unshakable integrity.

Our personal histories no doubt helped John and I connect. My mother was the youngest daughter of immigrant parents and she became a teacher. She constantly urged me never to settle for second best: "Always shoot for the stars."

John's father was hardworking but uneducated, and his mother, though educated, could only find work cleaning houses in their segregated Washington, D.C., neighborhood. In his book *Big Man on Campus*, Len Shapiro writes that John's mother had a similar message for her son: "You can do anything you think you can. It's all in the way you view it. It's all in the start you make, young man. You must feel that you are going to do it."

The fact that we were both outsiders may be what drew us together—John, a black man in the very white fraternity of major college coaches, and me, a Jewish kid with a mutt's pedigree. In any case, unlike Coach Smith at North Carolina, John Thompson preferred dealing with the underdog. At the time, we had a policy at ProServ that we would not represent coaches. I effectively created the rule because I was uncomfortable when coaches came to Donald asking him advice on their shoe deals or coaching contracts. Donald, either out of friendship or ego, really wanted to help them, but I was concerned it could adversely affect our ability to recruit players. My emphatic position was that if we helped the coach at Maryland, then the coach at Virginia might get upset. I thought we had to be neutral. Donald reluctantly heeded my advice and it became corporate policy.

That all changed in 1982 during a lunch with John. Like other coaches, he would ask me questions about business matters. While I was happy to provide some insight, I told him, "John, I would love to help you with these things, but you know we have a policy against representing coaches." Typical of him, John said, "I don't give a damn about your policy. I'd love you to represent me." He said this with such vehemence that I was floored. For one of the first times in my life, I had nothing to say. I was tongue-tied and all I could get out was "Well, okay. I'd love to do it." After my impassioned argument to Donald against representing coaches, I broke the policy.

The arrangement also allowed John to break from the rest of the Big East coaching fraternity. Dave Gavett, then the Big East commissioner, negotiated group deals for the coaches for product endorsements. A coach might get $3,000 to $4,000 as part of supporting a Big East official basketball deal, or something similar. I signed John with Wilson for $25,000 a year, which infuriated the other coaches and in turn delighted John. He wanted to be his own person and felt it was no different than competing against other coaches for wins. One of his lines was "Why do you want to live in the same apartment complex with people you're competing with? You don't want them to know what you're doing."

The relationship worked on every level. John loved the idea of turning his success into business opportunities apart from the rest of the fraternity. I enjoyed the process because I thought we were not only doing a good job, but helping John to become a unique brand. It all worked to help John recruit great players. Mostly, however, the relationship provided me with insight into the human spirit. I learned about relationships, human nature, and how the nature of race affects both of them.

While John came to represent one of the closest relationships of my life, he was also part of some of my most memorably stressful moments. John is a wise and devoted mentor, but he is also blunt, demanding, and unapologetic about what he understands to be right and wrong. For example, on an otherwise uneventful day in May 1983, I stopped by Georgetown to see John on my way home from the office. We discussed a few business issues, nothing unusual. Then, out of left field, John asked, "What do you think about this guy Bill Strickland?" I had met Bill following a speech I delivered in Houston at the American Bar Association Committee Forum on Entertainment and Sports. Bill was an African American lawyer interested in getting into the agent business. At the time, I knew we needed another lawyer to help me with the basketball business. Craighill and Fentress had just bolted ProServ to form Advantage International and a lot of ProServ's staff had followed them. Though we had retained twenty-three of the twenty-seven basketball players we represented, we were thinly staffed. What I didn't know at the time was that Strickland had gone to John Thompson to see if John could put in a good word for him at ProServ, hence the question.

"I really like the guy," I told John. "He's got an MBA from UCLA and a law degree from Georgetown. He played college basketball and baseball. He's pretty sharp."

"Well, are you going to hire him?"

"I really don't know, John."

"Well, David. You just gave me a eulogy about the guy. Why wouldn't you hire him?"

"You know, John, it's a very interesting time," I said. "At ProServ, we've had African American people in marketing. We've had African American people in accounting. But we've never had a lawyer who's African American and for some reason, unbeknownst to me, it seems to be very important to clients that we have one. Because of that, I think whoever we hire first will be under a spotlight. I want to make sure that the person we hire—that first African American lawyer—will be able to stand up to the scrutiny."

That's exactly how I felt. And to me, that's how the landscape looked. It seemed to me that it was the hand we had been dealt and I thought I had provided a very reasoned, unemotional response.

John thought otherwise.

"Really? That's how you feel?"

"Yes," I said.

"You know, people have used that excuse for a hundred years to keep black people from jobs."

"Well, John, I understand that. I don't make the rules. I'm not the one who's going to put a spotlight on him. But because he would be the first, he'd be like a pioneer and subject to a different level of scrutiny than the person who comes after him."

We proceeded into a long conversation, with John surgically carving me into small pieces, to say the least. As we continued to debate the issue, I quickly realized that a relationship that had taken three and a half years to build was being destroyed in thirty very emotional minutes. After an hour with John, I had gone from considering myself broad-minded and inclusive, with very few biases, to feeling like a leading candidate for the Klan.

At the climax of this emotional debate, I was about to cry. The realization that our relationship could crumble on this subject was nearly too much to contemplate. At that moment, John put his hands on my shoulders just as a priest might.

"David," he said, "I'm not trying to be difficult with you. But you're Jewish, and you should be used to people discriminating against you because you're Jewish. But a lot of people who meet you don't know you're Jewish. I'm black. Every person I have ever met or ever will meet knows that I am black. I just want you to be sensitive to how a black person feels about the potential for being discriminated against."

That was the end of the conversation. We didn't say another word except "Good-bye." I walked to the parking lot, got into my Volkswagen Rabbit, and drove home.

I did hire Bill Strickland, who turned out to be great. More importantly, that day changed my life. The conversation and John's passion touched me in a way I have never forgotten. It made me question my values and my most fundamental beliefs. The way John presented his argument, together with the power of his conviction, made me feel as if I had been touched by God. It was a bit like an out-of-body experience. He made a profound impact on me because he cared enough to want me to understand.

John made me see what many of us in America do not: that there are very strong cultural differences between black and white America, and that many of them turn on nuances and experiences often foreign to one side or the other. He helped me understand the true nature of exclusion and the idea of needing to be twice as good as the next guy just to be equal.

For more than twenty-five years, John and I have had dozens of intensely personal discussions like that one. He's looked me in the eye and told me things, taught me things that wouldn't have been the same coming from anyone else. That's why I've always found it ironic that he hired me to be his advisor when, in so many ways, he has been mine. Among his insights I've adopted as my own:

- Don't be a prisoner of your reputation.
- Don't try to be a spiritual advisor.
- Don't try to run a democracy.
- It's better to have a good enemy than a neutral friend.

It's a good thing I've followed these principles; while dealing with John made me a stronger person and helped me with other people and situations, I never had to be stronger than when I dealt with him.

In the spring of 1984, we had another one of our "heart-to-heart" talks. Two things had happened to Patrick Ewing that spring while he was at Georgetown. His mother had died and Patrick had led the Hoyas to the national championship against Houston's Hakeem Olajuwon. Ewing and Olajuwon were juniors and within hours of the title game there was speculation that both would leave college early and enter the NBA draft.

John called and wanted to know my opinion about Patrick passing up his senior season at Georgetown. I told him I thought it was a terrible idea. To start with, I had read in the *Washington Post* that Patrick promised his mother he would finish his education and graduate. I thought it was important that he honor that commitment.

"Really?" John said. "Well, I can see why you feel that way, but let me tell you how I feel. For a million dollars a year, he can get plenty of education."

"I respect that, John, but there aren't a lot of Patrick Ewings coming out of college every year. The fact that he and Olajuwon are both juniors is a fluke. He is a very rare commodity, and for those kinds of players, the salaries will never go down. I mean never, no matter how long he stays in school."

"Well, that's interesting," John said, "but what if he gets hurt?"

"You could buy an insurance policy to protect that," I responded.

We went back and forth on the issues surrounding the decision: the nuances of the draft and why I firmly believed Patrick should stay another year. I held my ground while John cursed me out like a truck driver. That's John, God love him. I've had Georgetown players tell me they thought their first name was "Motherf—er" because that's what John always called them. Even with that knowledge and being well aware of John's style, the verbal abuse was distressing. I started thinking, just as I had a year earlier, that in thirty short minutes our relationship was quickly deteriorating. I remember thinking, How could this be happening?

"I thought you were my friend and I'm asking you for your best advice," he said, "but it's obvious to me you're just telling me what you think I want to hear. But you are wrong. I don't want him to stay in school. I want him to leave. I don't want the responsibility on my shoulders if he gets hurt. His mother is dead. His family is depending on him. What if he does get hurt?"

John's voice was booming. Finally, after enduring his abuse, I had had enough.

"John, look, do whatever the hell you think is right," I told him. "But if you're asking my advice I'll tell you three things. Number one, Patrick will not even go number one in the draft. If Houston has the first pick, they're going to take Olajuwon. Number two, the money will never go down for franchise centers. And number three, in your system, you're going to protect him from injury. Even if something happens, Patrick's not going to get amnesia and forget how to play basketball. His value will be much higher a year from now than it would be today. That's how I feel, but do whatever the hell you want."

I was upset because the conversation had devolved from a conversation between two friends into a very emotional and abusive personal attack. I thought it was important for my integrity, for my relationship with John, and for my desire to eventually work for Patrick, that I be brutally frank and not cave in to the intensity. I had to make a very clear statement that if he was going to hire me to deal at the highest levels of the NBA, I couldn't let a college coach, even one as forceful as John Thompson intimidate me. As it turned out, John discussed the matter with Patrick, who never wanted to leave school in the first place.

While I was striving to develop a relationship with John, ProServ's most important college-coach relationship was with Dean Smith. During the 1970s and into the 1980s, Dean was instrumental in recommending players to ProServ. And we had done very well by all those players. We represented high first-round draft picks like Phil Ford and James Worthy, but part of the deal with Dean was that we also took care of the lesser players such as Rich Yonakor, Cecil Exum, and Tom Zaliagaris. For those players, we created opportunities in Europe and generally got them above-market deals.

The problem with Dean was that there was very little equity in the relationship. Every year we would start at square one despite the long-term relationship that existed between Donald Dell, Dean, and North Carolina.

In 1984, we found out just how vulnerable we were to the whims of a major college coach, particularly Dean Smith. Michael Jordan was the marquee player coming out of North Carolina heading into the 1984 NBA draft. Obviously he was a player ProServ coveted as a client. But we were also competing for the right to represent another North Carolina player and potential star, Sam Perkins, who went on to play seventeen years in the league. Dean screened agents and made "recommendations" to his players as to whom they should select. He broke the process into three categories: contract negotiation, marketing, and financial management. ProServ won all three components for Jordan, and two of the three for Perkins; Advantage International was selected to manage money for Sam. Less than a week after making his recommendations, Coach Smith called Donald and said Perkins had "changed his mind." The player had fired us, according to Dean, because Donald hadn't spent enough time with him on the phone during our six days of officially representing him.

Sam is a very laid-back guy and it is unlikely he would have made that kind of decision on his own in such a short amount of time. Moreover, Sam was sequestered in Bobby Knight's Olympic training camp, in which players' calls were screened. Donald told Dean he had tried to reach Sam but that there was no way to do so during those six days. Donald was not only distraught at Dean's news but also shocked at the way it happened. Donald challenged Dean about the real issue for the change. Dean challenged Donald to produce telephone records that would verify that Donald had in fact tried to reach Sam. Donald was furious.

"Look, after all we've been through together, can't you trust me?" said Donald. "I left a message for Sam, but I'm not on trial here. I'm not going to produce my phone records."

Perkins went to Advantage and the relationship between Dean and Donald, and eventually between Dean and ProServ, began to deteriorate. Michael Jordan was the last player ProServ ever got from North Carolina.

Coach Thompson's approach was in stark contrast to Coach Smith's. With John, your relationship was the sum total of all that had happened previously. He didn't demand that people continue to prove what they had already proven. Those things were a given. There was less quibbling over little things and therefore an increased focus on the larger and more meaningful decisions. That ultimately made me more effective for his players.

A Combination of Creativity and Preparation Is Essential

The net result of me standing my ground on Patrick staying in school was that everyone came out ahead. My relationship with John became stronger, Patrick's bargaining position turned out to be unprecedented, and I was able to negotiate not only my first contract for the No. 1 pick in the draft but also a groundbreaking deal with the New York Knicks. Thanks to John, I had primacy on representing Patrick. I made ProServ's presentation (Donald was in Japan at the time) and I was the one John lauded in strongly recommending our services to Patrick.

Until that point, Donald had been the firm's lead contract negotiator. I serviced players and handled their marketing, but Donald was the deal maker. I hadn't even been in the room when Donald negotiated Michael Jordan's rookie contract with the Chicago Bulls. But this time, John made it clear to everyone just who would be handling the negotiations. He even became furious when I told him Donald would be attending the first meeting with Gulf+Western, the conglomerate that owned the Knicks in 1985.

"What do you mean?" John demanded. "I didn't pick Donald to represent Patrick. I want you to go to New York and pitch Patrick."

I explained that while I appreciated his support, the Knicks were a unique team because a large corporation, Gulf+Western, owned it. There was an understood corporate protocol that chairmen, vice chairmen, and senior vice presidents expected to deal with people at their same level. But John exploded.

"I don't give a f—k how it works in corporate America," he boomed. "This is basketball. I didn't pick Donald. I don't like Donald. I want you to do it."

I finally had to say, "Look, John, if you picked me to be the coach, let me freaking coach the game. I really appreciate your support, more than I could ever express to you. Dean Smith never would do what you have done. He would have gone with the top dog. But as much as I'd like to do it alone, this is the best way for Patrick. Donald and I have to go together."

There was no question in my mind that I would take the lead, and I felt the stars had lined up in a way for us to break the existing NBA salary model. For one thing, the NBA draft lottery system debuted in 1985. Prior to 1985, a coin flip between the league's two worst teams decided the first and second picks in the draft. One of the most famous of these was the 1979 flip between Chicago and the Los Angeles Lakers. Chicago lost and took David Greenwood with the second pick while the Lakers selected Magic Johnson as No. 1. Now, however, all seven teams that had failed to make the playoffs had a shot at the No. 1 pick through a drawing held forty-five days before the actual draft. As an economics major, I understood how the new system dramatically increased the leverage and thus the value of the first pick. When a team goes from having a 50 percent chance of acquiring the No. 1 pick via a coin flip to having just a 1-in-7 chance through the lottery, the asset has become significantly more scarce and therefore more valuable. Eventually the odds dropped to 1-in-14 as the lottery expanded.

Still, we couldn't have created a better scenario than the one that emerged for Patrick. The New York Knicks had won a total of forty-six games the previous two seasons in the league's largest market. The team had passionate fans, a history of success, and owners with deep pockets. Fans demanded a better team and the local media drove those demands. Gulf+Western not only knew what it had to do, it also had the financial means to get it done.

Our asset, Patrick Ewing, arguably became more valuable than any player in the history of team sports to that point.

As a result, I couldn't benchmark our contractual demands to past rookie contracts or even to the existing wage scale for the league's highest-paid players. That was the traditional approach, as expressed earlier that year by Bob Woolf, a highly respected player agent, in an article in *Sports Illustrated*. Asked what Patrick could command, Woolf said, "I'd start with Olajuwon (whose 1983 rookie contract paid him $1.2 million per year) and I'd go up."

I had no intention of starting with anybody. Circumstance and my own analysis demanded we create a new market for Patrick, framing his value against his future and that of the franchise. As a point of reference to support my position, I looked at Kareem Abdul-Jabbar, who was making $2 million a year in the twilight of his career, and decided Patrick was worth $3 million a year. I put together a ten-year proposal worth $30 million with a unique protection against the usual hazard of a long-term contract. Patrick would have the right to terminate the deal after six years if the salary structure changed to the point where four players were more highly paid.

I had spent more than a month working out the terms of the proposal when Donald asked me what I thought Patrick was worth.

"Here's what I'm thinking about," I said. I handed Donald a three-page memo I had prepared for the Knicks, outlining the offer. When Donald finished, he said, "David, I would love to be the Knicks when you walk in there and ask for thirty million dollars for a rookie."

"Really?" I replied. "What would you say?"

"I would tell you that you must be smoking pot, and when you get serious, come back and we'll talk."

"You would say that?" I asked.

"Yes," said Donald. "And how would you reply?"

"I'd say, 'Hey, no problem. I'll come back. In fact, I think I'll have Patrick enroll in graduate school at Georgetown. Since you've won a grand total of forty-six games over two years, having the number one pick, and a franchise center that has played in three Final Fours probably isn't important to you. Not in a *small* market like New York where you have all these fans. So we'll just go to grad school for a year and go back into the lottery next year and you can explain to the fans of New York why Gulf and Western didn't have enough money to sign Patrick Ewing."

I was making a point as much as testing the argument on Donald. At the same time I was sensing a shift. I was about to take the game to another level and Donald was still in the Bob Woolf mode. After eleven years of working for Donald, for the first time I felt I'd moved beyond him. He just didn't see what I saw. He couldn't comprehend the paradigm shift the lottery presented and the unique combination of circumstances that had come together. He simply didn't understand how any player, much less Patrick, could be worth $1 million more than the highest-paid player in the league and nearly three times as much as the previous year's No. 1 pick, who also happened to be a franchise center.

That said, Donald was dead-on with regard to the Knicks reaction. When I presented the proposal in New York inside the highly styled corporate conference room of Gulf+Western, they said verbatim what Donald had predicted: "When you get serious, come back."

I asked them how season ticket sales had gone since the lottery. They told me the team had sold $6 million in new tickets.

I said, "If you think his value is roughly $1 million to $1.2 million as a basketball player, and you sold $6 million of additional tickets, then maybe we are asking for half as much as he's worth. Maybe he's really worth $6 million because this is a unique set of circumstances. There are very few players who can sell $6 million worth of tickets, particularly before they play a single game."

We could have asked for $6 million a year based on ticket sales alone and had a cogent economic argument to make. I knew my demands did not reflect the salary structure at the time, but I was beginning to believe my job wasn't to interpret the salary structure and negotiate accordingly. I believed that when you had unique players combined with unique circumstances, players like Patrick and Michael, my job was to understand their economic impact independent of the existing marketplace. For those players, comparisons to Olajuwon, Ralph Sampson, or just about anyone else were irrelevant. And I think Magic Johnson proved that point in a way he no doubt regrets.

Magic was never paid his true value because no one around him understood the breadth of his value. Magic signed a five-year contract for $460,000 per year with the Lakers as the No. 1 pick in 1979. But because Jerry Buss, the team's owner, was an expert at deferred compensation, the deal paid Magic in even monthly installments over thirteen years so the contract had a present value in the low $300,000s. In 1982, Magic renegotiated his contract, but the salary cap made its debut that season for the six teams with the highest salary structure, the Lakers being one of them. The cap went into effect for the rest of the league a year later, in 1983.

Because they were over the salary cap, the Lakers couldn't change the two remaining years on Magic's rookie contract, so they agreed to pay him $25 million over twenty-five years starting at the end of the first contract. Thus Magic, who had led the Lakers to a championship as a rookie and was clearly one of the game's greatest players, had to wait two more years before the deal even kicked in. Buss was a financial genius who had predicted the increase in mortgage rates and he had bought millions of dollars in mortgages. He bought a $3.5 million mortgage with a 20 percent interest rate that effectively paid Magic's entire contract for twenty-five years.

CNN interviewed me in 1982 and asked if I thought the deal would set a new trend for player contracts. Based on the same philosophy I would apply to Patrick, I told the interviewer that while it sounded amazing, within three years Magic was going to be crying for locking himself into a long-term deal while the salary structure escalated around him. Three short years later, Patrick was headed toward signing for $3 million a year while Magic was making a third of that. He never made the kind of money he deserved because the people around him didn't have the foresight to see where the market was heading. They were looking backward instead of into the future. That, as well as competing with Buss's genius, meant Magic never came close to making what he deserved. The league believed the contract was designed to circumvent the spirit of the cap. Accordingly, the $25 million, twenty-five-year deal was interpreted as a ten-year contract paying him $1 million in cash and $1.5 million in deferred money annually. The Lakers were never allowed to change the total contract value ($25 million), though they did pay the deferred earlier. So all told, Magic never made more than $2.5 million a year despite being one of the most talented and unique athletes in the history of team sports.

We had experienced a similar fate with Buck Williams in 1981. We negotiated what appeared to be a huge contract that ended up making Buck underpaid by the third year. So my experience heading into Patrick's negotiations was that the league was growing so quickly and the salary structure was changing so fast that it was difficult to create a long-term contract that didn't have potentially significant downside risk for the player. I was not going to repeat the mistake Magic's people made in 1979 even on a ten-year deal, so I created a new device: an early termination option.

I told the Knicks I was serious about getting Patrick $3 million a year and that I wasn't trying to shock them: "This is really what I believe based on the development of the salary structure. If you don't feel he's worth three million dollars a year, then maybe you should consider trading his rights, or he'll probably go back to Georgetown for a year. We have a very unique relationship at Georgetown where John Thompson is the coach, the teacher, the father figure, and his players believe in him completely."

I knew John respected me and what we were trying to do for Patrick, and I understood that the Knicks ownership could not withstand losing the asset value represented by the first lottery pick, a franchise center no less, and coming away with nothing. There was literally no chance the Knicks weren't going to sign Patrick. A tremendous amount of season tickets had been sold and Patrick's picture had been on the cover of the season ticket brochure. What were they going to do, call up all the fans that had already laid out money relying on "Saint Patrick" and tell them they couldn't afford to sign him? They had effectively paid for the contract with the increase in season ticket revenue.

The summer passed and we remained in a stalemate, a state I've often faced. Though familiar, the situation can test the relationship between the player and agent. I worked for Patrick and he wanted to be updated on the progress of the negotiations. But I knew it was better for him to be unaware of the Knicks position. When the team has made an offer in the neighborhood of $1.2 million a year and I was asking for $3 million, we were more than a tad apart. In fact, we were so far apart that the distance between the two offers was nearly as large as the biggest contract in league history. There are at least two bad outcomes if the client comes to understand the distance between the two sides. One, the client can get extremely nervous that no deal will ever be made. In the player's mind there are only two reasons for such an impasse: either I didn't know what I was doing, or the team didn't believe in the player's value. Two, if the team finally does agree to $3 million and the player knows it really wanted to pay a third of that amount, he's naturally going to think the team was out to cheat him. In that case, the player might get what he wants but the entire relationship starts off on shaky ground.

This is where the integrity and trust of John Thompson became invaluable. I asked John for his permission, as the parental patriarch, to defer informing Patrick of the details of his own negotiations until we were at least "in the ballpark." I was afraid of the potential ill will implicit in the chasm between our demand for a deal unprecedented in size and scope and the Knicks' desire to "slot" him relative to Olajuwon. For all of John's reputation as a tough guy, he is extremely smart. John understood the wisdom in keeping quiet on the particulars. Without John, I doubt I would have been able to withhold status reports to Patrick, not because he was so demanding but because he was so damn nice.

I remember the first time Patrick called me at home, soon after I had signed him. He left a message on my answering machine that went something like this: "Good evening Mr. Falk. This is Patrick. I really hate to bother you at home. But I wondered if it was possible for you to give me a buzz back. I just wanted to ask you a question."

I looked at my wife and said, "Was that a joke? Could that possibly have been Patrick Ewing leaving that message? Could the guy in a hundred years possibly be that polite and that considerate to think he's imposing on my time when he just let me represent the best player in the country?"

As I came to find out, that was Patrick. To this day he is respectful, thoughtful, considerate, charming, and warm. His personality was at odds with the intensity and power he displayed on the court. It always drove me crazy hearing how fans or writers would refer so negatively to Patrick, and how badly they misunderstood him as a human being. He was more like a big teddy bear, which was exactly how my children and family felt about him.

True to his kindness, Patrick never pressed me for information on the negotiations. It was John, who finally knew it was time to lay out the cards for Patrick. I told John that we had made some progress and that I was more comfortable briefing Patrick on both parties' position.

After all of my analysis of Patrick's negotiating position, I got an unexpected but incredibly fortuitous break. And, as it would turn out, the Knicks had virtually handed me the key to the vault within hours of learning they had won the first lottery. Jim Trecker, the Knicks' vice president of promotions, called to ask me for permission to use Patrick's picture on the team's season ticket brochure. I thought he was kidding. Why would anyone want to put themselves in that position before the contract was completed? So I said, "Sure."

By the middle of the summer the Knicks had started to digest the reality of the situation. They reluctantly came to recognize the unprecedented leverage Patrick had and understood the unique circumstances that demanded they sign him. I had told the Knicks that if they attempted to "wait Patrick out," instead of my demands going down, they would go up. I didn't want to be unfair, but we had all the leverage and the longer the deal dragged on the stronger our position became.

At that point, in mid-August, New York had gotten into the $2.5 million a year range and I passionately believed that if I waited, Patrick would get exactly what we wanted. Naturally Patrick was nervous, but John understood all the pressure was on the team. John is a very intelligent man who clearly understood and completely supported my position. It was one of those truly rare times when the franchise literally could not afford *not* to pay just about whatever it took to sign the player. The Philadelphia Eagles could afford to cut loose Terrell Owens with nothing in return. The Knicks could not do the same with Patrick.

The head of Gulf+Western Entertainment, Arthur Barron, called Donald and told him that if we wanted to make a deal it had to be done immediately. However, I had taken Coach Thompson, Mary Fenlon, who was Georgetown's academic advisor, and Patrick to Nike in Portland, Oregon, so I couldn't physically make the last-minute meeting in New York. (Patrick ended up signing with Adidas, which was ironic because that's who Michael had his heart set on before he finally agreed to a deal with Nike.)

Donald met with Barron and, to my great disappointment, essentially conceded the remaining open issues so he could close the deal. Patrick ended up making more than $30 million for ten years with a unique twist. They gave him a $5 million signing bonus collateralized against salary in the last four years, which created some interesting tax situations. Thankfully, we had retained the option of voiding the deal after six years. The early termination clause provided that if four players passed Patrick in annual salary, Patrick could terminate the deal and become a free agent. The Knicks didn't understand why I would want that kind of protection when they were paying Patrick a 50 percent premium over the current market rate. I explained that while I understood it sounded crazy, I truly didn't believe the contract would stand the test of time. Based on the prevailing salary structure, they didn't believe that was possible so they finally agreed to the clause.

On August 20, 1985, Patrick signed the contract and Dave DeBusschere, the Knicks' general manager, presented him with a $5 million check. Ralph Sampson's entire four-year contract as the No. 1 pick in 1983 paid him a total of less than $4 million. Olajuwon's contract in 1984 had a total value of $7.2 million. Patrick got $5 million before he played a single game.

I made him endorse the check "for deposit only," and then I brought it back to Washington, D.C., took it to a photo engraver, and had three bronze plaques made of it. I gave one to John accompanied by a note: "Dear John, I told you so. Love and kisses, David." The plaque made it onto John's office wall, but not the note.

The entire process taught me more about business and negotiation than I had learned to that point. It validated my approach to negotiations and it confirmed the value of preparation combined with creativity. Most negotiators are concerned with precedent. I realized you had to look into the future, not back into the past. That approach is more difficult because it requires a vision of the future. It's not unlike playing music by ear rather than by reading notes. You might not know what notes are called and maybe you don't even know exactly how the song is supposed to sound, but you have a feel for how you want it to sound.

John Thompson's integrity, which informed his confidence, provided me with the room to create. It also confirmed what I knew to be true of the greatest players, two of whom I represented in Michael and Patrick: money never drives those who want to be the best. Although Patrick's deal put me over the top professionally and established me as a force in my own right, the money I made at ProServ, which was minuscule compared to the deals I was making, never drove me. And it's a good thing. I still wasn't making much more than $100,000 a year.

That element of my character or personality came from my mother, who believed that the reward for trying to be the best was in the process itself. And it was cemented by my relationship with John, and the examples of people like Arthur Ashe, Michael Jordan, and Patrick Ewing. Beyond the business applications of John's lessons, I had also learned what it means to be a true friend.

A year later, John lifted me onto his shoulders again, this time in front of Donald Dell, Duke coach Mike Krzyzewski, and Johnny Dawkins, who had been the college player of the year. Coach K had prevailed upon Johnny to allow ProServ to make a presentation in our offices to represent him, and so the two of them flew up to Washington to meet with us.

The meeting took place in Donald's office, and in the middle of our presentation John called me. I had standing orders that there were four or five people that I always wanted to be interrupted for when they called. Of course, John was one of them. So when John called that morning to see if I wanted to have lunch, my secretary got very nervous. "Well, coach, please hold on. Let me go get David. He's making a presentation to Johnny Dawkins."

John said, "No, no. It's not necessary."

Moments later, John barged straight into Donald's office with Georgetown's academic advisor, Mary Fenlon, a former nun whom John called his "academic conscience." He walked over to Johnny Dawkins, put a hand on his shoulder, and asked, "How are you doing?" Then he said hello to Mike. Finally, he came over to me and said to Johnny, "This is my man. I really like him. I love him. And, I trust him." He pointed to Donald and said, "This guy I don't like. Screw him."

With that, John and Mary walked out of the room. I didn't know what to say. Donald chose to believe John was fooling around, joking. I wasn't so sure. But I was embarrassed because it all looked so staged.

I looked at Coach K and said, "Mike, I apologize. I had no idea John was coming over." He looked at me incredulously and said, "David, there's not a human being on earth who could have made John Thompson do what he just did if he didn't want to do it."

Johnny signed on as a client and stayed one throughout his ten-year career and is still a great friend twenty years later. Coach K became a client of mine, too, as well as a very special friend.

Seeing the world on the shoulders of giants like John Thompson provides a view like no other.

FALK'S FUNDAMENTALS

Don't be a prisoner of your reputation.

A well-known PGA professional once advised me, "If you normally hit a draw but when you get to the range you hit a fade, play the fade." Successful people remain consistent in their value system but flexible in reaction to changing market conditions.

Don't try to be a spiritual advisor.

A leopard doesn't change its spots. People don't change leopards.

Don't try to run a democracy.

Treat everyone fairly but don't treat everyone equally.

It's better to have a good enemy than a neutral friend.

In crunch time you must know how the people around you will react. The most dangerous enemy is an ally who deserts you.

A combination of creativity and preparation is essential.

Practice makes perfect as long as you don't do it the same way every time. Preparing for a major negotiation or presentation develops confidence, but preparation without inspiration limits your ability to adapt your performance to unexpected challenges.

It's a Long Horse Race

For thirteen months I waited anxiously for Donald Dell to offer me a full-time position at the firm. After he offered to pay me $13,000 a year in 1975 for the privilege of working eighty to one hundred hours a week, it took me thirteen seconds to formulate my next goal: I wanted to be the best. My focus was singular and I believe that trait gave me a common bond with many of the great athletes I would be privileged to represent. I had many setbacks in my career, but I never allowed obstacles, perceived or otherwise, to distract me from my ultimate goal.

Ironically, being the best had nothing to do with money. Some people might find that proposition difficult to accept. But throughout my formative years, my mother, who was the principal influence in my life, always urged me never to settle for second best. While I was aware of what money meant and its impact, particularly for my clients, it never drove me. In sports, and in the business of sports, the best are not defined by how much money they make.

As I have said, my intensity and competitiveness created a very natural commonality with the professional athletes I've worked with, especially the stars. I truly loved the "game" I played and it was obvious to my clients. Moreover, early in my career I recognized an important, indeed a critical truth about life, one that became a fundamental part of my business philosophy: It's a long horse race.

I've probably used this expression a thousand times, as my clients can attest. I am very clear about what it means: "It doesn't matter where you are at the quarter pole, or the halfway pole. It doesn't matter who breaks out of the pack first. What matters is who finishes the race first."

Staying true to this philosophy is not only helpful, it's also often essential in guiding you through difficult circumstances. It allowed me to absorb near-term setbacks because I was committed to the long-term plan. It's easier not to compromise long-term interests for short-term gains when you have a longer view. It's what Michael said about "letting the game come to him" rather than forcing the action. It's about rhythm, pace, and patience. The same tools the greatest basketball player of all time used on the court can be used to drive success in business.

Sacrifice Short-Term Benefits for Long-Term Success

In 1974, ProServ had well-seasoned and deeply pedigreed part-ners in Donald Dell, Frank Craighill, and Lee Fentress. It had become a global power in the tennis business by representing some of the biggest stars of the day, Arthur Ashe and Stan Smith among them. Craighill and Donald were very close to Horst Dassler, the head of Adidas and arguably the most powerful man in global sports at the time. Fentress had a long-standing rela-tionship with Converse, the major domestic brand and the domi-nant player in the basketball shoe market. Fentress had at least ten tennis players signed to shoe deals with Converse.

To carve a niche for myself in that environment demanded a long view with a singular focus. That's probably true in virtually any business environment and particularly so for newcomers. I was twenty-three years old, a "rookie" just coming into the busi-ness, and I recognized that the chances of my making an impact with those companies on behalf of the firm were slim.

So I looked for opportunities elsewhere, with the idea of build-ing my own relationships within the shoe industry, which was still in its infancy in the early to mid-1970s. In fact sports mar-keting as a concept, much less as a corporate application, barely existed for players of team sports and effectively did not exist at all for African American players. Over time, a long time, the world shifted, though ever so slightly at first. To put the long horse race into perspective, Michael Jordan's groundbreaking deal with Nike in 1984 was a direct result of a relationship I had nurtured over the previous decade. As for the kind of sports marketing and player endorsement opportunities that exist in 2008, very few offered significant economic rewards as late as the middle 1980s.

By looking beyond Adidas and Converse, and searching for a young company with plenty to prove, I found Nike. And I found my fit. The company was young, driven, incredibly entrepreneurial, willing and able to make decisions on the fly, and guided by the idiosyncratic genius of a former runner named Phil Knight. The business had been born and raised on running with Steve Prefontaine, an almost perfect combination of talent, style, and attitude, as the face of Nike in the early 1970s.

In 1971, Phil famously paid a graphic design student $35 for creating the Nike "swoosh." A year later, the first Nike basketball shoes—the Bruin and the Blazer—debuted. In 1978, Blue Ribbon Sports, which was the company's official name, was changed to Nike, Inc. That same year, Nike made John McEnroe its next great signing, which provides insight into the swashbuckling nature of the enterprise.

In 1974, Nike was still six years away from becoming a public company and more than a decade away from becoming a force in basketball.

I recognized that someone of my stature, or lack thereof, could exert more influence with a small, independently minded company in a town (Beaverton, Oregon) barely on the map than I ever could at Converse or Adidas. As it turned out, that reality worked against both companies to their great detriment, Converse in particular. Still, it took time to develop the trust of a company devoted to track and field. My sense was that a company like Nike would jump at the chance to sign ProServ clients, particularly basketball players. One problem, however, aside from Nike's initial disinterest, was with the players themselves. Adidas had a better product and Converse had a much deeper history in the game. Another issue was the game itself. The visibility and public perception of the NBA in the early to mid-1970s was similar to professional hockey in 2006, with two significant differences: a majority of the players were African American, and a majority of the teams were failing.

I met Rob Strasser, the head of Nike's marketing, in 1975. Strasser had a creative flair and a gambler's instincts, though it took a while to appreciate both of those traits as he turned down the first five or six players I proposed to the company.

By the time I introduced Adrian Dantley to Strasser in 1976, the horse race had already become long and decidedly one-sided. Dantley had been an all-American at Notre Dame and the sixth player chosen in the 1976 NBA draft before winning a gold medal at the Olympics in Montreal later that summer. I gave Strasser an ultimatum: "If you turn me down on this one, I'll never come back. You say you need players and I'm trying to give you players."

Dantley became the first ProServ athlete to sign with Nike. Though the numbers appear insignificant now, Nike paid Dantley $6,000 for one year and provided him with free shoes. For an NBA player in 1976, the deal was considered substantial, though still peanuts compared to tennis players. The first shoe deal I ever negotiated paid Hank Pfister, a tennis player, $25,000. I was so proud of myself about that one that I couldn't wait to get home and tell my wife, Rhonda, who had an entirely different perspective on my "success."

"You mean he's making more money for lacing up his shoes for a two-hour match than you're making in two years working hundred-hour weeks?"

She had a point. After two years, I was still making $16,000 a year at ProServ, a sum that trailed even college friends working for the government. I wasn't blind to the economics, but as I said, they didn't drive me. Michael Jordan always said he would have played the game for free. I felt the same way at ProServ; the only difference was that I was a lot closer to working for nothing than Michael ever would be.

Tennis players and golfers were naturals for endorsing generic sports products—tennis rackets and shoes, golf clubs and balls. They were individuals playing upscale sports on an international stage. And virtually all of them were white, educated, and possessing a social if not intellectual pedigree that matched their profession. European players in either sport who didn't even rank in the top ten had their own product deals. The stars, like our top tennis clients, commanded premiums. Ashe had a racket deal with Head that paid six-figure annual royalties. He also had two shoe deals: one in America with Head and another in Europe with Adidas. And he collected a nice salary with perks and equity to be the touring professional of the Doral Country Club in Miami. Oh yes—he also won money playing tennis.

To put basketball's place in the sports marketing universe in perspective, the average NBA salary in 1976 had yet to reach $200,000 a year. The first player selected in the draft was paid $1,500 by Converse to wear their shoes. Conversely (no pun intended), Stan Smith, one of the top tennis players in the world, earned more than $200,000 a year endorsing Adidas tennis shoes and clothing. In 2006, thirty years after he ceased to be the top player in the world, Adidas was still making and selling Stan Smith–branded tennis shoes.

It would have been an easy justification in those days to abort the long horse race and travel a more traditional path. Basketball, particularly the professional game, was barely national. The most intense interest was generated regionally between geographic rivals like New York, Philadelphia, and Boston. And while tennis was all about individual players—who had become self-contained business enterprises, separate from the governing bodies of the sport—basketball players were defined by team and team geography. It was beyond anyone's imagination at the time, or even years later for that matter, that any one player could transcend his team much less the sport.

That was particularly true in the 1970s. The league was headed straight downhill and gathering momentum even with the folding of the rival American Basketball Association in 1976. There were reports that up to 75 percent of the players were on drugs, suggestions that the league was "too black," and rumors that maybe as many as a third of the teams would fold. Economically at least, the rumors were well founded. The NBA was in trouble and more clouds were rolling in.

At ProServ, Michael Cardozo left to run the Connecticut operation in Jimmy Carter's presidential bid. He came back briefly following Carter's victory but soon departed for the White House as one of the president's four legal counsels. For me, Carter's success couldn't have been more opportune. I was handed Cardozo's clients, which included a number of basketball players and a few tennis players. At the time, just out of law school and working up to one hundred hours a week, I was writing all the firm's contracts when I took over Mike's players.

Meanwhile, I was convinced Nike could raise its profile in the NBA and that the investment matched the opportunity. After Dantley, I began doing more deals with Nike. Though they remained very small, with each one I was developing a deeper level of trust and connection with Rob Strasser. He was a bear of a man, six feet two with reddish-blond hair, tremendously overweight, and even more tremendously filled with enthusiasm. He was Knight's right-hand man for promotions and I had become Donald Dell's point person on basketball. Rob and I were two young lawyers with at least three things in common: very little stature, an intense desire to define ourselves professionally, and an appreciation for the creative process.

I remember standing with Strasser in Portland during the parade celebrating the Trail Blazers' 1977 NBA championship. I had two clients on the team: Wally Walker, who in 2004 would become president and part owner of the Seattle SuperSonics, and Maurice Lucas. As the parade passed by us, with thousands of fans lining the streets, it occurred to me that Rob and I might have been the only two people in town working that day. I was trying to put three of our rookie clients—Marques Johnson, Kenny Carr, and Bernard King, who were the third, sixth, and seventh picks in the 1977 draft—together with Nike. We were negotiating away amid the chaos of the celebration when Rob suddenly stopped, looked at me, and said, "What the hell are we doing sitting here doing deals in the middle of a championship parade?"

Well, I knew what *I* was doing. I was trying to change the economics of an industry one deal at a time. But for the most part, and particularly in the world of professional basketball, the world was still flat. Ernie and Chris Severn were two graying veterans and the heads of Adidas U.S. basketball promotions. They operated out of Westlake Village in Southern California, so they were tuned in to Marques Johnson's considerable success at UCLA. In fact, Johnson had been the college player of the year and was considered a future NBA star. The Severns offered him slightly more than the standard deal at the time: $1,500 a year.

So as the parade rolled on that day in Portland, I had Rob up to $6,000 for Marques. That offer was comparable to $1 million a year in 2008. I had successfully convinced Nike that because of its size and presence in the sport, the company had to be significantly more aggressive financially. I was pitching what would become the mantra for Avis a decade or so later—we're number two so we have to try harder. And try harder, though that was certainly relative, is what Nike did. They agreed to pay Marques Johnson, and doubled the standard $1,000-a-year deal for Carr and King.

In the end, however, the offer wasn't high enough for Nike to land Johnson. ProServ's relationship with Adidas allowed it to convince Horst Dassler to pay Johnson $10,000 a year, plus a royalty, and to create an Adidas "Top 10 Club" of NBA stars. Adidas made a special shoe and put ten NBA stars into it, including Marques. Michael Jordan was fifteen when he fell in love with the Adidas brand, the Top 10s in particular. Years later, Michael's love for Adidas would be put to the test and that test would change the athletic shoe market forever.

Long-Term Success
Demands Discipline and Accountability

Nike lost out on the Marques Johnson deal in 1977, but like Horst Dassler, Rob "got it" and understood the potential value of the basketball business. As the years passed, I continued to do smaller deals with Nike. We had built so much trust into the relationship that Rob would look to me to set the price. There weren't a lot of negotiations. I would tell him about the player, the deal would get done very quickly, and then, at the end of every one he'd ask: "Am I getting f—d on this deal?"

He never was and I made sure he never did. It's a key element of the long horse race: Done correctly, with honesty and integrity, each deal should build upon the one previous. It got to the point that Rob signed some of our players not only sight unseen, but even sport unknown. In 1984 and just ahead of Michael's deal with Nike, I made a deal for quarterback Boomer Esiason—two years at $15,000 and $25,000. Boomer had been a second-round pick of the Cincinnati Bengals in the 1984 NFL draft. After I completed his shoe deal with Nike, Rob asked, "By the way, what position does he play? Is he a guard or a forward?"

I said, "Are you serious? He's a quarterback."

Rob's response was, "Oh my God."

"Relax, Rob," I said. "You aren't getting f—d on this deal."

It is essential to protect relationships in business. And I worked hard to do that with Nike, which wasn't easy when you were working for Donald Dell. He had tunnel vision when it came to making deals. It was at once his greatest strength and his greatest weakness. Not only did he lack a long view, but often he didn't even appreciate the potential near-term impact of one deal upon another. He would fixate on trying to squeeze an additional $10,000 out of a deal that down the road might cost him hundreds of thousands, or even millions of dollars in business. His approach, which was directly opposite mine, was that when you found a company willing to spend money, try to get them to spend as much as possible. Whether the deal was in a company's best interest or in the long-term best interests of the firm was secondary to closing the deal. In other words, Donald believed in riding a horse to death. Getting to the finish line ahead of everyone else was an idea that existed out there in the future and as such never entered the current debate.

In 1985, after Michael Jordan had established himself as an NBA prodigy and a marketing phenomenon, I received a call from Michael Bozic, who was the president of Sears at the time. He wanted Michael to make an appearance at a Chicago Boys & Girls Club. It's a great organization and I told him I'd discuss it with Michael, who liked the idea. I mentioned my conversation with Bozic to Donald, who then begged me to put something else on the agenda. ProServ was running a tennis tournament in Chicago called the Volvo of Chicago and the company needed a presenting sponsor for about $100,000. Donald wanted me to convince Sears to become that sponsor. He no doubt thought I could leverage their desire for Michael into something more.

I met Bozic in his Chicago office, which seemed to occupy the entire top floor of the Sears Tower. I told him Michael was willing to do the appearance, and Bozic was very appreciative. We talked about various other things for thirty minutes or so before I asked him if he could do me a favor. I explained that ProServ managed a tennis tournament in Chicago only three weeks away and that we really needed a title sponsor. Since Sears was a Chicago company, I told him it would be reasonable exposure at a limited cost.

"Look," said Bozic, "I really don't like tennis and with the event just three weeks off, there are really not a lot of benefits for us. But I really appreciate Michael doing the appearance, and if it would help you out, I could give you seventy-five thousand dollars."

I was thrilled and after the meeting ended I left word with Donald that Sears was on board. But a few hours later I received another call from Bozic. This time he was fried.

"What are you so upset about?" I asked.

"Look, were you listening to me this morning? I told you I don't like tennis. There's not enough time to promote the tournament, and I'm just doing this as a favor. And your damn office calls and asks me if I want to sponsor three more."

It's a classic case of short-term thinking that has cost businesses large and small.

For years I had kept Donald and the tennis people away from Nike. I knew Phil Knight detested the idea of being the official "shoe" or "apparel" of anything. He was building an iconoclastic, independent company out in Oregon. He placed his first big bets on people like Prefontaine and McEnroe, whose fearless self-expression provided clues to the company Nike would become. Knight's Nike wasn't going to "Just Do It" like the rest of them. Phil Knight not only understood the notion of a long horse race, it was part of his DNA and it informed his vision.

Unfortunately for me, the Nike culture Knight created involved not just rebellion but rotation. Knight felt that managers got stale if they did the same job over and over, year in and year out. Even the best of them could be shipped off to another "challenge." And people did move around, particularly if they earned Knight's disfavor. That's how Rob Strasser ended up being "reassigned" to Germany in the mid-1980s.

For me it was an object lesson in the value of relationships. All the equity I had built up at Nike was invested in an executive who was recycled to Europe just as the economics of just about everything was starting to change. The NBA, thanks to the arrival of Larry Bird, Magic Johnson, and Commissioner David Stern, suddenly seemed capable of resurrection. The larger economy was on the same trajectory. Nike itself had gone public in 1980 and had amassed an amazing collection of international track and field athletes, fifty-six of whom would win a total of sixty-five medals in the 1984 Olympics in Los Angeles.

But the worm was only beginning to turn when Strasser headed to Germany. At ProServ we had helped escalate the market price for basketball players. Starting in the late 1970s, and thanks to very close relations with North Carolina's Dean Smith, Georgetown's John Thompson, and a number of other major college coaches, the firm started to represent a number of high first-round draft picks. When Bird and Johnson came into the league together in 1979 and instantly turned their teams into title contenders—Johnson led the Lakers to a championship in his first season, 1979–80—the profile and value of high draft picks increased on and off the court.

James Worthy was the breakthrough player. In 1982 he became the first No. 1 overall pick to be selected by an NBA defending champion. The combination made Worthy the highest-paid rookie in league history, getting more than twice what Johnson had received as the No. 1 pick three years earlier.

For Worthy, Coach Smith recommended ProServ to negotiate the Lakers contract but he told us James really didn't need marketing services because Puma had already made an enormous offer: $55,000. The backstory to that offer involved the formation of Adidas. Brothers Adi and Rudi Dassler cofounded Adidas in the 1920s, in Herzogenaurach, Germany. Following World War II, the brothers had a falling out and Rudi left Adidas to start Puma, whose corporate headquarters he established on the opposite bank of Adidas on the River Aurach. The rivalry continued even after the deaths of the brothers when Horst, Adi's son, took over Adidas and kept it miles ahead of Puma. The Worthy offer was part of an effort to close the gap between the two companies.

Although the deal was large for the times, I knew the economics for Worthy defied the established market parameters. I headed out to Nike to meet with Ken O'Neal, Strasser's successor as director of basketball promotions. I explained the unique nature of Worthy's arrival in Los Angeles and told him we were looking for a six-figure deal. He said, "Well, give me a feel for what it would take for you to just say, 'Okay, we have a deal.'" I told him $800,000 for six years, or in other words, $133,333 a year. He came right back and said he thought Nike could do $125,000 for six years, or $750,000. Needless to say, I was thrilled on a number of counts. First, we had dramatically altered the economic landscape for players. Second, I thought all the time and trust I had built with Rob had not in fact been wasted upon his departure. And finally, I knew Coach Smith would be blown away by what we were able to do for James.

My first call was to North Carolina. "We have an unbelievable opportunity," I told Coach Smith. "Nike is prepared to sign James for $750,000, which is more than twice what Puma is offering."

Then another aspect of the long horse race came into play. Relationships are critical to a long-term view in business. It's about people, not corporations. A couple of days later, O'Neal called to say he'd changed his mind. He suddenly didn't think Nike could offer that much money.

"Well, sorry, it's too late," I said. "I've already discussed it with Coach Smith."

From my perspective, I had invoked the name of God. North Carolina had the finest and most respected program in the country, and Coach Smith represented ProServ's most prominent college basketball relationship.

O'Neal's response: "Well, I'm really sorry."

I tried another tack, which would have allowed me to create a similar deal elsewhere. "We have a relationship with your company," I said. "At the minimum, leave the offer on the table and let me use it with other companies. I won't call you on it." O'Neal said he couldn't do that, but he thought he could do a smaller number, $90,000 a year. Then, a couple of weeks later, he lowered the offer a second time. I was angry and called Strasser in Germany to explain what had happened.

Because of the way the winds were blowing at Nike at the time, we couldn't get the deal done. The experience, however, made at least two things painfully clear. First, Nike was still an immature company, relatively small in scope and in this case shortsighted. Second, if I hadn't understood the importance or the nature of my relationship with Strasser, I certainly did now. His replacement tried to pick a fight over $30,000 to $40,000 a year. Nike won the battle but lost the war with Worthy, who would go on to be selected one of the fifty greatest players in NBA history.

We still wound up making a landmark shoe deal for James worth one and a half to two times what Magic Johnson and Larry Bird were being paid by Converse. The fact we were able to make that deal was a direct result of what had happened at Nike. I changed my approach and as a result changed the market. Instead of giving companies a dollar figure, I put the burden on them. I told everyone I would accept offers starting at $100,000 a year. Most of them responded by asking me if I was crazy. According to the majority, no one was going to pay a rookie that kind of money.

I held my ground: "If you don't think he's worth it, don't make a bid."

It worked for two reasons. One, James did have a unique set of attributes. He had played on a national championship team at North Carolina and had been the college player of the year in 1982. He was going to the defending NBA champion in the league's best market at the time, Los Angeles, and joining a team that would become known as "Showtime." He also was everything any coach would want in a player, on and off the court. Second, we had a motivated buyer in New Balance, a running shoe company that wanted to break into basketball.

Worthy got $1.2 million, $150,000 a year for eight years. The deal changed the basketball shoe market overnight. More players began to realize better shoe deals, but they still had very limited opportunities for other product endorsements. For professional team sport athletes in the early 1980s, identity revolved around the team, not an individual. In other words, the world was still flat when Michael Jordan came into the NBA in 1984. And no one predicted he would change its shape.

Be True to Yourself

Experts questioned Michael's shooting ability and ball handling skills. Although they acknowledged his athletic ability, the consensus seemed to be that Michael would be more of a showman than a franchise player in the NBA. The franchise players, at least according to Houston and Portland, were Hakeem Olajuwon, the No. 1 pick in the 1984 draft; and Sam Bowie, who went to Portland as the second pick. Portland had Clyde Drexler, who had averaged 7.7 points per game in his rookie season playing behind Jim Paxson, an all-star shooting guard who had averaged more than twenty points a game during the 1983–84 season. The Trail Blazers figured Drexler would end up being at least as good as Jordan and chose Bowie, who despite suffering from chronic leg problems, appeared to have the potential to be a long-term solution at center.

All that changed in Los Angeles. On the world stage in the 1984 Olympics, Michael became the star of stars. U.S.A. coach Bobby Knight said he thought Michael could become as great a player as he had ever seen. Despite the presence of players like Patrick Ewing, Michael levitated above and beyond all of them. As he came into focus for the rest of the world, so too did my vision for him.

I met with James and Delores Jordan, Michael's parents, following the Olympics and laid out the plan. I still didn't understand the degree to which he would become an NBA superstar almost from the opening tip, but I recognized the Olympics had changed the game. Michael had worldwide exposure and tremendous credibility and would come to be seen as an all-American hero. I recommended a plan that would concentrate solely on American-based companies with global sales. I suggested we pass on such giants as Toyota and Nissan, or anything foreign. I felt Michael was as American as apple pie: McDonald's, Chevrolet, and Coca-Cola. And while Michael agreed, he also thought he was Adidas. The long horse race told me he was Nike.

From my perspective, the key to Michael's marketing plan was his shoe contract because it would not only be his first partnership but also would have to drive the rest of the plan. If we could get a company to start marketing Michael as an individual personality, much as they would market a tennis player, then the plan had a unique foundation from which we could expand its range. Keep in mind that Converse still ruled the domestic basketball market and Adidas, whose shoes Michael had worn off the court for years, probably had the best product.

To refine the strategy I developed for Worthy, I met with the shoe companies and asked them not for a financial offer but for a presentation of their concepts for promoting Michael. The fit I was looking for had to be outside the box that every company had erected for itself in basketball. The approach was the culmination of all of my business experience since 1974 and thousands of hours preparing, negotiating, and closing deals. I had seen the tennis business from the inside out. What Michael Jordan did in Los Angeles was no different than what John McEnroe had done at the U.S. Open. Michael had jumped to the head of the class with a rare combination of style and substance. The fact that he played on a team was irrelevant. On the world's biggest stage in the glitter capital of the world, a Dean Smith–coached player had not only wowed fans with extraordinary dunks and moves, but he had made a deep impression on Knight, the antithesis of individual style, and like Smith, the embodiment of substance.

I wanted the shoe companies to present their marketing platforms, but I also needed them to commit to how much money they would invest in Michael Jordan product lines. At that time none of the companies had given significant thought beyond the basketball shoe and they didn't exercise a lot of imagination in designing new products, either. I wanted to move players beyond sneakers. Worthy received a great deal of money and exposure with New Balance, but it was a traditional endorsement. He wouldn't have his own line of clothing and accessories for several more years. He wasn't a tennis player. Michael represented the natural evolution.

Instinctively, I knew Michael was a better fit for an upstart company not afraid to take on Adidas and Converse. But I made the rounds, including Converse and Adidas, emphasizing how an electrifying player could give their businesses a jolt. I told them to think of a flashy player like Dominique Wilkins, who came out in 1982 and quickly became known as "the human highlight film." Michael Jordan, with his North Carolina pedigree and Olympic gold medal, was that and more.

My standard would not be how much they were willing to pay Michael, but how much they were willing to spend promoting his branded products. The kind of up-and-coming company I wanted could have been Pony or Puma; I met with both of them. But I believed the best fit was with Nike. First, Rob Strasser had returned from exile and was back leading basketball promotions at Nike. Second, I knew Jordan intrigued him. Rob had vision and no fear of upsetting the status quo. Finally, he had an intense dislike for Adidas, "the Germans."

I gave Strasser the John F. Kennedy speech following the Olympics: Don't ask what Michael can do for you; tell me what you can do for Michael. "If you sign this player," I said, "then you need to know we are looking for something radically different than anything we've done in the past. We want him treated like a tennis player. We want him to have his own line of products, which would be promoted individually and apart from the team." Then I told him what it would take: a million-dollar marketing commitment in the first six months. Rob never flinched.

While I talked, Peter Moore, a brilliant designer who had accompanied Strasser, started sketching. Both of them seemed taken by the brand name that had popped into my head: Air Jordan. Before the meeting ended, Peter showed me the sketch of a basketball with wings coming out the sides. The first Air Jordan logo had been produced on the spot. We quickly scheduled a meeting for September at Nike headquarters, where Strasser would lay out his vision for Michael Jordan–branded shoes and products.

The one wrinkle in an otherwise monumental meeting was that Michael had no interest in Nike. No interest in even getting on the plane to visit the company. The Olympic team had been all over the country playing exhibitions ahead of the games and Michael was worn out. He made it very clear that he wanted to stay home and hang out with his friends. And besides, even though Michael wore Converse at North Carolina, he considered himself an Adidas guy. He had told Nike recruiters exactly that. And he told Phil Vukicevich, who was the head of Adidas U.S. basketball, to "get close and I'll go with you."

I didn't have much of a relationship with Michael at that time, never mind influence. I had met him only twice—once when ProServ made its presentation to represent him and then following an Olympic exhibition game against a group of NBA all-stars in Greensboro, North Carolina. I hardly knew him and he barely listened.

The opportunity was saved only by one of the many gifts that make Michael unique—his parents. He is a combination of both of them: disciplined, charismatic, fearless, and competitive to a degree few could appreciate at the time. James and Delores had been involved in every aspect of Michael's decision to leave school early, then to choose ProServ for representation. They were caring and wise, and Michael deferred to them. James and Delores became an important bridge between Michael and me in the early years with Nike representing the first crossing. They literally forced Michael onto the plane with them to Nike.

The presentation got off to a less than inspiring start. Nike had created a video of Michael's highlights from college to the Olympics, with music from the Pointer Sisters' song "Jump." Strasser was so nervous that he literally couldn't get the VCR to work. Rob could sweat in a snowstorm, but inside the conference room that day, wearing a dress shirt with a thin yellow tie, he could have drowned. As if that weren't enough, Howard White, one of Nike's senior basketball executives and the only African American in the room, arrived thirty-five minutes late. Meanwhile, Michael sat at the end of the table with absolutely no expression other than abject boredom.

The video finally began and it was quite well done by 1984 standards. Compared to what Nike does today, it probably looked like a home video, but for its time the video was impressive. Most importantly, it conveyed their interest, imagination, and creativity. It ended with the logo: "Air Jordan, Basketball by Nike."

I couldn't have been happier. No one had ever put that much thought into marketing a player from a team sport, particularly a basketball player. Michael, however, remained implacable. Rob just kept working it, trying to get Michael to warm up. One of Nike's recruiters had told Strasser that Michael loved cars. As Rob finished describing what Nike would do for Michael, he said, "And we know you like cars, so if you come with us . . ."

Strasser reached into his breast pocket. Phil Knight, who had come in toward the end of the presentation, clutched his heart. He was in shock. Knight knew Strasser's boldness well and he thought Rob was reaching into his pocket to present Michael with keys to a car. Instead Rob pulled out two miniature Mercedes models. Phil regained his pulse and we all roared.

I had no idea how to read Michael during the presentation. As I said, I hardly knew him and he never cracked a smile. For all I knew, he still resented being dragged across the country for a show he had no interest in seeing. As I would come to learn and appreciate, Michael had put on his "business face" for the meeting. It wasn't until we had left Nike, finished dinner, and headed to the hotel that I finally asked him what he thought.

"I don't want to see anybody else," he said.

I took Michael and his father, James, to one meeting after that in Boston with Converse, which might as well have been the anti-Nike. In retrospect, that meeting was even more prophetic of the future. Its marketing people made it clear they weren't about to give a rookie guard the royal treatment, not when they had Julius Erving, Larry Bird, Magic Johnson, Isiah Thomas, Mark Aguirre, and Bernard King under contract. Instead they told us about how they had sixty employees at the company who were six-feet-six or taller, all of them former players, as if to impress upon us the depth of their basketball culture. They would treat Michael just as they treated their superstars, which, according to Converse, should be nirvana for an untested rookie.

James Jordan had attended a few meetings by this point and he had very quickly developed a high level of sophistication and in this case, annoyance.

"Don't you have any new, creative ideas?" he asked.

In fairness, Converse only reflected the conventional wisdom of corporate America in 1984. The idea of a single player transcending the existing model for product endorsements was beyond anyone's imagination. It also was threatening.

Some years later, Nike bought Converse out of bankruptcy. By

2006, the brand had regained its footing under the Nike umbrella and once more was becoming a presence in professional basketball with a street credibility based on its unique history and the retro feel of its Chuck Taylor line.

Rod Thorn, the Chicago Bulls general manager in 1984, pulled me aside and said, "What are you trying to do, David, turn this guy into a tennis player?"

"Rod," I replied, "that's precisely what we're trying to do."

Rod thought our approach could alienate Michael from the rest of the players, which didn't happen, at least not on his team. His approach to the game and the success that followed eliminated that question quickly.

Bridging the gap with corporate America was another matter. Outside of the shoe business, there was virtually no interest in Michael Jordan in 1984. No one believes that today. But back then it was like swimming upstream against white-water rapids. And it was partly racial. Consumer companies didn't believe an African American athlete could be a valuable ambassador in promoting its products, especially one on a mediocre team in a struggling sport. It seems like ancient history now, but the NBA of 1984 had become the first league to institute a salary cap for the purpose of saving up to a third of its franchises from bankruptcy.

Another factor was the mind-set of those making decisions within the corporate bureaucracy. When marketing departments considered athletes they only considered established performers. Their criteria were based on performance. I argued against that approach for a number of reasons, not the least of which is that it made no sense.

I asked Coke if they were going to buy a team. Of course not, they replied. Then why do you care about a player's performance? You are selling soft drinks, not a team's performance. It really didn't matter how well a player did on the court. What mattered, or should have mattered to Coke was how good that player was at selling soft drinks. To this day, many companies never even ask the question. The assumption is that the best players most positively affect consumer purchase decisions.

Tim Duncan might be the best all-around player in the NBA. He's also a very classy person with not a hint of negative press. But does he have the personality to sell your product? Companies are not so sure.

In 1985, Patrick Ewing joined the Knicks after being an even bigger college star than Michael and heading into a significantly better market in New York. Strasser gave me a hard time. "What's it going to be with Patrick, Air Ewing?" he asked.

"No, you don't get it Rob," I said. "Michael's the air force and Patrick's the infantry."

I couldn't try to replicate Michael with Patrick or anyone else because it wouldn't have been authentic. Michael and Patrick have opposite personalities. Michael is a tremendously public person, comfortable no matter how bright the light shines. Patrick is warm but inherently private. It wouldn't have made sense trying to fit Patrick into roles that were written for Michael. Patrick needed his own identity and ironically he got one with Adidas. To a great degree, that's why everything worked with Michael in a way that no one has been able to replicate. From the outset the marketing was authentic, true to Michael's personality, spirit, and style. The fact that he was deeply involved in the design of the shoes, from 1984 to the present, is in and of itself uniquely different than any other athlete and his or her relationship to a product. No one, however, seems to understand the importance or the depth of that reality. Even the NBA at the height of its prowess didn't understand that Michael had created a slot that was his alone. It wasn't a new space that could be filled by the next star. There's a long line of players whom either the league or a shoe company, including Nike, has tried to leverage into a similar model. This list includes Larry Johnson, Anfernee Hardaway, and Shaquille O'Neal—and none of them have come close.

Everything was custom-made for Michael with a long view in mind. Even when Michael did the movie *Space Jam* in 1996, we didn't just drop him into a film. We created a movie in which Michael Jordan played Michael Jordan.

There will never be and should never be another Michael. Everything he did on the court and off was authentic to who he was and fundamental to his core values and beliefs. Michael never tried to be the next Dr. J or Connie Hawkins, although those comparisons were made. He wasn't trying to retrofit something else to work for him. He created an empire because he never tried to be anyone other than who he is. It's why Brand Jordan is on its way to becoming a $1 billion entity more than twenty-three years after the first shoe launched. Michael's style always was and always will be authentic.

Know When the Race Is Over

In 1988, after I had negotiated Michael's second deal with the Chicago Bulls, I realized how far we had come together and how far he might go on the court. For all that we had done in re-creating the sports marketing landscape, the future looked even brighter. When Michael came to Washington to review the contract, I proposed a fee for negotiating the deal. Michael thought it was too high. I was crushed. So right in front of my boss, Donald Dell, I asked the one question you are never supposed to ask when negotiating: What do you think is fair? He came back with an amount about half of what I had proposed.

"Okay, I'll accept your fee proposal with two conditions," I told him. "First, I want you to pay it all now. You have an eight-year contract and I never want to send you another bill. Second, I want to reduce our marketing fee from twenty percent to a lesser amount."

Michael was as smart and shrewd off the court as on. He knew my penchant for negotiation and he was convinced this was a bad deal for him. Paying the negotiating fee up front provided a benefit to ProServ, but a limited one. I wanted to reward Michael for his loyalty and for never demanding we cut our marketing fee or otherwise using the leverage he had in a way that hurt the company. To that point, a lot of players with considerably less stature had thought it reasonable to ask for a cost savings. Tennis players, as a breed, always tried to slice the fees they paid or skimp in any way they could. Michael's reaction was to refuse my offer to cut our marketing fees.

"I don't want to lower the fee on the marketing," said Michael. "I think what you got me from the Bulls is because of what I do on the court. I think what you get me in marketing is really because of you."

I told him I was flattered, but in reality, most everything I was able to do for him was because of Michael. I said I would put the proposal in writing and asked him to have an accounting firm in Chicago provide an analysis based on what he was currently earning and paying in fees. And then I wanted him to have the firm analyze the benefit of a reduced marketing fee against the cost of prepaying the negotiating fee on his contract. Based on my own analysis, the estimated cost to prepay the negotiating fee was $25,000 versus a savings of $10 million or more in reduced marketing fees starting in 1988.

When Michael left, Donald was stunned. "What was that all about?" he asked. "Why on earth did you propose reducing the fee when the client told you he was happy paying it?"

"You know, Donald, that's your problem," I said. "You wait until the man comes in with a gun and says, 'I want to pay one percent' and there's no goodwill or trust left. I want to get in front of it and say to him, 'Thanks Michael.' I want him to know I understand what his presence has meant to this firm."

Michael did hire an accounting firm and realized the impact of the voluntary fee reduction. Our relationship changed forever. For the first time, he knew he could completely trust me. He prepaid the negotiating fee, I cut our marketing commissions, and the show went onward and upward beyond anything that had come before in sports marketing. There wasn't anything better I could have done with $10 million at that time.

At that point in my career, representing Michael's best interests, even to the seeming detriment to my company, was the best move I had ever made. It cemented the most important relationship in my career. And it affirmed to me that in the long horse race, an investment that might seem expensive in the short term has the capacity to pay off at a significant multiple down the road. Ten years later it did when I sold Falk Associates Marketing Enterprises, or FAME, for more than $100 million.

If Donald Dell had an Achilles' heel, it was his inability to take the longer view. He invariably waited for a crisis before responding; that tactic invariably means you have fewer options and less leverage than you might have had otherwise. Donald often failed to recognize that sometimes it's good business to do things you don't have to do.

Someone else I could never persuade to see the value of the long horse race, and who was in fact the most resistant to the concept, was the Washington Wizards owner, Abe Pollin. Abe had the view that I was an agent, he was management, and therefore we couldn't be partners. I believe that in a salary cap environment, where the players are guaranteed a percentage of the league revenues, players and owners are inherently partners. The very structure of the collective bargaining agreement makes owners partners with their players. If you own the Washington franchise, and you are trying to field a good team and sell tickets, and I represent the best players in the world, a lot of whom come from Georgetown and Maryland, how can we work more closely together so that if it's a close call, I can influence a player like Dikembe Mutombo or Alonzo Mourning to come back to Washington, a place they love, to play for the hometown team? How can we work more closely together to bring the assets to your team that make it fun for me to watch them play and fun for you to watch all those people in the stands? Nevertheless, Pollin essentially told me that helping the team ultimately was not my job. His position was that if he decided to bring in one of my clients to play for his team, my job was limited to negotiating his contract.

In contrast, Dave Checketts, former president and chief executive of Madison Square Garden, and I had battles royal when we were both young, but as we matured we actually became pretty good friends and I came to admire Dave. He's a smart guy. So when the Knicks traded Ewing in 2000 and the New York press jumped on Checketts, Dave came out and said that I had promised him Mutombo. Although I never made that promise, it was a very smart answer.

Other than Pollin, every owner in the league asked for my help getting great players like Mutombo, Mourning, or Juwan Howard to play for their team. We represented all these stars at the peak of their careers and everyone wanted them. General managers would ask how we might be able to help their team by influencing a player to go one place or another.

Pollin was the only owner who felt that persuading your clients to play for a specific team and working with that team to execute the transaction is outside of what an agent should do. That was Abe's prerogative, but as a result, he had lousy attendance and his teams rarely made the playoffs. In the height of irony, without ever talking to Abe once, who did we bring him but Michael Jordan? In a deal with Ted Leonsis, who was a minority owner of the team and heir apparent, we brought in perhaps the greatest marquee player in the history of sports, yet Abe never acknowledged we even had a role in making it happen. Nor did he even publicly acknowledge that Ted had a role. In that kind of an environment there could be no relationship, because Abe viewed agents as the enemy. And it has cost him a lot of money.

In the 1993 NBA draft, the Washington Bullets drafted Calbert Cheaney with the sixth pick. My partner, Mike Higgins, represented Calbert. Mike went to meet with John Nash, who was the general manager of the Bullets. I felt it was important for my partners and younger lawyers to get experience so I wasn't the one making all the deals all the time. I said to Mike, "Go first, meet with John, and I'll come down in a few hours. If I can help out, I will." By the time I got to the meeting the negotiations were over. Mike had done a great job negotiating a six-year contract worth $18 million, fully guaranteed. It was very friendly. Calbert had been the college player of the year at Indiana and he was our first Bob Knight player. We wanted to show Coach Knight that we could do a good job.

A year later, we signed our first rookie client from Michigan: Juwan Howard. The Bullets drafted Juwan with the fifth pick. I had enjoyed a very good relationship with John Nash and based on the experience with Calbert, I expected it would be a very friendly negotiation. Nevertheless, I did a lot of homework, and from all the parameters I studied, I determined that Juwan's market value was slightly in excess of $4 million per year. At the time, the NBA had a rule that if a player's contract expired and his team did not re-sign that player, then the team could use the last year of that player's contract as an exception to the salary cap and apply it to the first year of a new contract for a different player. Purvis Ellison had completed his contract with the Bullets at the end of the 1993–94 season and in the last year he was paid $2.3 million. So the Bullets could take Ellison's $2.3 million "slot" and use that money for the first year of a contract for Juwan with the ability to increase it by an amount equal to 30 percent of the first year's salary, or $690,000 a year. So that's exactly what we proposed for Juwan, a six-year guaranteed contract for $4,025,000 with no signing bonus, no performance bonus. Just a plain-vanilla contract using Ellison's slot, which, by good fortune, represented almost to the penny what I felt the fifth pick in the draft should get in 1994.

Unfortunately, the first player in that draft was Glenn "Big Dog" Robinson from Purdue. His agent asked the Milwaukee Bucks for $100 million and Herb Kohl, a United States senator from Wisconsin and owner of the Bucks, told Big Dog that he could have the whole team if Robinson would pay him $100 million. Thus Abe Pollin came out publicly and said he was outraged at the level of rookie salaries. As the league's senior owner, Pollin said he felt a responsibility to show the rest of the league what he termed "the right way to deal with rookies." So he instructed John Nash to offer Juwan a three-year contract for approximately $3 million per year, which was too short and too low based on his market value. The Bullets then proceeded to use Purvis's $2.3 million slot to sign a journeyman guard, Scott Skiles.

Now the team no longer had an exception, which meant they could only pay Juwan a contract starting at $1.3 million a year. I told them I didn't care how they did it, whether by trading players or waiving players, but they needed to clear enough room under the salary cap to sign Juwan to his market value, which meant a deal starting at $2.3 million. So the entire summer went by without getting a contract negotiated. Juwan actually missed the first seven games of the regular season because players aren't allowed to report until they have a contract.

Meanwhile, Juwan's coach at Michigan, Steve Fisher, who is a lovely man, was becoming very nervous that we weren't doing a good job. At some point late in the summer, to make the situation even more difficult, the Bullets offered a ten-year contract for $30 million, or $3 million a year, which was still under the market. We didn't want to tie Juwan into such a long deal because it meant betting against his talent. We turned it down. It was a very unpleasant situation.

I sent a message to Abe saying that if you want to change the salary structure, please don't do it in my hometown, Washington, with me. I'm the senior agent. I have the most top rookies. We had a very pleasant dealing last year. Why are you choosing this fight now? Start it next year with someone else. After seven games, the Bullets were off to a terrible start thanks to injuries and Juwan's absence. We finally agreed to a twelve-year contract that guaranteed Juwan $42 million but more importantly gave him the right to terminate the contract for any reason at the end of the second year. I wasn't happy with the contract and I didn't think it reflected his market value, but since we were only looking for $24 million of security with our initial proposal, the deal gave him almost twice the economic security with the flexibility to get out after two years. Remember, we had been willing to lock him in for six years at $4 million a year. Ironically after all the players signed, the average of what Juwan should have received if he were merely slotted between the picks ahead and behind him came in at $4,000,000 and change, so we were off by less than one-half of one percent from what we originally proposed.

In one of the most incredible achievements in the NBA, Juwan, who had left Michigan as a junior, finished his degree on time while completing his rookie year. I thought that was an extremely special achievement and one that I know made his grandmother very proud. He trained very hard over the summer and had a great second season. He averaged 22.1 points and 8.1 rebounds a game, and made the Eastern Conference all-star team. At the conclusion of his second season, Juwan opted out of the contract to become a free agent. I've always believed in the maxim that good things happen to good people. The collective bargaining rules changed effective at the end of Juwan's second year. For the first time in the history of the NBA, unrestricted free agency was created. Now, when a player completed his contract and received an offer from another team, his old team could no longer match the offer and retain the player.

After Juwan's rookie year, the Bullets had signed Chris Webber, Juwan's college teammate, who was considered one of the best players in the league, to a six-year contract worth $9.5 million a year, making him the highest-paid forward in the league. Juwan's second season performance resulted in a number of teams having strong interest in him: Detroit, Cleveland, New York, and Miami among them. I made a habit of never discussing negotiations publicly before they were completed; I thought it put undue pressure on all the parties and I didn't think it was professional. But in this one instance, right before the start of the free agency period, the *Washington Post* asked me what I thought it would take to keep Juwan with the Bullets; I said I thought it would take $15 million to $20 million a year. I then called Wes Unseld, who was the Bullets' general manager. I reminded him that while I never negotiated in the press, he should read the *Post* when he woke up in the morning so he'd be prepared for our negotiations.

Juwan ended up signing a seven-year contract for $105 million, averaging $15 million a year, 60 percent more than Webber. At the end of Juwan's first six years in the league, instead of making the $24,150,000 we originally asked for, he made around $52 million. I came out publicly and said, "I guess Mr. Pollin showed the rest of the league the right way to deal with rookies. He paid Juwan more than double what we asked for because he didn't follow a basic rule of business—it's a long horse race." Abe's experts had picked Juwan Howard as one of the top players coming out of college. We didn't select Juwan in the draft. Abe wasn't willing to pay him what the team had paid Calbert Cheaney the year before, even though Cheaney had gone No. 6 and there had been inflation in the marketplace. I thought it was a dramatic illustration of the old Fram oil filter slogan: "You can pay me now, or you can pay me later." You can buy an oil filter for ten dollars today or you can pay thousands of dollars for a new engine later.

An epilogue to the story: The contract put tremendous pressure on Juwan. The fans had great expectations because he was being paid so much money. I always thought Abe compounded the felony by never taking responsibility. Abe didn't pay him in the beginning, and then he paid him an enormous amount of money because he lost a bet that Juwan's value would go down. Abe went short on Juwan Howard, which was a mistake because instead of $24 million it cost him $52 million. But Juwan remained an asset of the franchise and when the fans were critical, Abe should have had the character to step up and tell them, "Don't be mad at Juwan because he's making so much money. Be mad at me because I didn't believe he would be this good. He proved me wrong and I'm happy to pay him." But he didn't do that. He didn't protect his own asset.

In the long horse race the only object is to be leading at the end.

FALK'S FUNDAMENTALS

Sacrifice short-term benefits for long-term success.

The most successful NBA team for the past ten years has been the San Antonio Spurs, winning four titles. In order to maintain their high level of performance, the Spurs have learned how to lose games during the regular season in order to be well rested and primed mentally in the postseason. Don't win the battle; win the war.

Long-term success demands discipline and accountability.

There's an entertaining television commercial for T. Rowe Price that shows a runner pounding the course with a measured pace. Midway to the finish line another runner literally blows by him, but his ultrafast pace tires him out and the Price runner eventually passes him. Winning a marathon requires complete discipline mentally and physically. If you alter the strategy in response to short-term bumps, you probably won't even finish the race.

Be true to yourself.

A jack of all trades and a master of none is known as a dilettante. Play to your strengths and don't be afraid to seek help when you need it. Be authentic.

Know when the race is over.

Great coaches learn to not run up the score. Whatever temporary satisfaction you might derive from a rout you will likely pay for the next time you face your opponent. Win the game and then walk away gracefully.

THREE

Blunt Is Beautiful—Stay True to You

When the truth becomes hard to tell, people start running from you instead of running for you. Often it's difficult for people to tell the truth, for any one of a variety of reasons. Sometimes they are afraid of hurting another's feelings. Sometimes they are embarrassed by something they have done or by their inability to perform something that requires skill. Regardless, failing to tell the truth is not simply dishonest, it's ineffectual. I have come to believe that not only is being blunt important, but that "blunt is beautiful."

As a Jewish lawyer in a Waspy all-white Washington, D.C., firm with a heavily African American client base, it didn't take a doctorate in psychology to know that in order to be viewed as "one of the boys," I would have to contort my personality. The thought of hanging out at clubs with players, adopting their lingo, aligning with their fashion preferences, and generally trying to be one of the crew was ridiculous to me, though certainly not out of the question for many other agents.

Most players have been on the receiving end of sales pitches since eighth grade. There is a "Dr. Feelgood" at every level to tell them what they want to hear and to reassure them that yes, "You are the man." I never wanted to be selling anything but the best track record in the industry based on a history of success with the top players. I am in the business of dispensing advice based on fundamental analysis, applied creativity, and establishing my own market. Those are my skills. My intentions have always been simple—do the best possible job—and every client I ever represented knows that. I make deals with their best interests in mind. There is no other agenda.

But it took a while to establish that level of trust even with players who selected me to represent them. In retrospect, it probably took all of five years before Michael Jordan understood and trusted where I was coming from.

So when I meet players today, some of them no doubt perceive me as a spoiled rich kid, because of my success. I want to tell them that while I didn't grow up in the projects, I wasn't as far away from them in an economic sense as it might appear. But it's an impossible bridge to cross for most of them, the idea that I didn't come out of the womb with a silver spoon in my mouth and a Ferrari in my garage. I've had to earn everything I've gotten. No one gave me anything. I never received money from anyone other than what I earned. I put myself through law school, and partially through college before that. I owe loyalty and friendship to people who helped me professionally, but there aren't a lot of people who have markers to collect from me. All of this has allowed me to pursue business and relationships with a long-term horizon. I've never been forced to compromise my values to settle an old score or to pay off a new one.

In that respect, I'm not much different from many of the players I represent. With few exceptions, Danny Ferry and Michael Jordan among them, many came from nothing or next to nothing and made their own way. I could appreciate the chip on a player's shoulder when he entered my world full of lawyers, MBAs, and assorted "suits." I might not have grown up with the daily pressures they had, but I understood what it meant to be from one place and then work hard to get to another.

In my case, my mother was my first mentor. She finished her undergraduate studies at nineteen and went on to graduate school. She earned two masters, one in education, the other in foreign languages. Before my parents were married, my mother worked as an interpreter for Nelson Rockefeller in the Bureau of Latin American Affairs in Washington, D.C., during World War II. She was well read and highly educated. She majored in Greek and Latin and spoke Spanish, Italian, German, Russian, and Hebrew. She was one of five children and every one of them went to college, something far from the norm in the 1930s, particularly for women. She taught Spanish, Italian, Latin, and Hebrew at the junior high and high school when I was growing up.

My father's family was the polar opposite. Every one of them ended up in the meat business, none of them going to college. I'm not even sure any of them graduated from high school. It was an amazing oil-and-water marriage proving the old adage that opposites attract. I don't think they were particularly well suited to each other, but like most parents of their generation, by the time they realized it wasn't working they decided to stay together for the children. Children are very perceptive, however, and I certainly sensed the discord.

Because my father didn't have an education, he lived vicariously through his children and always stressed education. My mother, because she was very achievement oriented, stressed education as well.

We moved to Long Island when I was eight, and while we actually lived in Seaford, I went to school in Levittown, where William Levitt built affordable housing for the GIs returning from World War II. My parents bought the house we grew up in for $17,500 in 1959. The mortgage was forty dollars a month. I can remember talking to two of my very close friends and wondering what it would be like to have a house that cost $100,000. In some ways it was beyond our imagination. Where I grew up, all the houses were split-level, cookie-cutter homes, and my father always had old cars because that's all he could afford. I wouldn't say we lived in low-income housing, but it was certainly at the lower end of middle income.

The fathers of most of my classmates were laborers, steamfitters, carpenters, and plumbers. My father owned a retail butcher shop and from the time I was nine years old, I worked there on weekends doing the worst jobs. I put the sawdust down to clean up blood from the meat. I cleaned what were called the fat cans, washed platters full of blood, and sometimes worked as a delivery boy. We didn't have a lot of money and I was cheap labor. In addition to working for my father, I had just about every kind of job available in a small town. I was a busboy at a local restaurant, worked at a soda fountain, flipped hamburgers, and worked in a warehouse. These odd jobs, along with the example of my father's life, gave me a great sense of working people. Even today, while some people might consider me a snob, I continue to see myself as a very blue-collar kind of guy. I knew about hard work, so when it came time to burn hundred-hour weeks for years on end, first at ProServ, then at Falk Associates Management Enterprises (FAME), the company I started in 1992, I had an appreciation and a very clear understanding of the process. I wasn't afraid of work. I knew the price and I had no aversion to paying it.

To this day I try to be mindful of people who do things for me, because I know what it is to be a working person. I don't think I'm a better person because I've been successful financially. But growing up the way I did gave me an appreciation for what it takes to be successful.

My father would leave home every day at four in the morning and once a week he would drive into the city to buy meat. He worked long hours and when he was home, he was exhausted. But he was an old-school guy when it came to running the family. He was the only boy of five kids. He grew up believing that the father was the czar. What the father said was the way it went around the house.

When I was in my early teens, I rebelled against the idea of following rules simply because they were my father's. Later on, when I got into business, I never wanted to be the person who walks into a room and tells someone they have to pay a player because "I say so." I wanted to have a reason, a well thought out rationale for what I was asking that team or company to do. Even as a kid I enjoyed the kind of intellectual stimulation that comes with a good debate.

I never went to camp. There were no music lessons. We worked, played ball, and we were happy. That's all I knew. It wasn't until I got to Syracuse University and was around a bunch of rich kids that I had any idea of how modestly we lived. I was a good student but I didn't kill myself. I worked enough to get good grades but not hard enough to get extraordinary grades. Still, I was extremely goal oriented, no doubt because of my mother's influence. I always wanted to go to college and when I went to college I knew I wanted to go to law school. When I was in law school I wanted to get a job and become a partner in a law firm. There was a natural linear progression to my goals, and I always had a strong sense of where I wanted to go.

Still, from my perspective, being successful was relative. It meant having a nice house with a nice lawn, maybe an above-ground pool in the backyard. Even a fraction of what I have today was completely outside my reality growing up. I had one aunt who belonged to a country club in Westchester and we thought she was Warren Buffett. But I never longed for things I didn't have, because no one else I knew had anything, either. I wasn't even aware they existed.

But it wasn't all innocence and roses. My father was a compulsive gambler who never earned a lot of money. He believed the next horse race would be the one to take him away from the meat business. He essentially lost everything he had ever earned at the track. So my mother became the family rock. Often she worked two or even three jobs, teaching and tutoring. I didn't realize all that was going on in my father's life when I was young. But as a result of his experience, I am very conservative financially. If I lost thousands of dollars in Las Vegas, I'd be ready to jump off a bridge. I can afford it, but I am just very conscious of what happened to my father and the possibility that that bad seed could be inside me, too.

As a result, when it comes to negotiations I don't gamble, and I never bluff. I don't believe in bluffing. In the closed environment that we live in, if you bluff once and get called, then the next time no one will believe what you say. And one of the reasons I don't bluff is directly related to growing up with a riverboat gambler who couldn't afford to be one. I have never lost sight of that history.

Say What You Mean, and Mean What You Say

My background and the reality of the world I was entering at ProServ led me to adopt a very straightforward approach. It took me a while but I came to recognize the beauty in being blunt. While I always tried to be respectful and mindful of the other person's feelings, I was also firm and to the point. I wasn't anyone's psychologist or spiritual advisor. In the case of my clients, I was an important part of their team, the business advisor hired to ensure their future by maximizing the present. Sooner or later I was going to have to counsel them on something important. I couldn't do that if I hadn't established a relationship based on shooting straight every time. I applied the same approach to those with whom I negotiated on my clients' behalf.

I believe that kind of approach is more than effective. In a world defined by twenty-four hour connectivity and access to massive amounts of data, getting to the point honestly and efficiently is a matter of survival. Whether you are recruiting a player or selling software, I think it's critical to say what you mean and mean what you say. Negotiation often demands nuance but you had better be prepared to live by the tale you are telling. In my world, honesty and consistency are essential to long-term success. The other side absolutely needs to know what to expect.

That's how I tried to conduct myself with general managers, owners, and the media. Some appreciated the approach, and others did not. But I believe it was an important aspect of my relationship with all those groups, most importantly with my clients.

Still, it was an evolution. In the beginning I approached negotiations as a zero sum game: one side wins, one side loses. As I got into my late thirties, I realized that was a gross error in judgment. Both sides had to win; otherwise success was relative. I had been in the business ten years by the time I started working for Michael Jordan, but I was still relatively young and representing Michael was a very heady experience. Undoubtedly some of the success went to my head. I'm sure I was arrogant at times and I'm equally sure I offended people. Blunt isn't always beautiful, particularly when it comes with a hammer, a point I no doubt proved early on.

It bothered me when someone didn't like me. I thought I exhibited integrity. I was conscious of being professional at all times.

I didn't lash out at anyone or scream and yell to get my points across during negotiations. I didn't do the recruiting dances some agents did. I might have been blunt, perhaps a little too much so in the early years, but I always tried to be fair.

It took another slice of wisdom from John Thompson to set me straight.

"Grow up," he told me one day inside his office at Georgetown. "This is not a business of popularity. If you want to be liked, don't be an agent. It's not a business where you're going to be liked, especially with the kind of outrageous money you ask for on behalf of your clients. The people you are negotiating with are going to hate your guts. Be satisfied that they *respect* you. Just make sure your clients like you."

Getting comfortable with myself and defining my approach was critical to my evolution at ProServ. I had to tell players, and sometimes their parents, that what I believed did not match their expectations. I accepted the possibility that I might lose some business. In some cases it was pretty clear I was cutting off my nose to spite my face. But I believe that approach built on itself and eventually contributed materially to the success of FAME.

To be sure, there were some players who were so used to being placated that they didn't respond well to my asking, "Do you want me to massage your ego or your wallet?" But I knew they would appreciate the honesty down the road. If you can't be honest at the front end, then there's not much sense hanging around for the back end because there isn't likely to be one.

Tommy Amaker, now the head basketball coach at Harvard, won the Henry Iba Corinthian Award as the nation's top defensive player at Duke in 1987. He had been a four-year starter as a point guard but was considered a little undersized and lacking offensively by many NBA general managers. I had known Tommy since he was ten years old because my first basketball client, John Lucas, was like a surrogate father to him. I also knew he was meeting with just two agents: Lee Fentress of Advantage International, and me.

I met with Tommy and Coach K, Mike Krzyzewski, who interrupted my presentation to say, "Tommy knows a lot about you. Tell us where you think he'll go in the draft."

I said, "Coach, because of his size, I think he'll go somewhere between the mid-second and mid-third round. [The NBA draft had three rounds in the late 1980s and eventually went to just two rounds.] What's most important to Tommy is not the number he is drafted, but the team that drafts him. He needs to end up with a team that will be flexible with a player of his size without an inherent bias against a slender six-foot-one point guard."

I could see Tommy's jaw drop. While I wouldn't say something I didn't believe to be true to win a client, it was important to be tuned in to the player's emotions during a presentation. In this case, I had to make the choice to adapt to his disappointment or continue with my frank and well-researched analysis. I decided to confront the situation head-on.

"Tommy, you look crestfallen," I said. "I know you've met some other people. What was their consensus?"

"Well, the last guy I met told me he thought there was a good chance I could go to the Houston Rockets in the first round at number twenty," Amaker said.

"Come on," I said chuckling. "He really said that to you?"

Tommy didn't appreciate the levity and got very upset. "Why do you think it's so funny that I could go to Houston at number twenty?" he demanded.

"Well, I only think it's funny because Houston doesn't have a first-round pick this year."

It was a fact, but an uncomfortable one in that environment. And there was an additional complication: I was also trying to sign Muggsy Bogues, the five-foot-three Wake Forest guard. I had the inside track on Bogues by virtue of relationships, specifically between his coach at Dunbar High School in Baltimore, Bob Wade (later at the University of Maryland), and John Thompson. To that point, ProServ had signed two other former Dunbar players: Reggie Williams of Georgetown and Reggie Lewis of Northeastern. Fentress challenged Tommy: how could he sign with me, as a small guard, when I also was trying to sign Bogues.

One night Tommy called me at home. "Look," he said, "I really like you and I know how close your relationship is with John Lucas. John acts like you're his father. But I really have a problem. How can you represent both me and Muggsy?"

I told him it was not a problem.

"Well, Lee Fentress told me that he's not going after Muggsy," Tommy said. "He's just going after me."

"Well, that's interesting," I replied. "Tomorrow afternoon, Lee Fentress will be visiting Muggsy Bogues at Wake Forest to pitch him."

"How do you know that?" asked Amaker.

"I know because it's my business to know," I said. "Look, I'm not here to say anything negative about Lee. I don't have a problem that Lee's pitching Muggsy Bogues. I'm just surprised that he would tell you he's not trying to get him. Why don't you call Muggsy and ask him? Call him tomorrow afternoon and ask him what he's doing."

The next day Tommy called Muggsy at a little past noon. Lee was there, meeting with Bogues. As a result we would end up signing both players because we were honest, informed, and not afraid to be blunt and to the point. If you try really hard to manipulate the facts and to change your approach to please every potential client, or to meet every potential criticism, then you will lose it all in the long term. Consistency is the kicker to an investment of talent, focus, and attention to detail. Tommy Amaker was not going to hire me because I was trying to sign Muggsy Bogues. And there wasn't any assurance he would sign with me if I agreed not to sign Bogues. I chose to address that potential problem straight on and let the chips fall where they may. Over the long term, I believe that's comforting to those with whom you do business. It's done in the light of day and not in the shadows. In a complex world with unexpected or changing market conditions, people want to know what to expect from a relationship, particularly one tied to their financial well-being.

The upshot? Tommy Amaker was drafted in the third round of the 1987 NBA draft but he never played a day in the league. He went on to become an important assistant to Coach K at Duke, and later the head coach at Seton Hall, Michigan, and Harvard. He has also remained a very good friend. When the Wolverines were put on probation due to infractions that occurred under a previous coach, Tommy told the media his program would work its way through the problem.

"It's a long horse race," he said.

I didn't have to wonder where that came from.

Business Is Not a Popularity Contest

One of the unique aspects of professional basketball is the nature of the majority of the players' backgrounds. Many come from inner cities with difficult economic and social environments. Most of them arrive without even a modicum of financial sophistication, which isn't surprising. But many also come into the league with a financial yolk constructed of family and friends. More than one high-profile player has seen millions of dollars in nonrecoverable income evaporate thanks to a long line of relatives with their hands out—or in some cases with their hands deep into his pockets.

It's a difficult position for an agent charged with dispensing prudent economic advice for the long term. In some cases, the player has grown up in abject poverty, or something very close to it. Others qualify as lower middle class, but still grew up without most of the basic goods and services even middle-class families take for granted. So when a young player and his family suddenly see a three-year guaranteed contract worth $1 million a year, the numbers appear much larger than what they really are for a person with an extremely limited number of high-earning years. Houses cost a lot more money than the down payment. Cars come with insurance demands. And with that kind of income, significant tax issues might arise, all of which can contribute to financial problems.

At FAME we created the most sophisticated money management practices in the industry. Even when a player was being squeezed by a mother, brother, or someone else in his extended group, we worked to set aside "untouchable" assets designed to be beyond the reach of anyone, sometimes even the player, though of course that was never truly possible.

At the same time, I never lost sight of my responsibility to the player and his future regardless of the outside pressures on his money. In two cases, among others, that responsibility required me to be blunt to the point of severing high-profile relationships. One of those involved New York Knicks guard Stephon Marbury, and the other player was Denver Nuggets guard Allen Iverson. These men, the No. 4 and No. 1 picks in the 1996 draft, respectively, parted company with FAME because of a similar set of issues.

We represented Iverson when he came out of Georgetown and we were able to get him a $50 million, ten-year shoe deal with Reebok. Other than Jordan's deal with Nike, the Iverson-Reebok relationship was one of the most successful in the history of the shoe business. Our business relationship ended three years later over money his mother wanted for first-class plane tickets to Seattle. A lot of Allen's money had gone to various members of his circle, an amount that concerned my partner, Curtis Polk, and me. Curtis was focused on doing his job well by protecting and preserving assets amid the normal wrangling and tug-of-war that goes on in the families of players over money. Allen's first contract with Philadelphia was about to end and a much larger deal hadn't yet kicked in when his mother called demanding that we release money to pay for the tickets or she would insist Allen fire us. We told Allen that given his financial situation at the time it wasn't prudent to be dispensing additional cash to pay for the tickets. On Monday he fired us.

Normally when an individual is fired in business, particularly in a public forum, there are reasons given for the termination. It might be lack of performance, dishonesty, or insubordination. In Allen's case, he was always positive about our relationship because he knew there was no good reason for us to have been terminated other than that we were too tight with his money. Despite the fact that he was very young and people questioned some of his behavior, I thought he showed a great deal of class, maturity, and loyalty by keeping the details of our separation private. He could have said he didn't get enough attention or that I was spending too much time with Patrick.

People criticize Iverson for all kinds of things, but I have always found him to be a very good person. He's loyal and has remained warm and friendly. I have told him many times how much I appreciated the classy way in which he handled the separation, though I think we could have done a lot more for him as he ascended into superstardom.

Marbury's case was quite the opposite. I resigned after Stephon turned down another marketing deal worth millions of dollars, money that he never saw. We had brought him nearly $10 million in deals over an eighteen-month period, and he complained that we did a poor job marketing him. To put that into perspective, there probably weren't ten players in the NBA in 2008 that made as much money off the court as Marbury turned down in 1998–99.

As I've said, I thought Allen showed a tremendous level of maturity and class in how he responded to our divorce. Marbury, from whom I asked for the separation, felt compelled to rail publicly against us. He even tried to call a press conference to announce he was firing us, but it was nixed by his team, the New Jersey Nets. In retrospect, those situations provide some insight into the maturity levels of those two players, a difference that is mirrored by their performance on the court.

I still consider Stephon a great talent who works extremely hard. I'm sure there was a natural competition between Stephon and Allen. They effectively played the same position, came out the same year, and very quickly became proven players at the NBA level.

We didn't represent Marbury when he came into the league and we didn't negotiate his first shoe deal with a company called "AND1," which paid him $400,000 to $500,000 a year.

Stephon called me one day and said he would be interested in having us represent him. By the time we got together, it was 1998 and the shoe market had softened considerably in two years. Still, he expected us to get him $4 million to $5 million a year for his next shoe deal. In fact, the market had softened to the point that no company was willing to pay even $1 million a year in 1998. I even told him I wasn't good enough to get him that kind of money in the prevailing atmosphere at the time. But I happened to be very close to AND1's president, Seth Berger. I told him Marbury had been their guy and people still connected him to the company. In fact, Stephon had been without a shoe deal since his first contract with the company ended. We eventually convinced AND1 to re-sign Stephon for $8 million over five years with not only a royalty on sales of several models of his autographed shoes, but also an equity stake in the entire company.

Marbury turned down the deal because he still thought the "real" market with him was at least $3 million a year. He really believed that if he waited a little longer someone would come across with $3 million to $4 million, if not more. I tried to explain the math as it applied to turning down the deal. If he waited a year, he'd have to get $8 million over four years, or a 25 percent increase over what AND1 was offering. The longer he waited, the more he had to make each year, which was a gamble with no upside.

He didn't budge. At the same time, Marbury's sister was managing a website called "Starbury." We negotiated a deal for another website that would pay Stephon $125,000 a year. That too was turned down because the exclusivity of the rights would have obliterated the "Starbury" site. So we went back to the company and made the rights nonexclusive. We not only increased the deal to $150,000 a year but also provided for a salary for Marbury's sister to manage both sites.

When we sought Stephon's approval for the revised website deal, he asked me to speak to his sister. She asked me if I was knowledgeable about the Internet. I had just come back from spending a day with Steve Ballmer, Microsoft's chief operating officer, who today is the company's chief executive. I could have made a billion dollars selling DVDs of that meeting. Steve had an incredible vision and insight into e-commerce and just about every other aspect of where the Internet was headed.

"I know very little," I said. "I'm in kindergarten trying to learn. I'm reading as much as I can and I'm meeting with some of the top people in the business. But no, I do not consider myself an expert at all."

Then she asked me if I understood the value of Stephon's website rights. "Yes," I told her. "They are worth between $125,000 and $150,000 a year. We've been negotiating with a company for six months and that's the market."

She responded emphatically, "No. Those rights are worth billions." I asked if she misspoke and really meant millions. No, she said, billions. I rarely lose my temper, but in this case I became incredibly frustrated. I was trying to figure out how to respond respectfully while making her realize just how unreasonable she was being.

Finally I said, "You know, there is a company in Redmond, Washington, named Microsoft. And you should call a guy there named Bill Gates because those people are up there scratching their heads trying to figure out how to get the commercial value out of e-commerce when all they need is for you to give them a call and explain it to them."

Two days later I resigned. Occasionally there are family situations that make dealing with players difficult. Prior to this episode, and to his credit, Stephon had largely insulated me from his family. But now I really felt he was losing valuable opportunities and significant dollars because Stephon was not comfortable turning down his family.

I wrote him a very personal letter explaining that I respected his talent and his work ethic and that I would like to maintain a positive relationship. At the same time I was frustrated and felt that I was wasting my time. Therefore I was resigning immediately. I told him that if he wanted to continue with me he could call me in the next seven days and agree to make fundamental changes in our working relationship. I sent the letter via FedEx on Friday for delivery the next Monday morning.

That Monday, writers from the *New York Times* and the *New York Post* called me for my reaction to being fired by Stephon Marbury. They told me he had called them to explain he was scheduling a press conference to announce he was firing me. I told the writers it was impossible to be fired since I had resigned the previous Friday. Ultimately, he signed with Steve & Barry's to produce a shoe that sold for $14.98 at retail. The deal received considerable publicity, but in July 2008, Steve & Barry's filed for bankruptcy.

The Truth, the Whole Truth, and Nothing but the Truth

It's necessary to understand and respect the pressures on high-profile people in any industry. With professional athletes, the pressures are magnified by the daily accounting to which they're subjected in the media. I appreciate the stresses that come with millions of dollars and the desire to take care of as many people as possible. Along the way, we make accommodations because blood is thicker than anything else, even money. But in the end, I believe being honest, even brutally so sometimes, creates the best atmosphere for long-term success.

In 1989, I traveled to Norman, Oklahoma, to meet with a top NBA draft prospect named Stacey King. Stacey had been a high-scoring all-American forward at the University of Oklahoma and was considered one of the most versatile power forwards in the country. Stacey brought his fiancée, Lisa, to the meeting and I brought one of my partners, Mike Higgins. The meeting went well. We discussed our track record of representing the most first-round draft choices and lottery picks. Stacey and Lisa peppered us with a lot of questions. At the conclusion of the meeting, I had a very good feeling about our opportunity to sign Stacey when he, Detective Colombo–style, popped a question from left field. He asked me how many times I had seen him play during his college career. I replied, "I've never seen you play live, but I've seen Oklahoma a number of times in nationally televised broadcasts."

Stacey was immediately put off and challenged me. "How can you represent me if you haven't watched me play?" I parried, "If you sign with me and get drafted in the lottery, what would you like for me to be doing for the next year, working on your business or spending ten weeks in Norman scouting the next great junior at the University of Oklahoma?" Stacey was stunned because the logic of my argument flew directly in the face of the emotional appeal every other agent had made to him—that he would be the top dog in their stable, and that they had followed his career virtually from the crib. I'm not certain that in the early years of my career I would have had the confidence to be as blunt with Stacey as I was in 1989. Nor am I confident that that approach would have worked effectively with a lot of today's ultrapampered young players. However, on that day blunt was truly beautiful and Stacey signed with us right on the spot.

Several years later I met a very personable, engaging young man in Cleveland named Desmond Howard. Desmond was an electrifying wide receiver and kick returner for the University of Michigan and on one of his many long touchdown runs he struck the Heisman Trophy pose in the end zone, a precursor to his winning the award that season at the Downtown Athletic Club in New York. Desmond's godmother was a secretary to a very senior partner at the law firm Jones, Day in Cleveland.

Jones, Day is one of the largest, if not *the* largest law firm in the United States. And Dick Sayler was a very senior partner who agreed to screen agents for Desmond. In performing his due diligence, Dick spoke to owners of teams in the NFL as well as the NBA and a number of them had urged him to hire me as Desmond's representative. We had a meeting in Dick's office in Cleveland that went very well.

However, at the very end of the meeting, Desmond popped "the question." In virtually every interview with a potential client who would be drafted in the top ten picks in the draft, the player would invariably ask, "Where do you think I'll be drafted?" It's similar to the question the same recruit probably asked prospective coaches when he was coming out of high school. "Do you think I'll start?" Heisman Trophy or not, only a handful of wide receivers have ever been selected with the No. 1 pick in the NFL draft. Ironically, the year before, Raghib "Rocket" Ismail, another spectacular wide receiver from the University of Notre Dame, would have been selected No. 1, but his agents negotiated him right into the Canadian Football League.

I knew that if I told Desmond he'd be drafted No. 1, or even No. 2 or No. 3, we could shake hands and go home as the representatives of the top wide receiver in the country. Unfortunately, it was my best judgment that Desmond would be drafted between Nos. 4 and 6. Despite my obvious desire to close the deal and my growing fondness for Desmond, his mother, godmother, and Dick Sayler, I gave him my most candid opinion about his draft position—that he'd be selected between the fourth and sixth pick.

Predictably, I received a call from Dick Sayler a week later telling me that Desmond had selected Leigh Steinberg, based on Leigh's track record of representing more players selected No. 1 in the NFL draft over the previous ten years. Leigh is both a friend and one of the few agents I have always respected. When the smoke cleared, Desmond decided to let Leigh negotiate his NFL contract and to let FAME handle his off-the-field marketing activities. On draft day, the Washington Redskins selected Desmond Howard with the fifth pick in the NFL draft. It's hard to describe the feelings of disappointment when you make a prediction that is 100 percent accurate and instead of being rewarded for your insight, you are penalized for your candor. However, the story was just beginning to unfold on draft day.

The Washington Redskins had three all-pro receivers—Art Monk, Gary Clark, and Ricky Sanders. Since Desmond did not go No. 1 or even in the top three, he challenged Leigh about the type of contract he could expect from Washington. Unfortunately, the Washington Redskins didn't feel the need to pay their rookie receiver more money than the four players drafted ahead of him, particularly when they already had three outstanding wide receivers who had played in the Pro Bowl.

For the next seven weeks negotiations between Desmond and the Redskins were stalled, and the growing discontent for Desmond by Redskins fans created a very significant obstacle to our efforts to market him in the Washington market. Eventually Dick Sayler called and asked Leigh and me to come to Cleveland to evaluate both the contract negotiations and their impact on Desmond's marketing activities. Despite my tremendous disappointment that Desmond picked Leigh primarily because Leigh answered "the question" in a more pleasing way than I did, I did not feel it was professional in "crunch time" to undermine Leigh's efforts to finalize the best deal possible for Desmond. And so when Sayler asked me if the Redskins negotiations were interfering with our marketing efforts, I explained that the marketing income Desmond could expect paled in comparison to the amount of his football signing bonus and salary, therefore Desmond should give Leigh the latitude he needed to negotiate the best possible contract.

In the end, Desmond got a contract that was slotted between what the fourth pick received ahead of him and what the sixth pick received behind him. By contrast, Stacey King, drafted by the Chicago Bulls—who already had a very talented young power forward on the roster named Horace Grant—received a greater contract than the one J.R. Reid obtained from the expansion Charlotte Hornets, one pick ahead of him.

The moral of the story is to try not to put yourself in a position where you lose important business opportunities. But when you are confronted with "the question"—and in business, prior to shaking hands to close a deal, there almost always is "the question"—don't sugarcoat the answer. Establishing the foundation for a long-term relationship requires that you let the client know that if you are not strong enough to stand up to his emotional needs and maintain your integrity, then you can't possibly do so in the undertow of business. And if you are on the other side asking "the question," be strong enough to accept an honest answer.

FALK'S FUNDAMENTALS

Say what you mean, and mean what you say.

If the truth is hard to find, players will run *from* the coach instead of running *for* the coach.

Business is not a popularity contest.

In the final analysis, it's not what they *want* to hear. It's what they *need* to hear.

The truth, the whole truth, and nothing but the truth.

The truth is the most powerful medium of persuasion. "Actually sir, it's not *like* a Xerox. It *is* a Xerox."

FOUR

See the Whole Court

Lawyers are trained to learn precedents because in law the past is prologue to the future. Yet in business, while it is nice to know the relevant history, you can become mired in precedents. It's possible to become so stuck in the past that you are unable to adapt to changing market forces, or become blind to the signposts showing where a particular issue is headed. People with foresight are able to see where markets are going and seize opportunity. In our business, we were the best at seeing where salaries were headed because we did not project past results into the future in an effort to determine where the market might go. We created the market by recognizing emerging forces that were changing the existing structure.

There's an old saying, "Some people read the news, some people make the news, and some people are the news." I always wanted

THE BALD TRUTH   **99**

to be the person making the news. In the process, I sometimes became the news, which can happen when you disavow the existing paradigm and seek your own path.

Don't Just See What Is Happening; Anticipate What Will Happen.

What makes Bill Gates who he is? Is he just intellectually more gifted than everyone else? No. He saw what was coming and got out ahead of the curve. In our business, as the salary structure in the NBA rose unabated year after year it became clear that I had to protect my players from signing contracts that could quickly put them behind the market. I created the concept of an opt-out clause that allowed players to opt out of long-term deals and become free agents. As a result, the No. 5 pick in the 1994 NBA draft, Juwan Howard, made $42 million more than the first pick, Glenn Robinson, in the same draft. I advised Alonzo Mourning to turn down the first $100 million contract in professional sports because there was a better deal to be done a year later and I negotiated Michael Jordan's final two contracts for an amount not likely to be surpassed. We sold FAME in 1998 because we could feel the winds changing due in part to flawed and ultimately failed collective bargaining negotiations between the National Basketball Players Association (NBPA) and the league.

In basketball parlance it's called seeing the whole court. Great point guards are able to see what is happening while simultaneously anticipating what is going to happen. That's different than simply reacting. The same principle applies to business.

Limitations Are Obstacles, Not Barriers

In 1979, when Magic Johnson led the Lakers to the NBA championship over Philadelphia, the finals were not broadcast live. Instead the games were tape delayed. It was a reflection of the strong concern in the broadcast world and on Madison Avenue that the NBA was "too black" and that the league had a very serious issue with a large number of players using drugs.

From an economic standpoint there were twenty-three NBA teams at the time and as many as six were on the edge of bankruptcy. Larry O'Brien was the commissioner, and the general counsel to the league was a bright young lawyer named David Stern. Larry Fleisher, the executive director of the NBPA, sat down with David and they agreed on a salary cap to limit the escalation of salaries and to protect the integrity of the league. The cap went into effect in 1982 for the six franchises with the highest payrolls. In that first year, the salary cap was $3.2 million for each team's entire roster. There were exceptions to the cap that enabled the team to replace a disabled player, for example. And teams could also exceed the cap to sign and retain their own players when they became free agents.

But the salary cap gave the patina of stability to the league. Larry Fleisher, as head of the union, agreed to the salary cap because he was focused on protecting the 286 player jobs. If the six economically challenged teams were to fold, that would result in the loss of seventy-two players' jobs. Fleisher balanced the restriction that the league was asking for against the danger that if he didn't grant the restriction, he would win the battle but lose 25 percent of his jobs. It was a savvy decision. A year later the cap was in place for every team.

The salary cap represented a ceiling on total team salaries, or rather a speed limit. I recognized very early on that no one drives the speed limit. Everyone goes seven to ten miles per hour over, or at whatever speed they think they can get away with. That same psychology applied to the cap because there were exceptions to the rules. It wasn't a hard cap, so a team could re-sign its own players even if its salaries exceeded the cap. In addition, if one player got hurt, the team could exceed the cap to sign a replacement.

To me the cap represented a guideline, and its increase provided a barometer for the degree to which salaries were going to rise. At the same time, I understood that salaries weren't going to increase uniformly. The best players were going to gobble up the largest portion of any increase. I came to view the cap as an indication of what the average salaries might become and, since our players were almost all above average, it became an interesting way to determine the market. Most agents looked at the cap as a constraint, or as an end point. We looked at it as a starting point.

In any regulated industry, smart people find gaps in the code and exploit them. The NBA went from an unfettered system where players had no limits on the amount of money they could earn, to one with an artificial constraint. My objective was to figure out how to take this constraint and make it work for my clients. With an economics background, I recognized the need to know the cap as well as anyone in the game on either side of the table.

Other than Gary Bettman, who managed the cap until 1993,

when he became commissioner of the National Hockey League, I might have been the only other person who had the cap memorized. Most agents didn't understand the salary cap even with the book in front of them, but I thought it was analogous to being an expert on the tax code. That person is able to make transactions others cannot because of specialized knowledge. I knew that to be a good agent I had to be a walking, talking expert before I could learn how to maneuver through the complexity of the salary cap.

Every year we would ask the league for exceptions that Bettman would ultimately deny on the basis of the collective bargaining agreement. I would offer to arbitrate the issue because I knew the worst thing that could occur would be that I was wrong. But if we succeeded, we would create a new exception to the cap. I had an entire notebook full of contract provisions we negotiated that the league permitted, though Bettman refused to allow them to become precedent for future deals.

The salary cap was designed to uniformly limit salaries at a time (1982) when several of the twenty-three teams were in danger of folding. The need for the cap was real. At the same time, the apparent limitations it created represented a challenge to a competitive person like me. I had to figure out a way to negotiate that minefield. In time, we became very adept at doing just that.

I represent Mike Krzyzewski, who is not only the head coach of Duke but was also the national coach for the 2008 U.S. men's Olympic basketball team. Mike is a gifted motivational speaker. Recently, I attended one of his appearances for Morgan Stanley in New York. He emphasized that successful individuals look at lim-

THE BALD TRUTH   103

itations as obstacles, not as barriers. They use their skills and creativity to overcome limitations that represent true boundaries to less talented people.

Later that afternoon, Mike thanked me for successfully concluding negotiations on a deal for him that I had spent a lot of time working on. He complimented me on the outcome, which exceeded his expectations. I was both flattered and amused and told him we had followed the philosophy of limitations he had outlined in his Morgan Stanley speech.

As someone fascinated by human nature, I have always recognized the importance of causal relationships. Consider the work of Anthony Downs, an economist at the Brookings Institution who studied traffic patterns and developed the theory that traffic expands to its maximum density. If a one-lane road becomes so clogged with traffic that the state decides to expand it into a two-lane road, people using other one-lane roads reroute to the new road and almost immediately it becomes as congested as it was as a one-lane road. No matter how many lanes are added to that road, traffic will expand to its limits. People will continue to be attracted to the road for any number of reasons: the perception that the road is better built, or that it provides more direct access, or because there are more services along the way.

The same dynamic can be found in virtually any artificially created limitation, including the salary cap. Take speed limits for example. There is a particular psychological approach to a speed limit set at 65 miles an hour. A driver understands that if he goes 70, then he probably won't get a ticket because he's traveling only five miles an hour over the limit. He doesn't think about slowing down to 60 miles an hour to protect himself from exceeding the speed limit. Most drivers are focused on how far over that limit they can go before it becomes a problem. Our nature is to push the envelope. That's who we are. So if you are an owner trying to win a championship, or an agent trying to negotiate a contract, you have to realize that a soft cap is not an absolute limit. I had to figure out how to safely allow my clients to drive 75 or 80 when the speed limit was 65. To me that's what business is all about. It's not as much a mathematical relationship as it is one of human nature. The law is intended to make sure we don't go faster than 65, but even those enforcing the law understand drivers are going to exceed the limit. The psychological reaction to artificial constraints and the human interaction with all these regulations is intriguing. The challenge became coming up with a rational, logical justification for speeding within the psychological behavior patterns of cap management.

One of the great aspects of professional basketball is that the business is so small. There are only fifteen players on each of the thirty teams and of those players, only a few are at the top end. We had the most first-round picks of anyone for twenty-five years, so we worked with the same owners over and over again. With the Bulls one year we might be dealing with management for Michael Jordan. The next year it might be Stacey King, the next year John Paxson. This situation was the great equalizer because neither side could afford to get over on the other. I wasn't interested in getting over on anyone anyway because that wasn't in the best interest of my clients. I wanted to be recognized as the best lawyer with the best brief in support of my case. I wanted to present the best insight into the facts, to the point that my argument was incontrovertible.

I've always considered myself a combination lawyer and economist, but I never considered myself a magician. The object of my approach was never to fool anybody. I searched for ways to persuade the other side to see the case as I did. For example, we pegged the growth of salaries to the growth in the salary cap. That allowed us to look into the future and determine a player's value and the appropriate length of any contract he signed. Why did Stacey King make 67 percent more in 1989 than Hersey Hawkins made in the same draft slot a year earlier? We were seeing the whole court and that allowed us to stay ahead of the curve.

Intuition and Ingenuity Define the Road Ahead

No one wants to make a mistake, but you can't be afraid of making one, either. I looked at where I thought the market would be and made my decisions based on the best analysis of the situation. If I was wrong, then I had to live with the decision. Most people get stuck in the past because they think it's the safest and most accurate guide to the future. That was just too mechanical for me. If it was possible to simply enter five years of salaries into a computer to determine the proper contract for a player today, then they didn't need me. Negotiation has never been a perfect science, which is one reason it's often called an art. Statistics and data provide guidelines, but intuition and ingenuity define the road that leads to where things are going.

Though we didn't sign him, I was a huge fan of Grant Hill

when he came out of Duke in 1994. The Detroit Pistons made him the third pick in the NBA draft. Anyone who followed basketball at the time knew the Pistons had fallen on hard times. Accordingly there was no question Grant would be the star of that team the minute he put on the uniform. There also was no question that the longer the contract term for a rookie of Grant's talents, the longer he'd have to wait to become a free agent and the less money he would make over the life of his career. In theory the best deal for Grant Hill would have been a one-year deal for the highest achievable salary and immediate free agency. On the other hand, and as turned out to be the case for Grant, an agent also has to consider the risk of injury.

With that in mind, the perfect deal would have been a long-term contract with the right to terminate the deal at the end of the first year and become a free agent. As it turned out, in 1996, veteran players obtained unrestricted free agency. As a rookie, Grant had signed a nine-year deal that didn't allow him to terminate until after his sixth season. The failure to negotiate an earlier out made it impossible for the contract to reflect the player's value in the market.

It wasn't hard to see that Grant was going to put up big numbers and improve the team. Ironically, the first pick in the 1994 draft, Glenn Robinson, had a ten-year contract and the second pick, Jason Kidd, had a nine-year deal; neither had early termination rights. The fourth pick was Donyell Marshall, who had an eight-year deal with a one-year option for a ninth year and no right to terminate. The fifth pick, Juwan Howard, who was our client, signed an eleven-year deal fully guaranteed with the right to terminate after the second season.

Who became the highest-paid player in the draft after nine seasons? Juwan Howard, by an average of $5 million a year. That's $45 million more than each of the four players selected ahead of him made. I knew we had to have enough protection built into Juwan's deal to cover him in the event of injury, but I also knew that the longer the contract kept him from free agency, the more it worked against his best interests.

In Grant's case no one saw the whole court. Rather than pay a 4 percent fee for our services, he selected a Washington lawyer, Lon Babby, who charged by the hour. As a result, Grant saved approximately $1 million in agent fees, a decision that cost him more than $45 million in salary during his first nine years in the league.

A year later I negotiated the first $100 million contact in the history of professional sports and then advised Alonzo Mourning to turn it down. Charlotte offered him a $99 million extension for eleven years, which came out to $9 million a year. Alonzo had two years remaining on his rookie contract so all told the new deal became worth in excess of $100 million. I really believed that as an unrestricted free agent one year later, he'd do even better. And he did. Alonzo ended up making $105 million for seven years, virtually the same amount of money for six fewer years.

There are no magic buttons to push in business. You have to be able to read the data and understand the facts. Most importantly, however, you have to understand the human nature dynamic. If we could put data into a computer and learn how to manage a business, then every business would be successful. But data by nature is old information. At the pace of today's world, even the best data might not reflect what is actually happening in a given market. So what do you hang your hat on when both sides have the same data? How do you present a case where the other side feels your argument is logical, rational, and fair? One answer is to use data as a guide while looking at all the other factors. Does the other side want to make a quick deal? Does the owner want to be friends with the player? I love facts, but at the end of the day they are just signposts. It always comes down to human nature. It's not a matter of manipulating these factual elements as much as it is recognizing the relationship between the data and what is actually happening in the marketplace.

After Patrick Ewing and Michael Jordan entered the NBA back-to-back in 1984 and 1985, we began to deal with owners almost exclusively. Patrick's rookie deal made me a marked man. I don't think owners were necessarily angry, but I was no longer operating under their radar. The owners wanted more control over what they were paying, as opposed to leaving those decisions to general managers.

Patrick's situation helped me to formulate a thought process. Traditionally an agent sat down with a general manager and negotiated a player's contract. The general manager was an expert in talent evaluation. He explained how the team evaluated the player's strengths and weaknesses and how that player fit into the team. Based on the general manager's evaluation, the team had an opinion as to what it should pay the player. With very few exceptions the average agent isn't competent enough to debate a player's skill level with a talent expert. I knew that if I allowed the negotiations to be predicated on talent, I was at a competitive disadvantage from the start. I never wanted to negotiate based on talent and I realized I didn't have to. The team's expert selected my client. My job was to attach a value to my client on that team.

In 1989 the Los Angeles Clippers selected Duke University's Danny Ferry with the second pick in the draft. In our business, the coaches at top schools like Duke, Georgetown, North Carolina, Indiana, Kentucky, and Kansas controlled the player-agent signing process. The coaches invited four or five qualified representatives to make their case. Those coaches—Mike Krzyzewski, John Thompson, Dean Smith, Bob Knight, Rick Pitino, and later on, Roy Williams—controlled college basketball. Agents didn't recruit the top players. They didn't write letters to the players or call their parents. The coach told agents to leave the players completely alone. If an agent called a player, that agent was out. And, unlike today, there was very little influence from the Amateur Athletic Union summer programs.

The AAU has been around for decades. It manages teams and leagues with players who compete without compensation. But in the last fifteen to twenty years, summer basketball under the auspices of the AAU has exploded in large measure because of the sponsorships provided by the shoe companies. Instead of a young player playing twenty to twenty-five games with his high school team, then heading off to college, he now might play as many as one hundred games a year, the vast majority of them with an AAU team. Teams travel all over the country, and the coaches recruit players much as a college coach recruits a high school player. Because of the sponsorships, AAU coaches have assumed in most cases a much greater degree of authority over the top players compared to the players' high school coaches. The result is that AAU coaches have become very influential in the college recruiting process.

For example, I met a young African American agent a few years ago and I asked him to give me his perspective on the AAU process. He told me a story about a player in New York named Charlie Villanueva (whom the Toronto Raptors subsequently selected with the seventh pick in the 2005 NBA draft). His AAU coach wanted Charlie to attend the University of Connecticut for one or two years, and then go to the NBA. But the AAU coach knew that Connecticut's Hall of Fame coach, Jim Calhoun, was represented by an agent named Jeff Schwartz, who also represents NBA players.

Like many college coaches who have agents who also represent NBA players, Calhoun obviously felt Jeff had done a good job for him and he recommended that most of his players consider Jeff. So this AAU coach called up Calhoun and said, "I'd like to give you Charlie Villanueva for one year. But I have a problem. I know at the end of that time you are going to recommend Charlie sign with Jeff Schwartz. I don't want him to go with Schwartz. I want him to go with an agent I select. I'm going to give you Villanueva, but if you have him go with Jeff Schwartz, you will never get another player from my program."

If that AAU coach had said this to Coach K or John Thompson, the response would have been: "Thank you. I hear what you are saying and I have only two words for you. Screw you. Don't tell me how to run my program. If you want to send a player here, send him. If you don't want to send him, then don't." Instead Calhoun took the player and apparently told him that he could go with any agent in the country except one—Jeff Schwartz. According to the story, Calhoun didn't want to incur the wrath of this AAU coach. That's the kind of power that some of the AAU coaches have assumed.

I think the AAU has some good aspects to it, taking kids off the streets in the summer and putting them in organized competition. But the political influences have become preponderant.

Danny Ferry came from Washington, D.C. He attended DeMatha Catholic High School in Hyattsville, Maryland, and played for coaching legend Morgan Wootten. We had represented almost every player from DeMatha starting in the mid-1970s, including Adrian Dantley, Kenny Carr, Hawkeye Whitney, Sidney Lowe, and Adrian Branch. And I had known Danny's father, Bob, who for years had been the general manager of the Washington Bullets, now known as the Wizards. Obviously I was dealing with a uniquely sophisticated parent. We had everything in the world going for us, but Danny wouldn't commit. Danny knew all the signs were pointing in one direction but he wanted to make his own decision.

Finally, two weeks after the draft he picked me. But Danny didn't want to play for the Clippers. Even before the draft, Bob had asked me to call the owner of the Clippers, Donald Sterling, and dissuade him from drafting Danny. I had a good relationship with Sterling even though he could be difficult.

I told Donald, "I just want you to know that Danny does not want to play for the Clippers. No disrespect."

He said, "David, if he just came to Los Angeles and sat on the balcony of my office overlooking Beverly Hills with the sunshine, the movie stars . . . He'd love it here."

I explained that Danny grew up in Bowie, Maryland, a small

blue-collar town. He's a very low-key, middle-class kind of guy. Ironically Danny fit better in Cleveland than he would have in Los Angeles. He came from solid stock and Danny didn't like the instability of a Clippers franchise that seemed to be in the lottery every year.

Meanwhile, Bob had received an invitation from a very wealthy Italian businessman named Raul Gardini, who owned the second-largest company in Italy, Gruppo Ferruzzi. He was fifty-six years old and one of the richest and most admired industrialists in Italy at the time. Gardini invited Bob and Danny to London, flying them over on the Concorde. Gardini explained that he owned the newspaper in Rome, *Il Messaggero,* and that he wanted to buy the local basketball team as well. I had signed a lot of players to teams in Italy. Dean Smith had created a system in which he recommended a top player like Phil Ford, who was the player of the year, and then "suggested" that you agree to also help a second-tier player like Tom Zaliagaris, who was a seventh-round pick. The price you paid for Dean's recommendation of the player you wanted to represent was helping a lesser player he needed to place in Europe. I always respected Dean for going to the trouble to protect all of his players, not just the high-profile stars headed to the NBA.

In talking to Gardini, Bob outlined a deal for Danny—five years at $2 million a year with the right to get out of the deal at the end of every season.

Until 1989, I would use Italy or one of the other Western European countries as a fallback during negotiations, but the money just wasn't there. And you were never completely confident your client would ever get paid by some of the foreign teams. But there were perks. Teams would provide a car, housing, a meal allowance, etc. In Italy, American players often lived in beautiful palazzi. And, unlike the grueling pace of the NBA, they played three games every two weeks, so the money was relative.

With Bob having outlined the basics of a deal with Gardini, I spent the rest of the summer trying to convince Donald Sterling to trade Danny's rights. Donald is an extremely optimistic guy. Despite the fact that the Clippers to that point had a very poor record, Donald looked at the sun shining in Beverly Hills and couldn't understand why guys didn't want to play for his team.

Finally, the day of reckoning came. I had been trying to engineer a trade to San Antonio or Cleveland because those were two teams that really liked Danny. But neither one could come to terms with Sterling. At the time, we represented Kenny Norman, who was the Clippers' starting small forward, and Charles Smith, who was the team's starting power forward. The Clippers had drafted Smith as the No. 3 pick the year before to play power forward and Norman was the best player on the team. Danny really would have been superfluous. He wasn't going to play center and there wasn't any room for him at either forward spot.

One day I got a call from the American representative of Gruppo Ferruzzi. He was an Italian gentleman named Enzo DeChiara who lived in Washington, D.C. Enzo asked if he could come over to the office to close the deal with *Il Messaggero,* which became the name of Gardini's team in the Italian League.

I knew we were playing the "four corners," which was essentially a stall tactic Dean Smith invented at North Carolina. We were trying to slow down the process in hopes of working out a trade that would satisfy the Clippers. Enzo came over about 7 P.M. I had made a laundry list of every perk I could imagine, from cooks, maids, bodyguards, and tickets on the Concorde for his parents, to disability insurance, life insurance, cars, and drivers. Given the list, I figured it would take weeks to get anything finalized, which in turn would buy us time. Enzo came in and said, "What is it going to take to close this deal?"

"Well," I responded, "you offered a house, but we'd like to have a palazzo. You've offered him a meal allowance, but we'd like to have two chefs." On and on I went and all Enzo said was "No problem."

After about thirty minutes I had exhausted the list. The only thing he turned down was a meal allowance because he had agreed to the chefs. In less than an hour I ran out of things to say. So Enzo asked the question: "Do we have a deal?"

I told him I had to call Danny. I left the room to make the call and Bob answered the phone. I told him about the meeting, the fact that I had asked for the moon and they had thrown in the stars as well. We either had to say yes or no. The clock had run out. As it turned out, Danny was on a date and unavailable. I thought, Thank God.

I went back into the other office and told Enzo that Danny wasn't available. I said, "You have been very generous, but let me sleep on it and get back to you in a day or two." Enzo looked at me. Then he asked, "Do you know who Raul Gardini is?"

I told him that I had heard of Mr. Gardini, but I really didn't know much about him.

"Let me tell you a little story about Raul Gardini," offered

Enzo. "Raul is called the peasant billionaire of Italy. There were two sisters from the Ferruzzi family and Raul and his brother-in-law, Carlo, married the sisters. Raul became an extremely wealthy and respected businessman. One day, he took a trip to Venice. He walked by this gorgeous villa and he thought to himself, I would like to buy this villa.

"He does some homework and Mr. Gardini finds the owner of the house. He returns to Venice, meets the owner, and on the spot offers to buy the house. The owner tells him the house really isn't for sale. It had been in the family for many years, he said, and it's just not for sale. So Raul did some more homework and he finds out the house is actually owned by an insurance company controlled by the owner of the house. There was a very complex financial structure, but the house was actually owned by the company.

"So Raul visits the owner in Venice and once again offers to buy the house. The owner tells Raul that while he knows who Mr. Gardini is and that while he appreciated Mr. Gardini's interest, the house was a family heirloom and it would never be sold. Mr. Gardini said, 'Well, in that case, I'd like to buy your insurance company.'

"The man says, 'That's very nice but the insurance company is not for sale.' Mr. Gardini assures him he would make a very generous offer. The man says, 'I appreciate that and I know you are very wealthy, but again, the company is not for sale.' So Raul says, 'I would like to offer you $325 million for your company.' The company must have been worth at least $100 million less and the man was no doubt astounded. So he says, 'Mr. Gardini, that's an extremely generous offer. Why don't you give me some time to think about it and I will get back to you.' Mr. Gardini replies, 'Take as much time as you need. My offer is good for twenty-two minutes.' "

With that the story was over. I looked at Enzo and said, "Is there a parallel between this story and our negotiations with Danny Ferry?"

"Yes," he said. "As a matter of fact it's now nine o'clock. I am leaving on vacation tonight and I have to tell Mr. Gardini we either have a deal or we do not have a deal by midnight. If we don't have a deal, there will be no hard feelings. But this offer will not stay open beyond midnight. Why don't you sign the contract with Danny's power of attorney?"

"I'd love to sign for Danny," I said, "but I don't have the power of attorney."

So we agreed I would sign the contract for Danny and that I had twenty-four hours to get his authorization. At that point I knew Danny didn't want to go to the Clippers. I didn't believe Donald Sterling was going to trade him. But with an Italian contract with an escape clause at the end of every year, the drill was simple. Danny was going to have to go to Italy for a year. At the end of the year we had a forty-five-day window to tell the Clippers, "Either trade Danny, or he's going back to Italy."

With the life insurance and all the perks, the value of the contract was worth almost $4 million a year, just off the charts. To put that number into perspective, in 1989 there had yet to be a $4 million a year player in the NBA. The life insurance alone was worth as much as the salary.

So Danny reluctantly agreed to the deal. I took him to a famous sports restaurant in Washington named Duke Zeibert's. Danny is the son of great parents. Bob and his wife, Rita, are dear friends of mine. They are a very close family with great values. Bob has won several world championships in basketball in the sixty-years-and-over age group and he's a fun guy to be around. Not surprisingly, Danny is one of the most well-adjusted people I have ever met.

We sat down at the restaurant and I told Danny, "This isn't the worst thing in the world. You're twenty-one years old. You are going to be living in an historic fourteenth-century villa with five bedrooms. It's a bachelor's dream. I know this isn't the way you thought your career would start, but I could think of a lot worse things in life. I wish I were you, heading off to Rome for nine months with cooks, maids, bodyguards, a BMW, learning a foreign language in a beautiful city."

He said, "Really? You think it's that great?"

"Yes."

"Great," said Danny. "I'll give you an hour to go home, pack your bags, and come with me."

I visited him about once a month and it was an amazing experience, though Italian basketball certainly wasn't the NBA. There were thirty-five-year-old guys on the team smoking cigarettes before the games. At the end of the year, and to my pleasant surprise, the Clippers finally cried uncle and traded Danny's rights to Cleveland in exchange for Ron Harper and two first-round draft picks. Harper was a young star on the rise and another in a long line considered to be the next Michael Jordan. The Cavaliers also received Reggie Williams, another one of our clients, in the deal. The team had made a huge commitment to Danny before we ever discussed a contract. Wayne Embry, the Cavaliers' general manager at the time, was a big Danny Ferry fan. Embry is a classy guy for whom I have a great deal of respect. He came to my office with an attorney named Dick Watson. Dick owned a small piece of the Cavaliers and might have been the smartest person I ever dealt with in the NBA. The man was a financial genius. Dick was a little eccentric because he was so bright, but he was a great guy.

The first time I met Dick Watson was in 1984, when we represented Mel Turpin, a center from Kentucky. We spent all night with present-value calculations all over the blackboard and what Dick called "decision trees." We made a very complex contract for Mel, who had a weight problem. I was doing my calculations on an original Hewlett-Packard calculator, and Dick had this new 12C model. It took me five minutes to do what he could do in three seconds. So the minute the deal was over I went out and bought a 12C myself. By contrast, Los Angeles Lakers owner Jerry Buss used to do present-value calculations in his head.

Five years later, Dick came into my office with Wayne to talk about Danny's contract. Now I had my own 12C, and I had figured out how to calculate present values fairly quickly. Dick walked in with a portable IBM computer. I would make offers and Dick would type everything into the computer. At one point we ran out of toner, and I didn't even know what toner was. This went on for hours. It was very friendly, but we were asking for another groundbreaking contract. I felt the way I had with Patrick and New York. Cleveland had given up Harper and two first-round picks, knowing they had a forty-five-day window to make a deal or lose everything. The Cavaliers absolutely had to sign Danny and I wanted to make him the first $4 million player in NBA history.

To his credit, Danny forbade me from reaching this threshold. He didn't want to be the $4 million man, particularly in a market like Cleveland.

"You're crazy," I told him. "You have the out with the Italian contract. They gave up Ron Harper and two first-round picks. They have got to sign you. There is no way they can't sign you."

Danny's response: "Great. Make sure the first number doesn't start with a four."

As we negotiated, Dick continued to input everything into his computer. After about four or five hours, I said, "Dick, what do I have to say to have your computer print out 'I accept'?"

It wasn't a long negotiation, perhaps three or four sessions. We ended up signing a deal similar to Ewing's, a ten-year contract worth about $34 million with a personal services contract attached that guaranteed Danny certain endorsement opportunities and another $3.5 million. He had a $37.5 million contract for ten years with some very complex adjustment provisions. It was an extremely intellectually stimulating process for me because of Watson, who taught me the decision tree concept, which was a process designed to produce the best decisions.

A decision tree is a diagram that graphically shows the impact of choosing different options. For example, you might have a branch coming out of the tree that says "six-year contract." There might be another branch that says if he makes the all-star team, he can terminate after four years. You might have another branch that says if the player leads the team to a championship, he can terminate after five years.

I honestly don't believe another human being could have picked up on the nuances of the Ferry deal just by reading the document because it was incredibly complex. But all the money was guaranteed.

Ironically, Cleveland had signed John "Hot Rod" Williams that year to a $34 million deal. Danny, on the same team, actually got more money, but because of his desire to be low-key about it all we never really publicized the total value of the deal. That's also why we split the contract into two parts. There probably wasn't another player in the league who wouldn't have wanted the bragging rights that go with having the largest contract.

We signed the contract and went to the press conference. The owner of the Cavaliers at the time was Gordon Gund, a smart, high-powered guy. Gordon explained to Danny that even though he'd just given him the largest contract in the history of basketball, he was in no way resentful. Gordon was very complimentary toward me for conducting the negotiations at what he termed a very high level. And Danny said, "Gordon, if you think this contract is a lot of money, you should have seen what David really wanted to ask for."

I was presented with extraordinary opportunities like these starting with James Worthy in 1982 (though I was really the junior person on that deal), then Patrick Ewing in 1985 and Danny Ferry in 1989. There were unique situations in the marketplace that demanded a unique response. I think the Ewing and Ferry deals, along with Michael's Nike deal, cemented my reputation not so much for being a hard-driving negotiator, but for being someone with a creative vision, or perspective on the value of players and where those valuations were going. Nobody ever believed Danny would be Larry Bird, and nobody believed Patrick would be Kareem, but Danny and Patrick made more as rookies than either Bird or Kareem was making at the time. And that's what was demanded in those situations.

Let's say a team selected Dennis Scott with the No. 4 pick. Now whether he should have been the No. 4 pick or the No. 44 pick is irrelevant. The team's decision connotes their evaluation of his ability. My job at that point is not to evaluate his talent. The question now becomes what is the fourth pick in the draft worth to that team? I developed a concept that stipulated there was a difference between talent and value.

A talented player on one team may not be worth as much as a less talented player on another team. James Worthy was a good example. He was a great player, one of the fifty greatest of all time, according to the league's experts. He was the first player selected in the 1982 draft, a remarkable performer in the playoffs, an all-star, a great teammate, and an extremely hard worker. Yet he was the third-best player on his team behind Magic Johnson and Ka-reem Abdul-Jabbar. James was probably one of the ten best play-ers in the league. Another player, let's say the twenty-fifth best player in the league, might have been the best player on his team. Even though that player wasn't as good as a James Worthy, with-out him his team would be in the lottery. On the other hand, the Lakers were going to be a great team with or without Worthy. Worthy's incremental impact wasn't as great on the Lakers as that of a lesser player on another team. As a result, the twenty-fifth-best player might have had a greater value to his team than Wor-thy did to the Lakers. There is a difference between talent and value and nowhere was it more apparent than in the case of Patrick Ewing. Independent of his talent, he was a franchise center, the first ever lottery pick in the league's biggest market on a team that had won a total of forty-six games combined over two seasons. He was a unique asset regardless of his talent. And with the lottery, the odds of getting that kind of player again were infinitesimal. Therefore his value was almost without limitation.

Dikembe Mutombo is another good example. We manipulated the 1991 draft to make sure he would be selected by Denver with the No. 4 pick. The owner of the team was Bruce Crockett, who also was president of a company called Comsat. He was a friend, and I had consulted with him when he bought the team. I really liked Bruce and he was very gracious. We made a fair deal for Dikembe as a rookie and after a few years he became an all-star, as well as a great shot blocker. Bernie Bickerstaff, who was the Nuggets' coach and general manager, approached me about negotiating a contract extension for Dikembe.

We made Bernie an offer and for the next two years we had an ongoing dialogue that never changed. It was like the movie *Groundhog Day.* Bernie would ask me if I thought Dikembe was as good as Patrick Ewing. I would consistently reply, No. He would ask me if I thought Dikembe was as good as Alonzo Mourning. I would say no. He would ask if I thought he was as good as Hakeem Olajuwon. I'd say no. Do you think he's as good as David Robinson? I'd say no. Do you think Dikembe is as good as Tim Duncan? I'd say no. But I also told him there were twenty-eight teams in the league (at that time) and that those five centers were unavailable to the Denver Nuggets because they weren't free agents and no team would trade them for Dikembe. So for Denver, Dikembe was Olajuwon, Ewing, Robinson, Mourning, and Duncan. He was the best center in the league but for those five players. So while he might not be as talented as those five, for each of the other twenty-three teams that can't get one of them, Dikembe Mutombo is the most valuable center in the league. Denver couldn't see the entire court. The Nuggets failed to sign him to a long-term deal and Dikembe went to Atlanta as a free agent in 1996.

The following year they lost their second-best player, Antonio McDyess, once again with nothing in return. I had told Bernie that would happen if they didn't keep Dikembe because the team could not get to the next level without a center of his caliber. By not signing Dikembe, Denver turned McDyess into the best player on the team and he expected to be paid accordingly.

I have always believed there are circumstances that can make anything more valuable. Let's say you are thirsty and you go to the local supermarket to buy a gallon of springwater. It costs $4. Suddenly the weather turns and it snows three feet. People hear they are going to be snowed in for four or five days so they go to the supermarket to load up on springwater. But now springwater costs $10 for the same gallon. Same package, same water, but what's changed? What changed are the circumstances.

In negotiations you have to be candid. That's why I always answered Bernie Bickerstaff the same way when he asked me whether I thought Dikembe was better than the top five big men in the league. No, I didn't think he was better than Hakeem Olajuwon, but to me that wasn't the question. The fact was that Denver could never get Olajuwon so whether Dikembe was better or not was moot. It's like asking a guy making $40,000 a year which car is better, a Ferrari or his Chevy. He can't afford to buy a Ferrari, so a Chevy is his Ferrari.

Understand the Long-Term Impact of Your Actions

In the early 1990s we began operating in an environment where players and owners were passing work rules without understanding the impact of those decisions. Neither side could see the whole court much less get out ahead of the curve. Imagine the government deciding from one day to the next that homeowners could no longer write off mortgage interest against their income. How many people would be able to purchase a home without that deduction? How would the stock market respond if capital gains suddenly were taxed at a 50 percent rate instead of 15 percent?

In basketball, changing the economic structure of the game has had a dramatic impact on the conduct of the players and the configuration of teams. In 1994, the NBA and the union agreed to a three-year rookie wage scale, which prescribed rookie salaries but also allowed young players to become free agents after just three years. This in turn forced teams to make significant financial decisions with limited information. Look at players like Tracy McGrady and Jermaine O'Neal. O'Neal, seventeen years old when he was drafted by Portland in 1996, is the youngest player ever to play in an NBA game. In his third season, O'Neal averaged only 8.9 minutes and 2.6 points per game. He also made $1,075,000. To retain his rights, Portland signed O'Neal to a four-year contract starting at $5,075,000 before trading him to Indiana. McGrady was eighteen when he was picked by Toronto in the first round of the 1997 draft. In his third season McGrady started less than half the team's games and averaged 15.4 points. Unsure of what he would become, Toronto traded McGrady to Orlando rather than re-sign him to a large deal. Maybe Indiana and Orlando had better insight into the futures of those two players. Or maybe no one knew what kind of players they would become and two teams simply got lucky. The point is there wasn't enough evidence to make an informed decision with the kind of money involved. (The players weren't very good with their original teams primarily because they were so young. McGrady became a star with Orlando and O'Neal became a star with Indiana.)

Neither side saw the downstream impact of the rookie wage scale, which resulted in unintended consequences for both sides.

During the 1980s and 1990s, player salaries continued to escalate despite the salary cap. We were signing rookies for what we believed to be terrific contracts with a reasonable escalation based on the economy, inflation, and an expected rise in the salary cap. But whatever we thought would be a high rate of escalation invariably was lower than the actual rate of increase, which was roughly 12 percent a year compounded annually. That was the *average*. For the top five picks in the draft it was even more pronounced. We signed Buck Williams and James Worthy to six- and seven-year deals for record amounts in 1981 and 1982. In less than three years they were behind the market.

By the time Juwan Howard came along in the 1994 NBA draft, it had become clear to me that even if we had to put him behind the curve for a couple of years—against our will—to gain total

free agency after two seasons, we could then make a deal way beyond anything we might have negotiated for him as a rookie.
That's one reason the rookie wage scale was so flawed. Rookies
were tying themselves into long-term deals. As a result, they were
forced into attempting to renegotiate contracts after three or four
years with very little leverage. As an owner, why would you ever
want to change that arrangement in a steadily rising market? Instead of tying up a player for a long time at relatively low dollars
before he ever played a game, the owners thought it was in their
economic interest to force players to become free agents.

The owners' mistake was not simply failing to recognize the
impact of their decision, it was also failing to understand the psychology of the players. The union unwittingly protected the young
players against the growing incompetence of the agents who were
engaged in a game I called "Match the Average Salary." The salary
cap prevented the vast majority of agents from negotiating contracts for their clients with an appropriate average salary without
agreeing to deals with terms as long as ten, twelve, or fifteen years.
Chris Webber, for example, was the first pick in the 1993 draft. In
order to obtain a contract averaging $4 million per year, Webber
signed a fifteen-year deal. When Juwan Howard was drafted one
year later, we knew his market value was $4 million a year. The
Wizards had $2.3 million in salary cap room. Accordingly it
would take a six-year contract to average $4 million per year.
When the team signed Scott Skiles as a free agent before coming
to terms with Juwan, its cap room dropped to $1.3 million. Now
it took a twelve-year contract to average $4 million. Agents would
agree to these deals because they never wanted to say they didn't

get their clients the appropriate average even if it meant tying up the player for a decade with no outs.

Prior to the rookie wage scale, the Dallas Mavericks locked up Jason Kidd for nine years with no outs. Detroit locked up Grant Hill for six years and Milwaukee locked up the No. 1 pick, Glenn Robinson, for ten years with no out. Why on earth would you ever want to change that system to one where you can only lock up the next Jason Kidd or Grant Hill for three years, then allow them to become free agents?

Was that the outcome the owners wanted? No. They would rather have given a player a contract that looked enormous but in actuality was much smaller because the money was pushed out a decade or more. Imagine if Juwan Howard didn't have the right to opt out of his first contract. He would have been stuck with a $41 million deal that stretched twelve years versus $109 million over nine years. From the owners' standpoint, changing the system in 1994 was a disaster. The rookie salaries really weren't high. The contracts were just too long. All they had to do was pass a rule that limited the length of the contracts to six or seven years, which is similar to what is in place now.

From the union's standpoint, it was an even bigger disaster. By making the rookie contracts shorter and thus forcing teams to pay players the maximum contract in the face of their imminent free agency, the union moved money away from proven veterans and transferred it to still-unproven players long before anyone really knew whether or not they were worth the $80 million to $100 million they were commanding.

Instead of paying the rookies $3 million or $4 million a year, teams were now paying them $14 million a year in their fourth season. In a capped environment, where do you think that money came from? It came from the veterans. That's exactly what I told Buck Williams, who was union president in 1994, before the union signed the deal.

The smart owners in the 1970s and 1980s, such as San Antonio's Angelo Drossos, recognized that the minute one player realized his teammate was making $100,000 a year more, that player would give up long-term security to move $1 ahead. That's why a player like Karl Malone, who constantly renegotiated his contract, ended up making $10 million a year less than Juwan Howard in 1998, the year Malone was named the league's most valuable player. Malone came out with his famous comment about how he didn't believe in agents and he didn't think players needed them. I responded, "I think Karl is one hundred percent right. If you want to be the MVP and earn ten million dollars a year less than a player who has made the all-star team once in his life, then I really don't think you need an agent to make a deal like that."

Salary cap rules provide that if a team is over the cap, it cannot renegotiate existing years on a player's contract. A player such as Karl Malone might have a six-year contract and at the end of two years feel the remaining years no longer reflect his market value, but if his team, in Malone's case the Utah Jazz, was over the cap they wouldn't be allowed to make any adjustments to those remaining years. The only way to adjust his compensation would be to add new years to the contract at a high enough level so that when those new years were blended with the remaining four years of the existing contract it would put him at a level commensurate with his market value.

As the salary structure grew faster than most people thought it would, many of the best players' salaries fell behind the curve. The only way to adjust those contracts was by adding additional years. In the most extreme example, Magic Johnson ended up with a twenty-five-year contract at what he thought was an incredible salary of $1 million a year only to find out a couple of years later that $1 million really wasn't a lot of money.

Malone was probably the most vivid example because he seemed to renegotiate almost every year. He would negotiate an extension for another two or three years and very quickly realize it still wasn't enough so he kept adding on more years. Because of Magic's contract and to keep teams from circumventing the cap, the league instituted a rule that no player could have a contract at any point in time longer than fifteen years. So there would come a point in time when players would run out of years to extend. That's exactly what happened to Malone. He kept fixing a bad tire and pretty soon there wasn't room for any more patches and all he had left was a worn tire. At the very end he finally made a significant amount of money, but he was never paid what he was worth.

The rookie wage scale was a classic failure of negotiation and reflected an absolute inability to see the entire court. A negotiation is supposed to produce a result that benefits both parties. The 1994 collective bargaining agreement created a result that penalized both parties. Neither party got what it really wanted. It was a cosmetic victory and neither side understood the future result of their actions.

The union has been around for forty-one years and for the first twenty-three, from 1965 to 1988, it won every war without a loss. For the last eighteen years it hasn't won a single battle.

Everything has been rolled back. The players have consistently taken a short-term view when the financial relationship between the players and management had made a long-term view the only option. The salary cap has been in place since 1982, which automatically makes the players and owners partners. At that point, whether the players received 59 percent of the defined revenues (what constitutes the pie) or 57 percent mattered a lot less than the size of the pot the two sides were splitting. It was the first attempt by the league to determine what monies they were going to count toward the split between the players and management.

It's analogous to the Jerry Stackhouse and Antwan Jamison deals. Who came out better: the player paying a 4 percent commission on a $14.7 million deal—Jamison—or the player paying 1 percent on a $6.8 million deal? Just like Stackhouse, the union has never understood that math. But Stackhouse isn't alone.

I remember asking Magic Johnson, "What if I could get you an average of ten million dollars more than you actually received per year over the life of your contract?"

He asked me what I would charge him. I told him 50 percent.

"Fifty percent?" he responded. "I'd never pay fifty percent."

It always amazed me that some people could never see the doughnut for the hole. Rather than pay a 50 percent commission and net an additional $5 million per year, Magic thought the better deal was to accept a much lower salary just so he didn't have to pay what he felt was a large fee. That's one reason there is still only one Michael Jordan.

In 1996, the Players Association agreed to what is called a "max contract," which put the first absolute percentage limitation on what players could be paid. A player with less than seven years of experience couldn't make more than 25 percent of the salary cap. A player with seven to ten years of service could make 30 percent and players with more than ten years could make up to 35 percent of the cap.

Once again the owners failed to understand the psychology of players. If players are told there is no ceiling on what they can be paid, but Michael Jordan makes $30 million because he is the best player in the league, that's fine. But when players know each team has a ceiling, then the best player on every team expects to be paid to that ceiling. The ceiling becomes the same as getting an A on your report card. If I worked really hard in school and the teacher gave me a B, that might be fine if Einstein got the only A. But if I'm the smartest kid in the class, then I want an A. Every player who considered himself the best player on his team wanted to be compensated with an A. It's not that the difference between $55 million and $65 million was going to change their lifestyle. They simply wanted to be paid what the best players were paid. The number really didn't matter. Players always wanted more money, but if a player knew he was being paid as the top dog in the pound, then he could live with whatever that number was.

Brand Your Product
to Differentiate It from the Competition

At the same time, it's important to understand boundaries and the impact of running up against them. There was no way, for example, to determine Michael Jordan's value when he finally became an unrestricted free agent in 1996. We were trying to accomplish something almost esoteric.

There was no relation whatsoever to supply and demand with regard to Michael. When Johnny Carson had the highest-rated show on network television, how did NBC decide what to pay him? There was no relationship to what Carson was being paid and his value to the network because the network could not afford to lose him at virtually any price. How could NBC not pay the *Friends* stars $1 million apiece per episode? NBC could not afford to lose that show, so it had to pay whatever the market dictated.

That's what happened with Michael and his last two contracts. I wanted to put him into a market all his own, which is what I thought he deserved. Michael had four contracts during his thirteen seasons with the Chicago Bulls. The first contract was for five years with a two-year option negotiated by Donald Dell, who was my boss at the time. In 1988, at the end of Michael's fourth season, I negotiated an eight-year deal worth $26 million, which he then played out. By the time he finally became a free agent, the Bulls had won four championships, Michael had won eight scoring titles, and he was an annual fixture on the All-NBA Defensive Team and the All-NBA Team. There was no question he was the greatest player in the game and by that point the consensus was building that he might be the greatest ever to play the game.

So what I wanted for Michael in 1996 wasn't simply money. He was going to make a lot of money. I wanted him to sign a contract that no one else could ever approach. If Rolls-Royce is the best car, it should be the most expensive, not the fourth most expensive. Everyone shouldn't be able to have one.

There is a concept in economics called the luxury curve. Ordinarily, if supply goes down and demand goes up, then prices rise. If the opposite occurs, prices fall. What happens when you have a unique product and there is no correlation between supply and demand? The first example was Johnny Carson in his prime on NBC. What do you pay him? No one can replace him. He is unique. At that point the luxury curve straightens out and becomes vertical. Supply and demand are no longer relevant. There wasn't a number that correlated to precedent. NBC had to come up with something that made Johnny happy.

Michael was in the luxury curve. There was no way of measuring what he was worth and if we could have come up with a figure there was no way the Bulls or anyone else could have paid him his actual value. He was probably worth $100 million a year. So what I wanted for him was a number that would position Michael where he belonged, as the highest-salaried player in the history of team sports. But I had one restriction on me. Michael did not want me to negotiate with Bulls owner Jerry Reinsdorf. Consistent with his philosophy of negotiations, he wanted to know not how much I could get Reinsdorf to pay, but how much Reinsdorf thought Michael was worth. The answer to that question was more important to Michael than the actual number. He wouldn't be satisfied knowing I had to wrangle with Reinsdorf into paying fair market value. After all he had done for the Chicago Bulls, he wanted to know exactly what the owner thought he was worth. He just wanted to know the number. He might not accept it, but he needed to know.

So I called Reinsdorf and told him that Michael would not allow me to negotiate the deal. It was the exact same position

Michael took with Coke and Gatorade in 1991. He told them to make their first offer their best offer. I told Jerry that Michael wanted him to make his best offer and that Michael would either say yes or no. It's an approach Michael developed on his own. But it's also an approach fraught with danger. If he really wanted to stay in Chicago, then he ran the risk of being forced to walk away.

All year Michael told me that he understood I was close to Jerry and that he knew we had dinner together often. But he also said, "If I ever catch you negotiating the deal before I hear Jerry's number, I'll fire you." He was underlining in permanent ink the point that he didn't care what I was capable of negotiating on his behalf. He just wanted to know how Reinsdorf planned to reward Michael's unique contribution. So crunch time came and Jerry and I were on the phone.

He said, "Are you nuts? How can you do a deal like that?"

I explained that I wasn't trying to be difficult but that Michael had been underpaid his entire career. This was like a rite of passage for him. He wanted to know what he was worth to the Bulls.

"I understand," Reinsdorf said, "but I really don't want to mess this up. So I'm going to ask you a very important question. Can you tell me what the first number starts with?"

I told him Michael probably would be upset with me if I said yes, but that I thought it was a fair question. I told him I wanted to provide enough guidance to make an informed decision.

Reinsdorf then asked the famous question: "Does it start with a two?"

I replied, simply, "No."

And that was it. There was a very long pause on the phone. He might have said something to the effect that if the number starts with a four, then we might as well hang up the phone.

"Jerry, I can't tell you what it is, but it doesn't start with a two."

I had made up my mind based on all my knowledge of the market, the psychology of the people involved, and all my homework that it really didn't matter to Michael whether he made $30 million or $50 million. At that point it was just showing off. The point was that I understood the salary cap rules as well as anybody and unless the rules changed dramatically I didn't think there would ever be a way for someone to make $30 million again.

I wanted Michael to be the only $30 million player ever in team sports. Both sides were making a statement. That's what the deal was about. It didn't matter whether someone came along who scored more points, won more rings, jumped higher, or even sold more shoes. No one was ever going to make more money. That's what I wanted.

Michael just wanted to know what the boss thought he was worth.

The next year, 1997, after the Bulls had won a fifth title and Michael had been the MVP of the NBA finals for a fifth time, the issue of what he would be paid came up again. Michael felt that he had done everything asked of him and he therefore deserved a raise. For Michael, just as it had been the previous year, the issue wasn't the money. It was the concept. If he had met all the performance expectations, then he deserved to be compensated in kind.

I wanted to get him $36 million and Reinsdorf wanted to pay

$30 million again. Michael ran out of patience and said let's just split the difference and go home. I was upset because I knew we would get $36 million, but that wasn't the point for Michael.

Michael was impatient but he had his ego in control. He didn't believe the issue should have been difficult to resolve. He felt that if he asked for $36 million after he led the team to a fifth championship, having been grossly underpaid for almost thirteen years, the answer should have been easy. And I didn't disagree. When it wasn't easy, Michael knew all he needed to know and the money was secondary.

It was as simple as seeing the whole court.

FALK'S FUNDAMENTALS

**Don't just see what is happening;
anticipate what will happen.**

In our interactive age we often don't have time to react. Changes are occurring so rapidly that by the time we analyze new information and prepare a response, the window for opportunity has closed. Individuals who can anticipate the next pitch will translate opportunity into success.

Limitations are obstacles, not barriers.

Even the most careful planning cannot preempt last-minute changes that challenge execution. Successful managers see these limitations, whether they be increased competition, regulatory changes, increased time constraints, or any one of a number of business issues, as challenges not barriers. Their ability to shift on the fly enables them to navigate these limitations that act as total obstructions to less nimble operators.

Intuition and ingenuity define the road ahead.

It's been more than five hundred years since Columbus taught us that the world is not linear. It is not always possible to carefully map out our journey from today's opportunities to tomorrow's successes. Since what lies ahead often can't be determined with certainty, successful managers will find their way paved only by creativity, feel, and ingenuity.

Understand the long-term impact of your actions.

The most basic law of physics dictates that every action has an equal and opposite reaction. But like the energy stored up in a volcano, the reactions sometimes take place years in the future and with unexpected force. Don't expect that the only impact of your decisions will be the knee-jerk variety. It is more likely to be the ripple effect across the entire pool of your business.

Brand your product
to differentiate it from the competition.

Imitation is the highest form of flattery. We live in an age of brand names that competitors try to mimic, and often the lines between a Bentley and a Chrysler are blurred. Learn how to separate your company from the competition through creative branding so that the boundary between your products or services and the competition will be so distinct as to require almost a separate language and customs.

FIVE

A Man's Got to Know His Limitations

R oles are played. Life is real.

    In business, as in life, trying to play a role or assume an unnatural identity is dangerous. At the very least it can be embarrassing when the spotlight shines down and the performance doesn't match the expectation. Long term, you will never realize the breadth of your potential because you have spent too much time adjusting your personality to fit constantly changing scenes. You won't know who you are and neither will anyone else.

Stay True to Who You Are

You might be able to adjust your personality on the fly to suit a particular situation, but sooner or later your real self is going to come through. The contrast of who you really are against who you are trying to be is going to make you look ridiculous. Those watching our performances are often much more perceptive than we realize. It's easy for others to see through the façade because very few people can consistently stay in character, particularly when it's outside their comfort zone. That's why it's essential to stay true to who you are. Or, more to the point: A man has got to know his limitations.

Consider Tiger Woods. Tiger has a picture-perfect swing. He has great posture, he's well built, he's six-foot-two and almost robotic in the consistency of his performance. Now take Jim Furyk, a highly skilled player with a bizarre loop in his swing. A coach might tell Furyk, who has been a great professional player, "Hey Jim, the Masters is coming up. You have to take the loop out of your swing." But no professional golf coach would ever really suggest that kind of change. They know that when Furyk wants to hit the most important shot of the tournament, he's going to revert to what's familiar. He's been hitting a golf ball with the same loopy swing his entire life, and under pressure that's the swing he will execute.

It's the same way in all walks of life. We develop certain habits, but we are who we are. Maybe you are laid-back and some people want you to become more outgoing. Maybe you are brash and people want you to become more understated. While I am sure I have a lot of quirks in my personality, the sum total of them is who I am. If people don't like me, then they are simply not going to like me. At one time I didn't understand the nature of limitations, much less my own. Over time and with experience, I have come to understand that limitations are just another data point when it comes to developing and executing a strategy.

The best and most elaborate illustration of that concept played out in a lawsuit brought against Michael Jordan by an aspiring filmmaker, Randy Fried, and his partner, Keith Bank, in 1993. No one on their side of the complaint, including the highly regarded law firm who handled the case, understood limitations. By contrast, I believe all those on our side of the table very clearly understood exactly what was at stake and how we had to proceed. Randy had won an award at the University of Southern California for a student film and he decided he wanted to make a movie based on the popular book *Heaven Is a Playground,* which was written by Chicago sportswriter Rick Telander. The story centered on the recruitment of legendary playground stars such as Fly Williams and Albert King, the younger brother of NBA great Bernard King. Randy and his group approached Michael in 1987 about starring in the film. Michael liked Randy and we entered into a very simple contract that gave them three months to raise the money to produce the film. Over a period of two years, Michael gave them three or four extensions, but they were never able to raise the necessary money.

In 1989, a day or two before the final deadline, they claimed to have raised the money but didn't provide any written evidence of that. Randy went ahead and made the movie with Bo Kimble, who had been an all-American at Loyola Marymount and led the NCAA in scoring during the 1989–90 season. While Michael didn't participate, Hakeem Olajuwon appeared in the film. The movie was about as successful as one of Shaq's films and quickly went to DVD.

In 1996, I was the executive producer of the Warner Bros. movie *Space Jam,* which featured Michael and various Looney

Tunes characters. That film did about $300 million worldwide at the box office and $1 billion in product-related sales. Around that time, Randy Fried sued us for breach of contract, claiming that he would have been—literally this was his claim—the next Steven Spielberg had Michael agreed to make *Heaven Is a Playground* in 1989. Fried said the movie would have been like *Jaws* and would have become one of the largest-grossing movies in history. All that, even though Fried had never made a full-length motion picture prior to that point.

Randy hired a large law firm in Chicago, D'Ancona & Pflaum. The senior litigator was a gentleman, and I use that term loosely, named Dean Dickie. We ended up in a trial that lasted from September 10 through October 15, 1998, in downtown Chicago. In many ways, though Michael was the defendant and he was being sued for $16 million, it was really my trial. I had negotiated the deal. I had memorialized the deal in writing and had represented Michael in his dealings with Randy and the Heaven Corporation. In many ways my credibility was on the line. It was the first time in a very public forum that I was truly being tested and it was happening right in front of Michael in the context of litigation. It was not a pleasant experience.

During pretrial preparation both sides go through a series of steps. Each side asks the other to provide written answers to questions, which are called interrogatories. Then each side takes oral testimony—depositions under oath. My deposition with Dean Dickie lasted eight days. Most of the others deposed spent two hours with him. It was clear from the first moment of our first session he was trying to set the table with me. He wanted me to know he was going to try to intimidate me in front of the jury. Conversely, being confident of the facts, I was trying to set the table with him. I wanted him to understand that the last thing on earth he wanted to do was to put me on the stand under oath because I would eat him for breakfast in open court. I think it's fair to say that both of us were being a little bit cocky, arrogant, probably even stupid.

Our lawyer was Fred Sperling, from another prestigious Chicago law firm, Schiff Hardin & Waite. Before a client is deposed, a good lawyer will advise his client that he cannot win a deposition. The purpose of a deposition is to give oral testimony so that later on, if your trial testimony differs from what you said in the deposition, the opposing side can then use the deposition to attack your credibility as a witness. A good lawyer also advises clients to keep answers as short as possible. I was admonished by Sperling to keep my answers limited to yes or no to the extent possible, but I knew Dickie would try to intimidate me by making my deposition a coming attraction of the trial. He wanted to make me uncomfortable to a degree that would lead me to recommend we settle the suit rather than go to trial. Conversely, I wanted Dickie to know that I was going to have every fact and every date at my fingertips and that I was going to be his worst nightmare if he was dumb enough to put me on the stand.

Prior to the deposition, neither of us had met. He obviously knew me by reputation and Dean no doubt had the expectation that as a high-profile sports agent I was going to be a tough hombre. His plan during the deposition was to break me like you break a stallion in the corral. I decided that I would throw him a change-up from the opening pitch—I wasn't going to give him fastballs. When the day came, we all sat down: Dean Dickie; the court reporter; Fred Sperling, my trial counsel; and Wayne McCoy, my personal lawyer, who also worked at Schiff Hardin & Waite. I was sworn in, and the battle started. To understand the psychology of the moment, listen to the first exchange:

Dean Dickie: "Will you please state your name for the record?"

I lowered my head and in a very soft, barely audible voice I told him my name. Dickie immediately jumped up and said, "Mr. Falk will you please speak more loudly? The court reporter can't hear you."

At this particular deposition the court reporter wasn't using a shorthand machine. She was typing on a computer in real time. So I replied: "Counselor, the court reporter can hear me fine. I'm watching her type my answers in real time."

Dickie: "I know that, Mr. Falk, but can you please speak louder?"

I told him I couldn't speak any louder.

Dickie: "Why is that, Mr. Falk?"

I said I wasn't feeling well.

Dickie: "Are you taking any medication that would impair your ability to answer these questions honestly and truthfully?"

"No, I am not," I replied.

Dickie: "So you are not taking any medications, even though you don't feel well?"

"No, counselor," I responded. "I am taking medication."

Dickie: "Mr. Falk, I just asked you under oath are you taking any medications?"

"No, counselor. If you ask the court reporter to read back the transcript, the question you asked me was whether I was taking any medication that would impair my ability to answer these questions honestly and truthfully."

So he repeated the question. "So are you taking any medications that would impair your ability to answer these questions honestly and truthfully?"

"No, I am not."

Dickie: "But you are taking medication?"

"Yes, I am."

"What medication are you taking?"

"I'm taking Sudafed."

"The orange box?"

"No, the white box."

Fred was dying of laughter at the realization that this was going to take a while and might not be pleasant. We had just gone through a testy exchange over something as silly as "How do you feel?" Over the course of the next seven days I spent six or seven hours a day answering questions. We continued to have these kinds of exchanges because Dean was a very poor questioner. In a deposition, questions should be so precise that the person being deposed can answer yes or no. He would ask compound questions and we would get into these confusing exchanges. Dean no doubt thought I would answer the question one way, and invariably I'd answer it another, which eventually made him very frustrated. But he never wanted to show he wasn't in control.

When the deposition ended, Fred told me I had done a great job, despite the fact that my answers were four thousand times longer than he would have liked. Over the last day or so of the deposition, our lawyers were working on other aspects of the case. I always had a strong belief that the "Heaven" people had never obtained financing for the movie, and that they had fraudulently given us notice telling us they had. Sure enough, there was documentation that suggested they did not receive the financing commitment before the deadline. So we filed a counterclaim for fraud, and Dickie scheduled an eighth day to depose me in connection with the counterclaim.

That deposition was conducted in Washington, D.C. Fred was concerned that I might be nervous, and as we walked into the building, he said, "David, today is going to be a little bit different. We're going to have a video deposition today. Instead of a court reporter transcribing your answers there will be a camera filming you."

"Why are they doing that?"

Fred told me that most people are antsy and uncomfortable in front of a camera.

"So Dean Dickie thinks I'm going to be nervous in front of a camera? I'm in front of a camera three or four days a week."

Once again the warfare was more psychological than verbal. I walked into the room and Dean was sitting there very smug with his arms folded across his chest. There was a long table in the middle of the room and he was at one side. I was sitting at the head of the table, opposite the camera.

A microphone was at my seat to record the audio, and a technician was there to operate the camera. Dickie watched my every move.

"Excuse me," I said. "What is that?"

The technician said, "Sir, that is the pickup that transcribes the audio portion of the tape."

"No, I know what it is. What kind of equipment are you using?"

Dickie was looking at me warily.

I looked at the technician and said, "Don't you know that's a high-impedance microphone, and when you put it next to a silk tie it's going to create a lot of interference and the audio quality won't be very good? We can't even use equipment like that on my weekly television show, which is a low-budget cable television program. I was just talking about that with the technical people when I was doing the *Larry King Live* show."

Dean Dickie had probably spent twenty-five thousand dollars on the video setup for the purpose of advancing his psychological war. Still, despite the contentiousness of the deposition, it was a minor-league version of the real game.

The one thing you learn when you are forced to be a witness is that the process of taking a deposition and subsequently testifying is very similar to the experience you have when you are about fourteen years old taking biology in high school. There's a rat in the maze that has to get to the water. Now if the rat takes a wrong turn and doesn't get to the water, what happens? The rat gets an electrical shock.

When the opposing lawyer pauses and heads over to a table to pick up a copy of the transcript of your deposition, you are about to get shocked. You become the rat in the maze and you have just made a wrong turn. By the third week in the trial, there had been hours and hours of testimony by Randy Freid about how he was going to be the next Steven Spielberg and how Michael hadn't honored his word and how the movie would have been a block-buster. Randy was effectively hallucinating on the stand, but the judge gave him very wide latitude because there was concern about anyone getting a fair trial in Chicago with Michael Jordan as the defendant. It was a legitimate concern, but at the same time we didn't ask them to bring the case and we didn't ask them to bring it in Chicago. Two months earlier, the Bulls had won a third straight championship for the second time. Since owners had locked out NBA players in an ongoing collective bargaining dispute, the trial was Michael's first real public appearance since the championship celebration.

Finally, the day everybody had been waiting for arrived: Dean Dickie had me on the stand for cross-examination. He had been working toward this day from the moment we sat down for my deposition. My deposition ran more than eighteen hundred pages. I had studied the document and reviewed it with my lawyers, which was appropriate. The first question Dean asked was whether I remembered I was under oath. I told him I did.

"You testified yesterday that the first time you learned that RCA Columbia was going to finance the movie was in July of 1989. Do you recall that testimony?"

"Yes, I do."

"Do you recall you are still under oath?"

"Yes, I do."

He walked to the table. I didn't have one deposition book like everyone else—I had three. He opened one of the books and handed me an entry. I knew I was about to get my first shock, and it was only the second question.

"Mr. Falk, could you please turn to page 709 and read line nineteen?"

Line nineteen indicated that I learned RCA Columbia was going to finance the movie in June 1989, rather than July, which was a very important point because of the June 30 deadline in the original contract.

"Does this refresh your recollection?"

"Counselor, I'm afraid it doesn't."

"Why is that, Mr. Falk?"

"If you turn to page 704, you see the transcript says July, and on page 709 there is a typographical mistake by the court reporter."

There was pandemonium in the courtroom.

"I'm not asking you about page 704. I'm asking you about page 709."

Fred Sperling made an objection and asked the judge to allow me to read page 704. Sure enough, on page 704 it was clear that I didn't learn about the financing until July. Dickie was really embarrassed. The critical point upon which the entire suit hinged was whether we knew prior to the deadline that they had financing. We hadn't known.

Dickie said, "Mr. Falk, are you aware of your obligation to read your deposition after you have completed it and check it for errors?"

I told him I had read the transcript. He asked why I had failed to point out the mistake.

"Counselor, there are over eighteen hundred pages in my deposition. I read them as carefully as I could, and I sincerely apologize to the court for missing Ju*ly* instead of Ju*ne* on page 709."

The trial was essentially over in the first hour. If the deposition was combative, this was high drama. After this initial exchange Dickie stepped up the heat, trying to trip me up and embarrass me.

The judge called a recess after about an hour. I gathered with my lawyers, Wayne McCoy and Fred, along with Michael. They told me I did very well in the first hour but that I was extremely combative. They wanted me to tone it down a bit and refrain from being so antagonistic in front of the jury. Fred told me I wasn't there to cross-examine Dean Dickie.

I went out for the next session and tried to dial it back a little. We went another sixty to seventy-five minutes and there was another recess. Now Fred and Michael said, "You acted like you were asleep out there. What happened? Give it more emotion."

"Is this a movie? Just leave me alone," I said. "There's a lot of pressure. I have to remember all these facts. I'm doing the best I can. The end of the first hour I was too abrasive. Now I'm too passive. Just let me be myself. I'll do the best job I can. I'm not trying out for a role in a Hollywood movie."

It was a classic example of why you can't try to project a role, particularly under pressure, because you are not going to appear sincere. Trials are about credibility. I was trying to show the jury I was a credible witness with command of the facts and that I was being honest and sincere. If I was like a shark smelling blood one hour, then like a rock star on Quaaludes the next, the jury was going to wonder who the real witness was.

The epilogue to the story is that we won the case both ways. They lost their claim for breach of contract and we won our counterclaim for fraud.

People were curious as to why Michael Jordan would spend five weeks of his life sitting in a courtroom in Chicago. That's simple. People were attacking Michael's integrity, which is above reproach. If he settled the case, then he was effectively admitting to a breach in his integrity. A settlement also invited others to sue him, no matter how baseless the claims, on the assumption he was not going to spend the time to defend himself and instead would write a check and walk away. I told Michael we couldn't settle the case—he had to make a statement. That's why it was so important that we not only won the case, but that we also went on the offensive and filed a counterclaim. We had to let people know that if you want to sue on a contingency, where the person making the claim really has no money in the case, then we would force that firm to spend the money necessary to bring the suit to trial. When D'Ancona & Pflaum sued us for $16 million, they probably were on a 30 percent to 40 percent contingency, which meant they stood to receive a significant piece of a settlement.

I was confident the facts were in our favor. And while the jury might have been enamored of Michael, they also wanted to know if he treated Randy Fried and his partners with respect, even though they were not big Hollywood filmmakers. Did Michael brush them off after making a commitment? The jury, even one sitting in a Chicago courtroom, wanted to know the answer to those questions.

The suit was absurd from the beginning. The idea that *Heaven*

Is a Playground would have outperformed a major release by Warner Bros. had Fried's group been given the money wasn't rational.
If I am driving a Chevy against Michael Schumacher in his Ferrari, can I win? The answer is no.

The larger point is that trying to play a role in a serious business situation can have catastrophic results. At some point you are
going to completely lose your credibility. You have to be yourself,
take your lumps, and remain sincere. No one on the other side of
the suit understood or respected that principle.

Not only do most people revert to form under pressure, they
also don't perform well when the heat is on. I believe pressure
brings out the stars. The trial wasn't about how smart I was. It
was truly about my credibility. Lawyers for the plaintiffs were attacking my credibility in front of a jury with court reporters taking down every word. A courtroom is a very public forum where
you are asked questions that go directly to your motivations and
integrity. It's a very intense environment and I was incredibly focused. So when I was told at the first break I was too assertive and
abrasive, I had to explain to everyone in that room that I was
under attack. I was in a heavyweight fight and at the end of the
first round my corner man was telling me, "You're a little too aggressive." Wait a minute. The other guy is trying to beat my
brains in. What do you mean "too aggressive"?

The fact is, everyone has limitations. Maybe you are really good
at presentations, but not quite as good at negotiations. Maybe
you're a great negotiator, but not so good at business development. There is a natural tendency to try to be good at everything.
When you are under pressure, sometimes you strive to do something or be someone that is really beyond your capabilities.

With experience, I learned to lead with my weaknesses. I would tell players, "I'm not here to become your best friend the first day you meet me." I don't believe anyone is your best friend on day one. When you meet someone the first time and they have a charming personality, you can be impressed or it can force you to question their sincerity. Is it the real thing or an act? I learned that I couldn't be anyone other than who I am. I told potential clients, "I'm an acquired taste. Over the course of time you will come to feel comfortable with the consistency of my performance and we'll become good friends. But I'm not here to sell you on friendship today or to compete on the basis of being your friend. I'm not interested in winning a Mr. Congeniality award in a beauty contest."

Those who are the best at anything stand the test of time. I have never been interested in competing in a beauty contest because I never thought beauty was my best asset. My track record is my number one asset. So if someone comes in and says, "I'm not a very good negotiator, but I'm really charming and good-looking," then that's how they are going to compete. But over the long term I'm going to outcompete anybody because I have the best track record. That is what I believe.

Tommy Amaker is like a son to me. I helped him get the head coaching job at the University of Michigan through an influential alumnus who happened to be a very good friend of mine. After six years at Michigan, and despite winning twenty-two games during the 2006–2007 season, Tommy was fired.

Out of the blue, he was approached by Harvard to become its head basketball coach. Tommy had been an assistant coach at Duke in the Atlantic Coast Conference, the head coach at Seton

Hall in the Big East, and the head coach at Michigan in the Big Ten, three of the top conferences in America. Now he was being courted by Harvard, which plays in the Ivy League, an atmosphere dramatically different than the ACC, Big East, or Big Ten. The school takes sports seriously, but the team travels on buses and plays mostly on weekends to accommodate the academic demands it places on its student athletes.

It was clear from the beginning that Tommy wasn't going to make the kind of money at Harvard that he had made at Michigan or Seton Hall. To be sure, there are some interesting challenges to coaching at Harvard. As I discussed a number of nonfinancial aspects of a contract for Tommy with Harvard's athletic director, Bob Scalise, he would repeatedly say, "We don't do things that way at Harvard."

Harvard is the oldest college in America and widely considered the Rolls-Royce of higher education. When the administration says it doesn't do things a certain way, it means something. After the fourth or fifth time, I said, "Bob, can I ask you a question? How many years has Harvard played intercollegiate basketball?"

He said more than one hundred years, the last fifty-two in the Ivy League.

"And during that period of time, how many championships have you won?"

He said, "David, we've won Ivy League championships in every sport at Harvard—men and women—except in men's basketball."

"So in one hundred years of basketball and fifty-two years in the Ivy League you've never won a championship in men's basketball?"

"No, David."

"Then maybe you should change the way you are doing things at Harvard."

If you are trying to spin your qualifications to meet a completely different set of criteria, eventually it's not going to work. Don't go into a marriage thinking you are going to change the other person. Don't continue taking the same approach to men's basketball at Harvard if it's not working. Despite my ribbing, Bob understood this implicitly. That's why he hired Tommy Amaker.

The simplicity of that advice is overwhelming, yet very few people follow it. People try to morph themselves into whatever they think the interviewer is looking for. You might be a good enough actor to get the job, but you will never be good enough to thrive in that position and keep the job. In the end, Tommy Amaker understood exactly what Harvard was and what Harvard was not. That's why he will be successful at Harvard.

When I came home from college following my junior year, I needed to find work for the summer, but school ended late at Syracuse University and I couldn't find a job. I went over to my best friend's house, and he was hanging out with his college roommate, Bob, who is now a well-known divorce lawyer in Los Angeles. Bob asked me what I was going to do. I told him I'd driven a truck the previous summer and worked at a warehouse the summer before that, but I was having a hard time finding a job.

He said, "You should find a job working in a summer camp. It's really fun. The pay's not great, but you don't spend any money. You can play basketball every day."

So I looked in the *New York Times* and found a couple of ads for camp counselors. It was an eight-week commitment for something like $200. The summer before, I probably took home $200 a week. I told Bob what the openings looked like, and he said, "Are you kidding? You don't want a job as a counselor. You want a job as a group leader or an assistant head counselor. That's where the money is."

I'd never done anything like that before. Bob grabbed the *Times*, found an ad for a group leader, and called the number. He told the person who answered that he was David Falk, and that he'd worked at Camp Cayuga as a group leader for three years. He got me an interview.

I drove to the interview, which was at the camp owner's house. I was totally uncomfortable because I was not a good liar. I was going to be a senior, but Bob had told the man I had just graduated from college and that I was headed to law school in the fall. I interviewed for about an hour. The man finally said, "Your credentials are terrific. I really like you, and I'd really like you to come join us. Just let me make a call to one of your references."

I was sitting in the man's living room. This was 1970, and he was making the call on a rotary phone. I kept telling him that I had another interview, but he told me to hang on because he just wanted to talk to the owner of the camp that I had supposedly worked at for three years. I could hear the phone ring six or seven times. There weren't answering machines in those days, so he never connected with the owner. So he offered me the job.

For the next eight weeks I was uncomfortable. People asked me questions about college. I had to filter almost every conversation because I had told a white lie or two. It wasn't as if I was a child molester and had lied about my background. But it was the only time in my life I misrepresented myself, and because I was so uncomfortable I vowed never to do it again.

This is an oversimplification, but if you are not confident about what you are selling, then you will take whatever approach necessary to make the sale. If you really believe in the product—and I really do believe in my abilities, my commitment, and my track record—then you don't have to bend yourself into a pretzel. You want to be able to say this is the product. It works. It's tried and true. This is Berkshire Hathaway, the number one performing security in America. Maybe you think it's too big, or maybe you think it should be in New York and not Omaha, but it's really done well. If you are Warren Buffett, you say, "I don't take business meetings; I just do business."

There was a popular TV commercial years ago that opened with an executive sitting behind his desk. A salesman came in to sell him a photocopier, and the salesman said, "This photocopier does two-sided copies, ten copies a minute. It's just like a Xerox." The next salesman came in with a different copier and told how it collated, did color copies, and he said, "And it's just like a Xerox." The third salesman came in and told how his copier could do everything. The executive said, "I know, it's just like a Xerox." The salesman straightened his tie and said, "Sir, this *is* a Xerox."

Don't Win the Battle Only to Lose the War

I don't want to suggest that it's simply a matter of the right way versus the wrong way. I think the question is, What is the best way? I believe the service I have provided has been the best service.

But knowing how to provide the best service has been an evolutionary process for me. When I was younger I didn't respect the fact that I had limitations. I thought I knew how a successful agent went about his business. He was tough, steadfast in his position, and demanding. I didn't appreciate the necessity of knowing one's limitations or the idea of being true to your own identity.

In 1985 I had a football client named Frank Reich, who was drafted by the Buffalo Bills in the third round of the NFL draft. Bill Polian was the Bill's general manager at the time, a good person, and a real hard-nosed football guy. Polian had found the team's second-string quarterback, Joe Dufek, at Yale. Dufek started five games in 1984, when the Bills went 2-14. Following the team's selection of Reich in 1985, Polian came to my office and we had a good meeting. I wanted to get Frank three years at $1 million, and we quickly got to three years and $900,000. I took Bill to lunch, we returned to the office, talked some more, and I got him to $950,000. But that was as far as he was willing to go.

Over the next seven weeks, I hammered Polian, trying to get that last $50,000, which came out to $17,500 a year, probably $7,000 net to Frank after taxes and commissions. One day Polian called me and said, "David, can I ask you a question? How many hours of film have you watched on your client?"

I said, "Zero hours. Why do you want to know?" I knew when he asked the question exactly where we were going. He was going to tell me that they had an absolute fix on how good Frank was going to be from watching film, and that I had no idea.

"We watch sometimes thousands of hours of film on players,"

Polian said. "We know their tendencies, their ability to move. We know all you can know about these players."

I asked him what they did with all that information.

"We use it to predict how successful a player will be transitioning from college to the pros."

"So you can take all that film, break it down, and accurately predict how well a player is going to perform?"

"David, we spend millions of dollars scouting games, looking at film, breaking down everything to its smallest detail."

Polian gave the whole history of scouting.

"So that really gives you an accurate representation?" I asked.

He said it did.

So I said, "Can I ask you a question? If it's that scientific, why did twenty-eight teams pass on your starting quarterback for fourteen rounds in the draft in 1983?"

Boom! Polian slammed down the phone. He was furious. Ultimately, he gave me the $50,000. But in the seven weeks it took to get the extra $50,000, Jim Kelly arrived in Buffalo from the USFL, and Frank Reich missed nearly the entire training camp. I'm not saying Frank would have beaten out Jim Kelly, who was subsequently elected to the Pro Football Hall of Fame, but any chance he had was lost by not being there seven weeks earlier, learning the offense and getting comfortable with the coaches. But in my immature desire to make this perfect number of $1 million, I kept Frank out of camp for seven weeks. I got the money, but I failed. I won the battle, but lost the war.

I had to learn that when the other side came up to $950,000—95 percent of where I wanted to be—and that the last $17,500 a year was going to cost seven weeks of camp and infuriate the coaches, I should have accepted the offer and sent Frank into camp early so he could get a jump on the season. I never made that mistake again.

If I had been 90 percent from where I needed to be, that would have been a different story. I would have had to wait. There is always going to be a certain level of pain, but I had to realize I couldn't win every battle. And I had to look at the big picture. Was Frank Reich the next Dan Marino? No. There were a number of other quarterbacks selected ahead of him. He needed to get into camp early to have a chance to compete. A lot of people might say that I won. I got the $1 million. But I lost.

I wasn't flexible. It was poor judgment. To be a good negotiator, to be a good advocate in court, to be a good salesman, good judgment is a critical quality. It's about picking up signals and adjusting your approach but not your personality. It's finding an effective approach that is going to win the game without changing your foundational beliefs. It's very easy, particularly as you become successful, to become institutionalized in your thinking.

A good example of that is Harvard. The school is a brand name. When you say "Harvard" the name stands on its own merits. So when somebody at Harvard tells you, "This is the way we do things at Harvard," it has a resounding ring to it. On the other hand, they have never won in one hundred years, so the way they are doing things with regard to men's basketball clearly is not working. There's an expression in sports: You have to change a losing game. If it's not working, then you have to find a fresh approach. When I was young I got fixated on my goal, which truly isn't important if you can walk away with 98 percent of what you were after. You have to be able to know when it's enough. It's a judgment call and my judgment sometimes wasn't very good when I was younger.

However, I always had a sense of what I thought was the right deal. The real question, however, is "What is the goal?" In a negotiation the goal is to make a deal. If you want to be an absolute perfectionist with zero tolerance and you set a goal to get $1 million, do you walk away from $999,000 or do you make the deal?

When I was young, I thought it was important that I receive recognition for deals I thought were innovative. Now I realize that it's enough just to be on Michael Jordan's team. If it's 99.9 percent Michael, and I have one speck of credit coming my way, that's fine. Who cares? It's been great fun and it's been a great ride.

Look at Kobe Bryant. If he and Shaquille O'Neal had stayed together on the Los Angeles Lakers and won ten rings, why would either care who got the credit? The goal is to win championships. If I'm Kobe and I win ten rings, I don't care if everyone thinks it was all because of Shaq.

Kobe and Shaq became diverted from the most fundamental goal in sports, which is to win. Kobe might have won the battle, but he's losing the war. People love to debate whether the Lakers won because of Shaq or because of Kobe. The given is that they won. The Lakers haven't won since Shaq left and they didn't get past the first round in 2007. Thanks to an absolute fluke prior to the trade deadline in 2008, the Lakers were able to add an all-star player at virtually no cost to the team and Kobe got what might be called a "do-over." The constraints of the salary cap made it unlikely that Kobe would ever win another championship with the Lakers, even if he averaged one hundred points a game. That is not a reflection of his desire, work ethic, or talent. It's simply a reflection of the fact that the salary cap makes it improbable that a team can replace a player of the caliber of Shaquille O'Neal or Kobe Bryant. But it happened for the Lakers.

The Memphis Grizzlies began as an expansion franchise in Vancouver, British Columbia, then moved to Memphis in 2001 because the experiment of basketball in western Canada simply wasn't working. Unfortunately, the size of the market in Memphis made it extremely difficult to make the business work there, too. The team's owner, Michael Heisley, is an astute businessman as well as a wonderful gentleman. From 2001 through 2006, he had Jerry West as president of his basketball operations. Jerry is undoubtedly one of the keenest judges of player talent in the history of professional basketball. Despite this combination of business acumen, the Grizzlies were struggling financially. Perhaps it was the size of the market, perhaps it was the heavy franchise relocation fee the NBA charged Heisley to move from Vancouver. The net result was that Heisley made a decision to trade his young all-star center, Pau Gasol, to reduce payroll. To make the trade work, however, he could *not* take back a player or players of equal talent because they would command the same salary as Gasol. Accordingly, Memphis acquired Kwame Brown; Javaris Crittenton, a rookie guard; and, using an archaic exception to the salary cap, Aaron McKie, who was not even playing in the league. The Lakers had to sign McKie to make the deal work under salary cap rules. While Gasol is not a dominating player like Shaq, his presence has reenergized the Lakers, taken Mitch Kupchak from the outhouse to the penthouse, and given Kobe a rare do-over with a great chance to utilize his extraordinary talent and drive to win a championship with Gasol.

Kobe didn't understand his own limitations relative to winning. If Jerry Buss did in fact tell Kobe that he was not going to sign Shaq, regardless of what it meant to Kobe's future with the Lakers, then Kobe had a choice. If he truly wanted to win championships, then re-signing with the Lakers probably wasn't the right choice. The same could be said of Shaq, though he did win in 2006 with Miami. If the goal is to win as many championships as possible, then the formula was in place in Los Angeles. Shaq wanted to be paid, Kobe wanted to be the man, and it's unlikely anyone involved will be as successful as they might have been had they stayed together.

Kobe lost sight of the goal. He and Shaq were a formula for success. There was no need to tinker with the formula. It worked.

When a player—even a player as great as Kobe is—loses sight of his limitations, then he can lose sight of the goal. When that happens, he can lose both ways—on the court and off. Ironically, Michael Jordan was forced to show he could carry an entire team to a championship because of the antics of his general manager. Instead of supplying Michael with playoff-hardened veterans or rookie stars, Jerry Krause, the Chicago Bulls general manager, always played the long shots. I used to compare what Michael did to Olympic diving. The first diver does a swan dive off the low board that equates to a degree of difficulty of two. By the end of the competition, divers are doing six-and-a-half twists off the thirty-meter platform and the degree of difficulty is nine. Every year, Krause would turn up the degree of difficulty by acquiring long shots through trades and draft choices.

The National Basketball Players Association is an excellent example of an entity being diverted from its stated goal because of leadership that does not recognize its limitations. The union leadership is charged with improving working conditions for its members, which includes raising salaries and increasing jobs. Instead, they have become obsessed with trying to prove that David Stern isn't manipulating them into bad deals. The irony is that in a salary-capped environment, the players are partners with the league because they are sharing revenue. Once that structure is in place, the only way both sides are ever going to make significantly more money is to increase the size of the revenue pool. To increase the size of the pool, you have to be on the same page in terms of marketing, age limitations, conduct, dress codes, dealing with fans and media, and all the issues the public sees. Both sides have to present a unified front to make sure the product on the floor is the best possible.

For years NFL players and owners had a contentious relationship. Today the two sides have positive relations, and the sport continues to grow exponentially. The union leader for thirty-five years was Gene Upshaw, a tough guy who played on the offensive line for the Oakland Raiders. He understood that his job was not so much to fight the NFL as it was to work with the league to grow the pie.

It comes back to the goal. What is the goal? Is it to win or to score more points? Is it to prove you are as smart as David Stern or to make more money?

Isiah Thomas might have been the quintessential example of how playing a role in real life isn't anything like being a role player on the basketball court. By the early 1990s, the NBA salary cap had been in place for eight or nine years. Thomas, as president of the Players Association, recognized that there were a number of former players unable to make it financially from the time they played their last game until pension benefits kicked in. Players were eligible for pension payments at age fifty-five, but they could start collecting at forty-five in exchange for reduced benefits. While the pension benefits were dramatically better than they had been in the 1960s, they still weren't enough to sustain a player. An even greater problem was that some players financially couldn't get from the end of their playing careers to age forty-five. It was a serious problem.

Thomas, in a classic example of not knowing one's limitations, came up with the Pre-Pension Benefit Plan (PPBP). The idea was to implement a second-tier, nonqualified pension fund, which meant contributions to the fund were not tax-deductible. The union would allow the league to reduce the salary cap by approximately 5 percent. Instead of that money flowing to the players, it would produce a pool worth roughly $300 million. Every player would receive a share of the pool, based on what the player earned. Patrick Ewing was earning $3 million a year and his salary represented 1 percent of the pool, so Patrick would receive 1 percent of the PPBP benefits upon retirement. A player earning $300,000 a year would receive one-tenth of what Patrick would get.

The plan was absurd. The intent to create a plan to help former players was noble, but the execution was fundamentally flawed across the board. If you are a player and your income is directly proportional to a defined metric, which is what the salary cap is all about, then the last thing you want to do is reduce the size of the cap, because any reduction will produce an automatic downward pressure on salaries. If the players wanted to achieve the desired result, then all they had to do was allow every player to negotiate his contract based on the full value of the cap and then assess each player a 5 percent tax. Same outcome, but a dramatically different impact on leaguewide salaries and player movement.

The second flaw should have been even more obvious: the plan wasn't socialistic enough. Isiah's plan gave the players who made the most money the largest share of the fund, while the players who needed the most help received the smallest share. There were other holes in the plan, as it was presented, but these two should have been enough to send everyone back to the drawing board.

I told my clients, many of whom were among the highest-paid players in the game, that the need was there but the execution was a terrible way to accomplish the intent.

In a predictable if not ridiculous response—typical of the Players Association under Isiah's leadership—I was accused of dismissing the plan out of self-interest. From Isiah's perspective, as an agent I was worried first and foremost about losing my 4 percent commission on the money that went into the plan. In other words, since it didn't pass through the players, no fees would pass through to the agents.

My response was that if the players weren't worried about losing 96 percent, or twenty-four times what I was going to lose, then I wasn't worried about my 4 percent fee. Patrick Ewing would have contributed $150,000—5 percent of his $3 million salary—and saved the commission he might otherwise have had to pay me on that money, which would amount to $6,000. Meanwhile, he would be out $144,000.

Charlie Grantham, executive director of the Players Association, whom I liked, allowed me to make a presentation to the players in Miami at the annual meeting in 1991. I asked Michael Jordan, Patrick Ewing, and James Worthy, my three highest-profile clients, to attend the meeting because they clearly understood the specific problems with the plan. Michael had other commitments, so James brought Magic Johnson. Everyone knew Magic had been Isiah's buddy. If nothing else the trip was worth it to see the look on Isiah's face when Magic walked into the room with me. Thomas had fire coming out of his eyes.

I stood up before the players and said, "If I told you I just negotiated a contract for you, you would say great, then ask me how much you were going to make. If I said I can't tell you, but it's a lot of money, you might ask me how long the contract is. If I said I couldn't tell you, but it's more than one year and less than twenty years, you might ask how much of the deal is guaranteed. If I told you a little bit was guaranteed, would you sign the contract? Of course not. Then how can you sign off on a plan that has so many holes in it? More importantly, the one thing you never want to do under any circumstances is to interfere with the size of the salary cap.

"Let's have a little pop quiz. Match up the following categories in baseball, basketball, and football in 1991. Which sport has the highest average salary? Baseball. Which sport has the lowest average salary? Football. Which sport has the best free agency? Baseball. Which sport has the worst free agency? Football. Of the three major sports, the one with the most free agency has the highest salaries, and the one with the least free agency has the lowest salaries. The more restrictions you put into the system the less money you are going to make, so the last thing you want to do is interfere with the cap."

The most striking memory I have of the experience was waiting for the players to call me into the room. I was sitting with Lafayette "Fat" Lever, who is a good guy and was vice president of the union. Some of the players were so anti-agent, it didn't matter what you said, because they considered agents the devil incarnate, which is a belief system I put at the feet of Isiah.

Fat said to me, "David, I respect you. You are a reasonable guy. Why are you against the plan?"

"Let me be crystal clear. I am not against the plan. I understand the rationale of having a plan. I'm just against the way you are implementing the plan. You do not want to lower the salary cap."

I explained how the plan could work, which left the cap in place and charged a 5 percent tax on all salaries. The money would go into a fund, and each player would have an account based on 5 percent of his salary. He was incredulous.

"But you don't understand," he said. "Then *we'd* be paying for it."

I asked him who he thought was paying for it under the current plan. He said the owners were paying. Right. The owners are paying for it with *your* money. Fat thought that by lowering the cap, the players weren't putting their own money into the fund. That's what the union was preaching. Their position was that if you reduced the cap by 5 percent, and that money went into a fund, then it was the owners, not the players, who were contributing the money. They couldn't understand why I was against the plan.

The other interesting memory I have of that time was talking with Rory Sparrow, a great guy and a client of mine who went to work for the league. Rory is very bright. He had been an electrical engineering major at Villanova University with a 3.8 grade point average. He was the New York Knicks player rep at the time. I told Rory that he had to change the way the plan was being implemented. He was conflicted. He knew I was right because intellectually he grasped the point. But he wanted to be pro-union so he supported the deal.

The union agreed to the plan. They invested the money, and what do you think the average return on that money was before they disbanded the plan four or five years later? One percent! If you went to a kindergarten class and asked them to throw darts at the stock tables in a newspaper, or you had them break open a piñata full of stocks, bonds, and mutual fund options, you would be hard-pressed to find anyone unable to earn more than 1 percent on that amount of money in the early 1990s.

Not only did they horribly execute a great idea, but the results were embarrassing all the way around. By trying to play the role of a CEO against a world-class management expert like David Stern, Isiah Thomas guaranteed that the players, his constituency, sustained another loss.

You Must Be Willing to Walk Away

For a long time, Los Angeles Clippers owner Donald Sterling did not recognize his own limitations. His game was to see if he could make a better deal, even at the cost of winning games. I'm not saying that was his goal. But if someone falls into a pattern of behavior they repeat over and over, there has to be a reason. It took Donald a long time to realize that paying the going rate to keep star players like Elton Brand was the only way he had a chance to be as successful in basketball as he was in real estate.

It's difficult to tell a person who has made a billion dollars in real estate that he's not running his basketball team the right way. By the same token, that's the point of this chapter: A man's got to know his limitations. What works in real estate doesn't necessarily translate to basketball. The fact that you are one of the most successful real estate investors in history is not an indicator of your ability to manage a professional sports franchise properly.

A lot of people get fixated on what they think the right deal should be and they lose sight of the importance of making the deal. That's what I did with Frank Reich. The irony in Sterling's situation is that by reputation he has never sold an investment property. Yet with the Clippers he had lost every important player—Danny Manning, Charles Smith, and Kenny Norman, to name only three. Rather than keep his best talent, Sterling let them go because he didn't believe their value matched the cost of keeping them. In the real estate business, he believed the exact opposite.

The most basic function of an agent or a lawyer is to be an advocate for your client. If you are advocating a position for your client with an owner, general manager, or coach and they aren't receptive to it, there is a tendency to become more passionate about your position. Donald Sterling in his own way has always been a great negotiator because he has always been willing to walk away regardless of the consequences, which is Rule 1 in negotiations. You have to be willing to walk away. He was always willing to walk away, even if it hurt him. The people advocating him to take a different position might be logical and even persuasive, but at the end of the day Donald was willing to walk away. It was a very powerful way of conducting business because that approach provided him with great leverage. As an agent, you knew Donald didn't feel the need to make a deal, regardless of the facts.

Can you imagine a team like the Lakers taking that approach with Kobe Bryant? It was life or death for the Lakers when Kobe was a free agent. Sterling, in a similar situation, insulated himself from all the potential fallout and stood his ground, no matter how negative the consequences. As a result, for a long time the Clippers were considered the worst franchise in professional sports.

Sterling is a very bright man—it wasn't that he was bumbling along. He simply wanted to do business his own way and was willing to accept the consequences. Most owners aren't willing to do that. They have rabbit ears, which is why criticism changes their position. But after dealing with Donald several times, I realized that what he really wanted you to do was try to convince him to do something that you didn't believe he was going to do in the first place. He enjoyed that game more than he enjoyed his team's success. When we started negotiating Elton Brand's deal, Sterling had never given a player a contract totaling more than $14 million. And of all people, that amount was paid to journeyman Eric Piatkowski, which is bizarre given all the great players who have moved through that franchise.

I knew Donald wanted to see if he could retain Elton without paying him the maximum salary. To preempt the entire conversation, I said, "Look, this is backwards. You know what the asset is and you want to see if you can get that asset below market value. The price is a max deal. You have to decide if the asset is worth the price. Elton is going to make the max whether you pay him or someone else does."

My position was simple: If you don't think the asset is worth the price, then don't buy it. But you can't get it cheaper. Here's a great analogy. When my clients want to buy a Ferrari, they'll call me and ask if I can help them. I tell them I know the Ferrari dealer in Washington very well. The player tells me the car costs roughly $210,000, then he asks me what price I can get it for. I tell him, $210,000. How am I helping? Well, it can take the average guy up to four years to get a new Ferrari, but I can get one in six months. That's how you discount the deal—how long it takes to get the car you want from the manufacturer in Italy. Ferrari isn't going to discount the price. Why? Because it's a Ferrari and they have a waiting list full of people who will pay full price. Elton Brand was a Ferrari. There would be no discount because there were other teams willing to pay full value.

I think Donald was surprised at how relaxed I was about whether he was going to keep Elton. I wanted him to know that I hoped Elton would remain with the Clippers, but at the same time I really didn't care. Elton was going to get the max from someone. It was that simple. I wasn't playing a role. That's exactly how I felt. Whether the Clippers paid him or not really became fundamental to the future direction of the franchise. I told Donald it would be a great public relations story for the team to step up and pay a player who really deserved to be paid. Elton has a great work ethic, he's a team player, and he's a great face for the franchise.

The Clippers didn't step up. Miami signed Elton to the max, but because he was a restricted free agent the Clippers could match the deal, which they did.

If you are an employer, the more you pay an employee the more you want him or her to feel you are being fair. The last thing you want is to be paying an employee a lot of money and having that person feel like he or she is being cheated. I had a woman working for me in an administrative job. She was very good. But I started to hear from companies I dealt with that she was bad-mouthing me. So I fired her. All the companies liked this woman and they wanted to know why I would let her go. When I told them why, they essentially told me to grow up. They didn't understand why I would fire someone for being critical of me when there were a hundred media people doing the same thing every day. I told them I didn't mind being bad-mouthed, but I wasn't going to pay someone to do it.

If you are an owner and you are paying a modern NBA player $80 million to $100 million, the one thing you want—assuming the player works hard and stays healthy—is for that player to know you didn't have to be arm-wrestled into the deal. Why lose goodwill, particularly when it's so easy to maintain?

As I became more successful, I realized I could always say no. And I could say it very quietly and calmly. I didn't have to scream or yell. I could simply be myself. Ultimately, much of the success we had at FAME, and a lot of the success I have had since selling the company, can be attributed to me becoming someone who clearly knows his limitations, and that knowledge has allowed me to remain focused on the goal rather than the show.

FALK'S FUNDAMENTALS

Stay true to who you are.

Managing a business for the long term is the polar opposite of adopting a role in a feature film that will be produced over a period of months. Long-term productivity requires that we operate within our strengths even if our critics find fault along the way. Changing your operating style to satisfy short-term criticisms threatens the long-term stability of your organization.

Don't win the battle only to lose the war.

In the history of the National Football League, only one team has ever enjoyed a perfect season, the 1972 Miami Dolphins. As recently as 2007, the New England Patriots didn't lose a single game in the regular season, but the pressure mounted to eclipse the Dolphins record and the Patriots lost in the Super Bowl. Success is generally defined by reaching specific goals but often we must sacrifice certain short-term successes in order to arrive at our desired destination. Did chasing a perfect season interfere with the ultimate goal of winning a championship?

You must be willing to walk away.

Negotiation 101: In order to attain the ultimate deal, you must be willing to walk away from intermediate opportunities. This necessitates an honest appraisal of the strength of your position. A man on life support can't very well afford to pull the plug.

SIX

Goodwill Hunting

When a business is audited in corporate America, its value is derived on the basis of its hard assets—inventory, real estate, cash in the bank—and soft assets such as accounts receivable, dollar-denominated investments, and the like. But there is also a component of value called goodwill, which is the name value of the business in the marketplace, or the reputation of the business. It's an intangible, but one way or another, it is of significant value in every business.

In conducting business, especially one that involves negotiations, the goodwill developed over a specific period of interaction will have a major impact on future dealings not only with that particular company, but throughout the entire industry. The more publicity generated by your dealings, good or bad, the more of an impact the manner in which you have conducted yourself will affect the amount of goodwill you generate in the future.

In the sports world, which is a very finite space—there are

thirty teams in the NBA, thirty-two teams in the NFL, and thirty teams in Major League Baseball—I deal with the same owners over and over. Whether it's for a veteran player coming up for a new contract, rookies I represent on a specific team, or free agents I am trying to sign to new teams, the names and faces are generally the same. When I was in my thirties, certainly by the time I hit forty, I realized that it was important to earn the respect of these people by being both protective and aggressive on behalf of my clients. At the same time, it was equally important to develop a level of goodwill with management. I came to understand how important establishing trust with ownership and management was to my ability to achieve successful results on behalf of my clients. It was crucial that they didn't think I was trying to push them over the edge of the boundaries of fairness.

Likewise, one of the most perplexing issues for me over the last twenty years has been trying to understand why owners, who are about to pay a player a salary upwards of $100 million in guaranteed money would not want their employee to feel as though ownership had gone to the mat to make sure they were well paid, cared for, and respected. Instead, they engage in complex, dragged-out negotiations that result in the player still earning $100 million but feeling the owner neither wanted to pay him the money nor felt good about paying him the money.

Goodwill Is the Currency of Relationships

I sold FAME in 1998. We had a very small company, twenty-four total employees including two business partners. Unfortunately, in our business everything becomes public. From the players' salaries to the value of their shoe contracts it becomes available for public consumption. Because we sold the company to a publicly traded company, SFX, the amount we received also became public.

As a result, we were faced with a number of interesting decisions. The first had to do with our personnel. Having never sold a company before, there were a lot of potential unknowns that could negatively affect the staff, including layoffs. For example, we had a chief financial officer named Eugene Mason. We were concerned that the parent company would say, "David, we have twenty-five accountants in our New York office. You no longer need to have a CFO. We'll take care of all your accounting from the home office." We had a general counsel named David Bauman, who is my wife's first cousin. We were concerned SFX would tell us about all the in-house lawyers it had in New York, the parent company's general counsel, and its relationships with outside law firms: "We don't need to be spending money on a salary and office space for a general counsel."

In order to protect some of our senior people, who had worked very hard and had been an important part of the team that made our company successful, we gave them all five-year employment contracts and increased their salaries. In some cases we doubled their salaries. We also gave them stock options that we believed, incorrectly as it turned out, would become very valuable. Invariably, as human nature would have it, everyone was happy when we explained our rationale. We tried to protect them against the unknowns such as compensation policies, requests by the parent company to cut staff, and any other corporate issues that might come up.

But when it was announced that we sold the company for more than $100 million, we suddenly had a new set of problems. If the number had been $20 million, everyone would have been thrilled with their new salaries and employment contracts. At $100 million, the number seemed so large that everyone felt they were entitled to an additional cash bonus as well. I worked seventeen and a half years for Donald Dell and in that time I made less money—combined—than I made in my first two years on my own. The last thing I wanted was for any employee to feel we were trying to cut corners or be stingy.

We considered creating a fund to pay cash bonuses to some of the top people. While we were bouncing this idea around I happened to offer a flight on my private jet to Jeff Wechsler, who was one of our five senior people. Jeff had been with us approximately six years and he had done a very good job as the senior manager for clients Glenn Rice, Kenny Anderson, and a few others. During the flight Jeff said to me, "You know, I've worked for a number of years for you and I think I've done a really good job. I've produced a lot of revenue for the company. Don't you think it's appropriate that I get a bonus?" Since I had given considerable thought to the idea prior to the conversation, his plea really hit a soft spot.

"Jeff, I'm going to ask a question that no lawyer worth his salt would ever ask." Lawyers are never supposed to ask an open-ended question that they don't know the answer to, especially in court. "If I were inclined to give you a cash bonus, what do you think would be appropriate?"

Now if he would have told me $100,000, $150,000, maybe even $200,000, I probably would have written him a check on the spot independent of whether my partners agreed or not.

He thought about it. "I think what would be appropriate is something between $3 million and $5 million."

I was stunned.

"Jeff, that amount of money represents one hundred percent of what all the clients you have managed are paying the firm. Do you think, in your estimation, that I, having signed all those clients and negotiated all their contracts, had any role in the generation of the fees they are producing? Do I deserve any portion of those fees, or should I give you one hundred percent of all the fees?"

I realized that I had a dilemma. If I gave Jeff a bonus, then whatever I gave him, based on his expectations, wouldn't satisfy him. I was conflicted. I wanted to do something, but I wanted to engender the goodwill that should go with the action. I now realized that the bonuses I thought might be appropriate would make Jeff and our other top people unhappy. Time went by and there came a point where I had an issue with the company over the interpretation of my contract. Eventually we agreed the parent company owed me approximately $650,000. The issue was resolved about a year after we sold the business. I told the company, "If you agree that $650,000 is fair, then I would like to direct that money to a group of people in the office as an extraordinary bonus."

I gave Jeff Wechsler and three other people $100,000 each. I gave our CFO, one of our senior investment people, our public relations director, and my former secretary, who I promoted to client services manager, each $50,000. I gave my new assistant, who had just started, $25,000. Then I sprinkled the rest of the money around the office to the remaining staff.

On a scale of one to ten, the gesture registered maybe a two at

Walking on Air in Phoenix.

M. J. signing his very first endorsement contract to create a line of shoes and apparel called Air Jordan (1984).

Photo by J. B. Strasser

Before he was known as the "Hoya Destroya," Patrick Ewing was known as "Boomer." Here he is with Boomer Esiason and me at Madison Square Garden.

Photo by George Kalinsky for Madison Square Garden

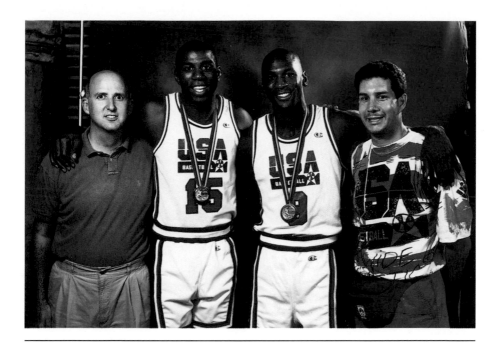

A golden moment at the Barcelona Olympics (1992) with Magic Johnson, Michael Jordan, and Magic's advisor, Lon Rosen.

© 1992 NBAE (Photo by Andrew D. Bernstein/NBAE/Getty Images)

A Mac Attack. With John McEnroe at the Garden.

Photo by George Kalinsky for Madison Square Garden

John Thompson encouraging Dikembe Mutombo at halftime of a Knicks game.

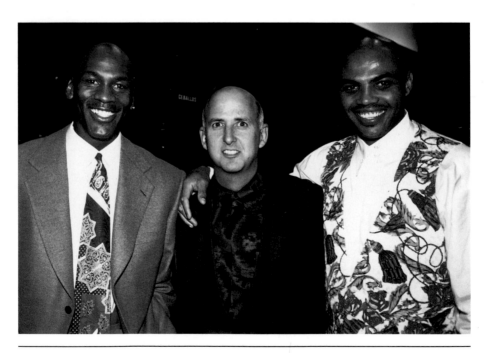

"Airing" it out with Charles Barkley in Phoenix.

The New York Times Magazine

NOVEMBER 17, 1996 / SECTIO'

Behind Michael Jordan™

David Falk is a
sports agent with a
vision – of sneaker
deals, movie deals,
restaurant deals.
Thanks to him,
pro athletes now
compete in a
whole new arena,
playing the
brand-name game.

By Lynn Hirschberg

I always wanted Michael to know that he could lean on me.

The New York Times, 11/17/1996 (Photo by Christian Witkin/NYT)

For David Falk—
with the bullish
best wishes of
Louis Rukeyser

After the final bell of *The Wall Street Report* with Curtis Polk and Louis Rukeyser.
Photo by Brian Slanger for Maryland Public Television

Hired assassin or retiring artist?
Bill Ballenberg (Photo by Bill Ballenberg/Sports Illustrated/Getty Images)

Sharing the moment with the guest of honor at Patrick Ewing's retirement at the Garden.

King for a day.

© 2002 NBAE (Photo by Rocky Widner/NBAE/Getty Images)

With visions of championships dancing in his head.

© 2008 NBAE (Photo by Garrett Ellwood/NBAE/Getty Images)

the top end for the four to whom I gave $100,000. They said thanks but it really didn't make much of an impact at all. By contrast, the last person I called in was Brenda, who had been my personal assistant from about 1994 to 1998. Brenda is a terrific person and she had recently sold a home at a loss and then purchased another one. Her finances were extremely tight.

One of my favorite Julia Roberts movies is *Erin Brockovich,* which is the true story of a single mom who loses a personal injury lawsuit and convinces her lawyer, played by Albert Finney, to give her a job in his law office. She has no legal background, but the lawyer agrees to hire her as a file clerk. Brockovich eventually comes across a case that was filed against Pacific Gas & Electric. She comes to believe that the facts of the case don't make sense and she convinces Finney to allow her to keep digging. Eventually she uncovers a vast conspiracy. The firm becomes involved in litigation against Pacific Gas & Electric over a plant that was knowingly emitting chromium into the ground where it entered the water supply and caused a tremendous number of serious medical conditions for local residents.

Finney promises to pay Erin a $2,000 to $3,000 bonus for her work. Single-handedly, she gets all the residents to sign a petition to join the class-action lawsuit the firm would manage. At the end of the movie, the firm wins the case and the members of the class action are awarded the largest amount of money ever in California for a class-action lawsuit, $333 million. Finney wants to give Erin a significant bonus for getting the residents to sign on to the class action. He calls her into his office. He has a check in his hand and he acknowledges promising her upwards of $2,000. Then he tells her that things have changed and as a result he feels he has to change the amount of the bonus. She becomes very upset and dresses him up and down about how lawyers are all the same, that they never keep their word. Finney is flabbergasted. Finally he says, "Here's the damn check." The check is for $2 million.

That's the exact experience I had with Brenda. She came into my office and I gave her a personal Christmas bonus and a raise. Then I told her that I wanted to give her a onetime founder's bonus for doing such a great job.

"So I'd like to give you fifty thousand dollars."

Right away she got very upset.

"That's really not funny, David. You know things are tight for me and I don't appreciate you making a joke out of my situation."

I was stunned. I didn't know if she was trying to be funny or really serious. "I'm not trying to make a joke," I said. "I am giving you a fifty-thousand-dollar check."

She got really angry.

"David, that's not funny. I told you. I lost money on my home. Things are really tight and I don't appreciate being the brunt of your jokes."

I pride myself on being a good communicator but I felt like Albert Finney in *Erin Brockovich*. Finally I said, "Look Brenda, here's the damn check."

She opened the envelope, saw the check for $50,000, and broke out crying. I was holding back the tears as well because it was such an emotional moment. I had the exact same experience with Alyson, who was the head of public relations, and Mary Ellen, who had recently joined the company as my assistant. Their appreciation made me feel happy that I'd given them the money.

By contrast, the $100,000 I gave to the four most senior executives didn't generate much if any goodwill.

As fate would have it, one of the people I had given $100,000 to, Nina Mitchell, was the number two person in our investment company, FINAD, which managed the financial affairs for our clients. She had the most seniority of anyone in the company except me, but Nina was neither a partner, nor a principal. Like Jeff, she was very vocal about the idea that she deserved $1 million, even though the entire financial division didn't generate $1 million in profits. She did a great job managing the clients once I brought them through the door, but she was a manager, not an income producer. I thought $100,000 on top of her salary increase, employment contract, and stock options was generous. She didn't agree.

Shortly afterward, we had a disagreement over a client whom I had tried to persuade to use FINAD. The client eventually chose Bob Mosberg, whom Nina and I both knew, to manage his money. Nina was surprised that Bob, who worked with very high net worth people but previously had never managed any athletes, had signed our client. She sent me an e-mail asking if I knew of Bob's plans to expand his money management business to include athletes. Since she happened to know Bob longer than I did, I told her to give him a call if she was so curious.

Clearly there was some tension between us. Finally I called her into my office.

"Nina, you've had a burr in your saddle for the last year or so since we sold the company. From the bottom of my heart, I am sorry you feel that way. We doubled your salary. We gave you more stock options than anyone else except the principals and recently I personally gave you a $100,000 bonus. I had hoped it would make you feel better that we had recompensed you appropriately for your service."

"You know, that's what really bothers me the most," she replied. "You dare to take credit for this $100,000 that I got from the company. You had nothing to do with it."

Once again, I was the lawyer in *Erin Brockovich*.

"You are too bright to be serious about what you are alleging. The company owed me money. Instead of the company paying me $100,000, and me personally paying $40,000 to $45,000 in taxes, and then paying you a bonus of $55,000, I told the company to send the entire amount to you."

It just didn't register. It was a total failure on my part. I made a gesture that I thought was significant in an attempt to make her feel appreciated and generate some goodwill from a person I liked and respected, who had been a very loyal, long-term employee. We didn't have the same economic view of her services because the investment part of the business was designed to protect our clients' money. It was a very labor-intensive, service-oriented business and was not a significant profit center. Despite all my ambitions, I failed. I didn't generate any goodwill by sacrificing $100,000 of my own money. Incredibly, I wasn't even able to convince Nina I was the one responsible for her bonus.

It was a great learning experience for me. I totally failed to generate goodwill from an action that was 100 percent a goodwill gesture.

If I could do it all over again I would call Brenda in and ask her what it had cost her to buy her new home. She would tell me that it had cost her about a quarter of a million dollars. Then I would say, "Here's a special founder's bonus for $250,000. I want you to pay your house off in full."

Why? She gave me the most value in goodwill. Seven years later, she still talks about that day. It made an impact on the rest of her life. It wasn't the amount of the money. She didn't gauge the value of the gift by the amount. It was just the thought that I would give her an extraordinary payment above her bonus, above her raise. She felt respected and valued by the gesture and it created millions of dollars of goodwill in our personal relationship. By contrast with Nina, who received twice the amount of money, the act registered zero. If anything it was a negative. She didn't feel it was enough and she didn't even give me credit as the originator of the gift.

Goodwill Is the Lubricant That Greases Deals

That story is a microcosm about how I feel about doing business in today's NBA. The salary structure continues to get polarized. The better players are making larger amounts of money, but because there is a luxury tax built into the system many of the middle-class players are getting squeezed. I tried to explain to owners that if they were going to pay a player upwards of $100 million guaranteed, the last thing they want is to be in the situation I was in with Nina Mitchell. She didn't feel that the person who gave the money deserved any credit. I tell owners, "If you are going to pay one of my clients $100 million, don't let me, as the agent, receive all the credit for wrangling the money out of you or otherwise forcing you to pay this amount of money. If you are going to pay $100 million, you want that player to walk out to center court and thank you in front of a full house. You want him to feel that much goodwill for you and the franchise based on your gesture."

Sadly, the process of negotiation often gets off track relative to that concept. Instead of compressing the time necessary to make a deal, some owners drag it out. When all is said and done, the player feels about the owner the way Nina Mitchell felt about me.

In sports, particularly when you do repeat business with the same people, I cannot overestimate the value of goodwill. It's the lubricant that greases deals, the emotional intangible that promotes relationships. I believe with the utmost conviction that most people with whom I do business are bright people. They have gone to college, business school, and maybe even law school. They have been extremely successful in their business just as I have in mine. When we sit down to discuss a deal, I am going to propose they do something—sign my client to a new contract, use my client in an endorsement deal, trade my client to another team, or take any one of a number of similar actions. My counterpart thinks about my idea, but he isn't quite comfortable.

In my entire life, I've met very few people who are so persuasive that they could convince me to do something I didn't want to do. Conversely, with as much success as I've been credited with in the sports world, I still don't consider myself to be a genie who can magically convince someone who doesn't want to spend $100 million to spend the $100 million. What happens is that you reach a point where both sides are close, but there is a gap between your position and the comfort level of the person on the other side of the table. What bridges that gap is not verbiage, PowerPoint presentations, brochures, or recommendations. It's goodwill.

That person may be thinking, I'm not quite there, but I've had a really great relationship with David over the last twenty-five years. There are four or five things he's recommended that have worked great, so I'm going to give him the benefit of the doubt.

The exact opposite happens when there is no goodwill. If you haven't generated goodwill from past dealings, then you are missing the ingredient that closes the vast majority of deals that get made every day all around the world. It's an intangible feeling of trust. You like the other person because you know that rather than trying to squeeze you for the last dollar, he is trying to work with you. He is trying to accomplish something for his client but it's not adverse to your interests. In situations where I've had that kind of goodwill, making deals is easy. In situations where goodwill doesn't exist, I don't think there are enough texts on negotiating or sales techniques to persuade the other person to do something because the comfort level that derives from goodwill is missing.

To generate goodwill you have to be honest. The other person has to know that when you tell him a particular player is good for him, you are not trying to close a deal that ultimately will negatively affect the franchise. If you have a positive track record of making sound recommendations, the next one becomes easy. The same is true for owners. One of the notable examples was Edward DeBartolo, who owned the San Francisco 49ers during the glory years with Joe Montana, Jerry Rice, and Roger Craig. Every player in the league wanted to play for the 49ers. San Francisco is a beautiful city, the team was winning, and DeBartolo was known for going the extra mile to make the players feel appreciated. Along with Bill Walsh and Carmen Policy, the team's coach and president, respectively, DeBartolo created what amounted to a family atmosphere not unlike the old Boston Celtics.

In the old days when Red Auerbach coached and managed the Celtics, his teams won eleven championships in thirteen years. When his players retired, Red found jobs for them with the franchise. In 2008, Bob Cousy, who hasn't dribbled a basketball in forty years, and Tom Heinsohn were still Celtics broadcasters. Red created a strong sense of loyalty, of goodwill. That intangible creates a magnet for players. Players wanted to play for the Celtics. Jerry Colangelo, who owned the Phoenix Suns and eventually the Arizona Diamondbacks, is a gentleman and purveyor of goodwill. He is charismatic, and he was a very successful owner. Players wanted to play in Phoenix because they knew Jerry would take care of them. He had a passion for basketball and I think he communicated that passion to the players, though he remained a great businessman. I think Colangelo and DeBartolo derived a greater joy from their sports franchises than they did from their other businesses.

I signed Elton Brand in 1999, when every agent in the country wanted him. Elton is a wonderful, intelligent person whom Chicago made the No. 1 pick in the 1999 draft. Following his second season, Elton was traded to the Los Angeles Clippers. I live in Washington, D.C., and while I travel extensively, it's not easy to see Elton more than once a month. I really enjoy Elton and we have a very close relationship. I try to act as part business advisor and part mentor, helping him develop a methodology for making sound business decisions. He's very bright with a high level of curiosity about business. We were out to dinner one night and I wondered whether geography affected our relationship.

"Elton, do you still get recruited by other agents? Do they still come up to you and try to persuade you to sign with them?"

He looked as if I had asked him if he brushed his teeth in the morning or worked out during the off-season.

"David, when I go out to dinner in Los Angeles I have on average six different agents come up to me and ask me, 'When was the last time David was in Los Angeles? Are you happy with the marketing? Is David taking care of you?' "

If I had to worry the other twenty-eight days that I'm not in Los Angeles that Elton was going to fire me and hire someone else, I would either lose my mind or I'd lose a client. What I hope is that the level of care and feeling is there. The level of performance is obvious. I would hope that the intangibles of caring, the friendship we have developed, and the passion I have put in above and beyond what's required in the job to help him develop as a businessman provide a reservoir of goodwill that carries him for the twenty-eight days I am not in Los Angeles while the piranhas in the business try to steal my client.

I signed Jeff Green from Georgetown in 2007, my first rookie since Elton. Jeff was drafted No. 5 by Seattle. Seattle is the longest flight in the continental United States from Washington, D.C. There is not another franchise anywhere in the NBA that is farther away from where I live than Seattle. Right after we signed the contract with the SuperSonics, I shared with him my experience with Elton. I told him I'd try to get to Seattle every six weeks or so and meet up with him on the road from time to time, and that he could call me every day if he needed to. I told him he would be approached by a lot of agents who live on the West Coast, some of whom might live an hour from the arena. I also told him I couldn't compete with geography.

"If you are looking for someone to be around all the time, then you should fire me. I only hope the work I've done preparing you for the draft, and helping you secure contracts with Nike, Vitamin Water, and some of the team's sponsors demonstrates that I am here for you when you need me. I can't come live with you. If that's what it takes for me to keep you as a client, then the relationship is going to fail."

Jeff expressed a quiet confidence and a high level of maturity and responded that he did not need someone to come live with him. In fact, even though many young players bring their parents and sometimes their entourages to live with them, Jeff moved to Seattle by himself. I made the comment to him not because I was challenging his maturity, but to condition him to the fact that he would be encountering many agents on the West Coast who would be attending games in Seattle and testing his commitment to me on a weekly basis.

I like Jeff immensely. He's very inquisitive and bright, but he's not very vocal. I truly believe we've started a bank of goodwill that will sustain our relationship in the years ahead.

You need that kind of goodwill in every relationship you have, business and personal, because it bridges the gap even when the gap is geographical. I've met some incredibly persuasive people in my lifetime. I've met Tony Robbins several times. He is one of the most successful motivational speakers in the world. He has multi-millionaires working in Wall Street brokerage firms tearing his walls down to get time with him. I say that with the utmost respect. But I don't think Tony Robbins could persuade me to do something I didn't want to do. If I was ambivalent, I might do it because I like Tony Robbins. He's a good guy and I don't think he would try to persuade me to do something that was detrimental to me just to prove that he could.

Goodwill Can Be Your Most Valuable Asset

Goodwill is like the *x* factor. It's difficult to put your finger on and sometimes it's even difficult to define. But it's an incredibly important intangible quality that's as valuable as any asset you can put on a balance sheet. Often it's more valuable. Yet it seems that for many people, it is a concept alien to their mind-set. They look at business in a nuts-and-bolts way, value for value, a winner and a loser. I think they miss the whole point.

In the summer of 2004, I received a call from Mitch Kupchak, general manager and head of basketball operations for the Los Angeles Lakers. Phil Jackson had decided to take time off from coaching, Shaquille O'Neal had been traded to Miami on July 14, and the Lakers were searching for a new coach. Mitch had been a marketing client of ProServ in the late 1970s and early 1980s when he played for Washington. He is someone I like immensely. He indicated to me that the Lakers were looking to hire a high-profile coach to replace Phil. And they were interested in Mike Krzyzewski.

It was an interesting dynamic because Mitch had gone to the

University of North Carolina, which is Duke's chief rival, six miles down the road. Mitch is also an absolute acolyte of Dean Smith, but was now talking to me about hiring the Duke coach. We set up a meeting at Mike's home.

Mitch was terrific: very candid and honest. He answered all of Mike's questions. We talked for about two hours and in the process of the conversation, I told Mitch that the only way Mike would consider the opportunity was if he was the only person they were talking to and if he became the highest-paid coach in the NBA. At the time, Larry Brown was the highest-paid coach in the NBA, making $9 million a year. After Mitch left, Mike, his wife Mickie—who is very involved in all his business decisions—and I batted around the idea. The offer definitely intrigued Mike. He had been offered NBA jobs previously, most notably by the Boston Celtics.

He asked me what I thought.

"Jerry Buss is a great owner, Kobe Bryant is the best young player in the league, maybe the best player in the game, but with the Shaq trade, I think the timing is really bad."

I knew Mike loved Duke. He views himself as much a teacher as he does a coach. For a number of reasons, coaching in the NBA is not the same as coaching in college, even at a major university. I thought it was a tremendous financial opportunity, but Mike has a beautiful home in Durham and lives near his kids and his four grandchildren. It's just a special environment and Mike has tremendous equity after being at Duke for nearly twenty-five years. In the end, we all agreed it was a great experience going through the process and understanding Mike's value in the market. While it was flattering to think he could become the highest-paid coach in the history of professional sports, I didn't think he truly had his heart in it. We ended up calling Mitch back and turning down the opportunity.

The minute we hung up the phone, I thought, Gosh, that's a lot of money to turn down.

"You know, Mike, I think you made a great decision for yourself. But now I have to really roll up my sleeves and get to work ramping up the marketing machine."

The very first deal we made was with American Express. Like most things in business—and this is why goodwill is so critically important—the deal came about due to a combination of people. One was a local consultant named Gary Stevenson, who had attended Duke and later worked for me in marketing at ProServ. The second person was Mark Dowley, who also worked for me at ProServ and went on to run the marketing department for a large Hollywood agency called Endeavor, which is run by my very good friend Ari Emanuel, the younger brother of Rahm, who is now a congressman from Illinois. American Express had a campaign in which it used longtime cardholders. After a number of discussions we ended up making the deal. It was a very short-term contract for a relatively small amount of money.

But they made a truly amazing commercial. It showed Mike on the Duke court, which is called the Coach K Court. It showed him in his office with pictures of great players such as Grant Hill hanging on the wall behind him. They bought so much commercial time during February and March that it seemed like the commercial was on every five minutes. In fact, it was so widely exposed that a lot of other coaches started complaining that the commercial was more like an infomercial for Duke. As always, the man who had the most insightful line about the campaign and the publicity generated was John Thompson, who called me one day and said, "I want you to know I am not jealous of Mike. He's earned it. But I am envious." Mike, John Thompson, and John Thompson III are the only coaches I've had a professional relationship with. In John Thompson's case we go back to 1982.

The American Express affiliation and the exposure Mike received were incredible. It was one of the few times in my career where I thought we probably should have paid the company for the relationship and not vice-versa. The frequency with which the commercial ran, combined with the class with which it was produced, showed Mike not as a highly competitive coach, but as a teacher and a friend. It was just tremendous.

In this one case, the intangible value of the goodwill generated by the commercial established a foundation upon which other companies became his long-term partners. It's an important example of the power of goodwill. It started with people with whom I had past experience and culminated with the execution of the program.

Goodwill Must Be Earned Before It Can Be Employed

Goodwill also flows downhill when a team or a player doesn't recognize an opportunity to generate goodwill. It's a lesson I have shared with my clients as well as others. Kevin Garnett is my favorite nonclient in the NBA. I love his competitiveness and intensity. While I don't believe there will ever be another Michael Jordan, on or off the court, Kevin has that same kind of compulsively competitive nature.

He came into the NBA straight out of high school. Because he's never had an agent who had the desire or the ability to teach him about business the way I was able to teach Michael, I sense Kevin doesn't have a mentor.

In the summer of 2006, I represented John Lucas III, the son of my very first client, John Lucas. John tried out for two teams that summer, the Cleveland Cavaliers and the Minnesota Timberwolves. He went to the summer league with Minnesota. Kevin invited John to stay at his house, gave John a car to drive, and really supported him. In turn, John really played well for Minnesota that summer. Kevin definitely thought the team needed a player like John, who could be a backup point guard who provides energy and speed off the bench. Management had other thoughts and released him.

I called Jim Stack, who is a very nice man and the general manager in Minnesota. He told me John had been cut in favor of a six-foot-ten power forward who ended up in the NBA Development League playing for one of my former clients, Jeff Malone. Jeff told me there was zero chance of the guy ever playing in the NBA and he was right. I called John at Kevin's house and explained the team's decision. Then I asked John if he would put Kevin on the phone.

"I really want to thank you for the support you showed John," I told Kevin. "It was very thoughtful of you to let him stay at your house. Your encouragement meant a lot. I don't want to extend myself to an inappropriate place, but I'd like to give you some free advice."

"What's that?"

"Did you ever watch *The Wizard of Oz*?"

Kevin laughed.

"Of course. Who hasn't seen *The Wizard of Oz*?"

"How did Dorothy get back to Kansas?"

He thought for a minute.

"She clicked the heels of her red shoes three times."

"Exactly. Now why did she wait until the end of the movie to click her heels? Why didn't she click them the minute she got to Oz?"

"Because she didn't know she had the power."

"Kevin, you're Dorothy. You are one of the top players in the league. You have the power to sit down with management once a year at least and say, 'There's a player I'd like to have on our team. You can sign him for the minimum.' It's not like you are asking management to sign a $10-million-a-year player, or to go out and sign Kobe Bryant for $20 million. You are asking them, as a favor to you, to keep John Lucas for one year at the NBA minimum, which is $400,000. Kevin, you have just agreed to a new contract paying you as much as $10 million less than you could have earned had you put yourself into the market. If you can't learn how to use the red shoes—the goodwill you have generated—once a year to enable management, without even thinking about it, to sign a player for one year at the minimum, then there is a problem. You shouldn't be playing for the Minnesota Timberwolves. If they don't have enough respect for you to agree to that request, then you should be playing elsewhere."

If you analyzed Kevin Garnett's mind-set, you would ask, Did he know how to use his power? I would say yes. I believe Kevin is an intelligent individual. I don't think he felt he needed to use his power. Because of who he was, the team should have recognized his status and come to him. I often use this analogy with players: If you won the lottery and a huge amount of money, let's say $500 million, whom would you hire to manage your money? They invariably tell me about their guy in New York, Chicago, or Los Angeles. No. Wrong answer. If you suddenly had that much money you should want to hire Warren Buffett, probably the top investment expert in the last hundred years in the United States. But Buffett is not going to read about you winning the lottery, then pick up the phone and call you to see if he can make a presentation. You have to make that effort, and even then it's unlikely that Warren Buffett is going to agree to help. Glen Taylor is the owner of the Minnesota Timberwolves. While he's not Warren Buffett, he is a billionaire and a very successful businessman. Like Buffett, he is not going to call Kevin Garnett and ask him if there is anything Kevin wants the team to do. He would expect that if Kevin has strong feelings about issues on the team, he will call the owner and ask to sit down and discuss them.

The converse of the situation is Kobe Bryant, who has been in the league since he was seventeen years old. Kobe has been extremely proactive publicly about trying to initiate certain movements within the Lakers. While I admire his desire to exercise his power, I think he's at the opposite end of the spectrum from Kevin. He has publicly put his reputation on the line to effectuate changes that should have been made behind the scenes. While Kobe clearly acknowledges the power he has as perhaps the best player in the

NBA in the post–Michael Jordan era, and as marketable as he is, nevertheless when he goes public with his demands and frustrations with management it undermines his popularity. It also puts such a spotlight on his relationship with the owner, Jerry Buss, that instead of making it easier to bring about these changes it makes it more difficult. Jerry is a highly intelligent individual and a successful businessman. I don't think he wants to run a team where the inmates are running the asylum. How to exercise power is a very difficult thing to learn. You have to learn how to use it and when. In Kevin's case, because his salary was so high it became very difficult for ownership to bring in the kinds of players who would allow the team to make a championship run. So they made the decision to start all over again. At the end of the day, Kevin got what he wanted regardless of which side initiated the change. I do think, however, he could have achieved the same result a few years earlier had he had the ability to sit down with Glen and have the kind of discussions they probably had at the end.

Kevin and young players like him shouldn't have to ask management for favors. Based on what they have accomplished, it should be a given. Conversely, management should have recognized the opportunity, at virtually no cost, to generate goodwill with its only superstar, a player who had essentially left $10 million on the table to help the team build a better roster.

A similar thing happened when Alvin Gentry became head coach of the Detroit Pistons. I have known Alvin since he was Larry Brown's assistant at the University of Kansas. The Pistons fired Doug Collins and on February 2, 1998, made Alvin the interim head coach. I happened to be in Boston on business staying in the same hotel as the Pistons, who were in town to play the Celtics. Of all the players I have ever met and not signed, the one who always disappointed me most was Grant Hill. I like and respect Grant and he comes from a great family. He went to Duke, where he had great success, and he's from Washington, D.C. Grant played at South Lakes High School, where he succeeded Michael Jackson, a dear friend of mine who went on to play at Georgetown and with the Sacramento Kings. Grant came out of Duke in 1994, exactly ten years after Michael Jordan went to the NBA from North Carolina. For a number of reasons, it would have been a perfect fit for both of us. But it never came to pass.

Once I realized the Pistons were in the same hotel, I gave Grant a buzz and he came up to my room. For the first time, we talked in depth about what happened in 1994 and why we had never gotten together. I asked him if he was happy in Detroit and we talked about the coaching change.

"Who would you like to see as the next coach?"

"I'd love to see Alvin get the job. He's really good with the players and I think he'd be good for our team."

I asked him how Joe Dumars felt. Joe was the senior member of the team at that time. Joe is a humble man and ironically, the polar opposite of his former backcourt mate, Isiah Thomas. While Joe, in his own quiet, dignified way, has done a masterful job running the Pistons and guiding them to an NBA title, Isiah, who is always willing to pump up himself and his abilities, managed the New York Knicks to an unmitigated disaster that will probably take years to correct.

"Yeah, Joe's on board," Grant said.

"I guess it's over then."

He looked at me quizzically.

"What do you mean?"

"Well, if you want Alvin to be the coach and Joe wants Alvin to be the coach, then it's a fait accompli. You just have to walk into management and tell Rick Sund [the general manager] or Tom Wilson [the team president] that you two would like Alvin to be the head coach and it's done."

I could tell there was a disconnect. He couldn't understand why I thought the decision was so automatic. We had another discussion, a bit like the one I had with Kevin. I tried to explain to him that one of the things a star player has to learn is that he has an inherent power—goodwill—as a result of his performance on the floor. A player has to learn how and when to use that power positively. Grant is a passive individual by nature. That is an endearing quality for a man with his looks, talent, and pedigree. He's very humble. But there are times as a leader when players have to take control of the situation. They have to step up to the plate, take a rip, and make things happen. Yet human nature often doesn't allow us to be very good at representing ourselves.

Kevin wasn't a very good agent for himself because he didn't understand how to express his desire to have John Lucas. He wasn't able to quantify or recognize the reservoir of goodwill he had built. Grant wasn't aware that the power of the goodwill he earned could be used to affect the team's head coaching decision. I think the reason in part is that players are used to having others, people such as myself, make those plays for them. None are more used to that than my clients. At the same time, I try to teach them that there are times when they have to be able to take that walk themselves, particularly when it's in the best interest of everyone involved.

Goodwill Cuts Both Ways

As I've said, goodwill cuts both ways. During my thirty-five years in business, I have come across few executives who better exemplify the positive results that come from investments in goodwill than Bill Schmidt, the former director of sports marketing for Gatorade. Bill was a modern-day Santa Claus who dispensed game tickets, T-shirts, Gatorade products, and a variety of other gifts that made people want to do repeat business with his company. Bill called me in the spring of 1993 and explained that Gatorade had planned a new ad campaign for Michael Jordan that featured the song "Be Like Him" from the Disney movie *Jungle Book.* Bill asked if I had any contacts at Disney who could assist Gatorade in obtaining the rights to use the song in Michael's new commercials. Coincidentally, I had just received an inquiry from a division of Disney that produced children's books, seeking to have Michael produce a series of interactive children's educational products.

I called the executive at Disney who made this inquiry and requested her assistance in obtaining clearance to use "Be Like Him" in Michael's Gatorade commercials. I explained that her assistance would create a more positive environment to discuss a potential Jordan affiliation with the children's learning products she was seeking. After checking with the appropriate people, she explained that the cost of clearing "Be Like Him" would be $350,000 for a thirty-second commercial. This was simply unworkable for Gatorade. So instead of using "Be Like Him," Gatorade hired a young, up-and-coming music group in Chicago to compose music for the new Jordan campaign. The group came up with a very catchy song called "Be Like Mike," which became one of the most popular and successful catchphrases in advertising history. The entire expense for composing and performing the song "Be Like Mike" and licensing it to Gatorade was $10,000.

Several months later, I received another call from Disney as the Bulls were about to wrap up their third consecutive NBA championship.

Disney wanted Michael to look into the camera as he ran off the court following the team's victory in the deciding game and utter the famous phrase "I'm Going to Disney World." Michael had produced a similar spot for Disney after the first championship (1991) and shared the $100,000 fee equally with the Bulls starters. Disney explained that the fee for the spot remained $100,000 and that no one had ever been paid more. I explained that Michael isn't like anyone else and that it would take considerably more than that to close a deal, especially after his third championship and our experience with "Be Like Him."

After a series of discussions I told them Michael would agree to do the spot for $200,000: $100,000 to Michael and $100,000 to a charity he designated.

When Disney responded to me, they said they would pay him $150,000, but all of it would go to Michael's charity of choice. The entire process was irritating for several reasons, not the least of which was that Michael did not really want to do the spot. But he was trying to accommodate Disney despite the fiasco with "Be Like Him." We had negotiated in good faith and after a seemingly endless amount of back-and-forth, not only did they fail to significantly change the deal, they now wanted to control where the money went.

I was furious. I told them, "After all this time this is the best you can do? The price is now $500,000."

Ironically, this final conversation took place in my hotel room in Chicago during a meeting with Dean Barrett, the head of sports marketing for the McDonald's Corporation. When I hung up from my unpleasant and unsuccessful conversation with Disney, Dean smiled and asked whether McDonald's could pay Michael $100,000 and make an additional $100,000 contribution to his chosen charity to produce a championship commercial for McDonald's. Dean proposed that as Michael walked off the court he would be asked, "Michael, are you hungry for a fourth championship?" to which Michael would reply, "No, I'm hungry for a Big Mac." We shook hands on the spot and made this championship commercial an amendment to Michael's long-standing relationship with McDonald's.

For a $100,000 contribution to charity, a minimal investment for a large corporation, Disney could have engendered significant goodwill with one of the most popular individuals on Earth and received the unprecedented promotional value he generated. Instead, it took a simple deal, overnegotiated it, and lost the opportunity to have Michael Jordan celebrate his third consecutive championship at Disney World.

Two situations for identical money. One company didn't embrace the concept of goodwill and as a result failed in its attempt to have the most popular and successful athlete participate in its celebrity campaign. Ironically, several years later we unsuccessfully approached Disney to produce Michael's movie *Space Jam,* which became a blockbuster hit for Warner Bros.

McDonald's, on the other hand, creatively and immediately exploited Disney's failure and was able not only to strengthen its long-term public affiliation with Jordan by enjoying the afterglow of the Bulls' "three-peat," but also to lampoon Disney's long-standing celebrity campaign. And Gatorade, using an unknown song from an unknown group, ended up with an ad campaign that still has resonance today.

From power to money to a long-term ability to do business, few intangibles stand the test of time as goodwill does.

FALK'S FUNDAMENTALS

Goodwill is the currency of relationships.

In an age of instant information and access, competing parties will frequently find themselves in very comparable negotiating positions. What enables them to cross the divide is goodwill.

Goodwill is the lubricant that greases deals.

Highly intelligent and successful people are unlikely to persuade colleagues and competitors of a similar bent through facts, figures, or even negotiating ability to do something they don't feel comfortable doing. What enables them to fuse two very powerful and competing forces is goodwill.

Goodwill can be your most valuable asset.

Unlike cash, inventory, real estate, or other hard assets that can be measured with traditional metrics, goodwill frequently can be the ultimate determinant of success and failure in business. Developing and maintaining a reservoir of goodwill among employees, colleagues, and even competitors is often more valuable than more tangible assets.

Goodwill must be earned before it can be employed.

Most highly successful competitors perform well under pressure. The challenge brings out their leadership abilities, their innate competitiveness, and turbocharges their skill set. By contrast, goodwill is most often earned by doing the right thing when there is no pressure to do it. By going the extra mile to be supportive, respectful, generous, and loyal, an executive earns this most valuable commodity.

Goodwill cuts both ways.

By failing to recognize natural opportunities to do the small things that create goodwill, executives often plant a negative seed that grows into reverse goodwill. When the leader most needs to call upon his troops for support, a vote of confidence, or double-duty mission, the obvious prior failure to do the right thing, to make the small gesture, rebounds with unexpected negative force.

SEVEN

The Customer Isn't Always Right

There's an age-old business axiom that says the customer is always right. The axiom is most often associated with services provided. If the customer doesn't like a hotel room, give him another. If he complains about the food, offer to take it off the bill. To maintain loyalty, the axiom demands accommodation. Do whatever is necessary to make the customer happy and you will maintain the relationship. The implication in a client-based business is that if the customer says he wants A, even if you know B is better for him, you acquiesce to the customer's wishes regardless of the outcome.

Often the opposite is true. If you are conscious that "it's a long horse race," you will have the confidence to tell a customer when he isn't right, particularly when the ramifications of a wrong decision, which might not be obvious to the customer at the time, are clear to you.

Don't Be Afraid to Let a Customer
Know When He's Wrong

In the summer of 2006, I bumped into an old friend, Heavy D, in the lobby of the L'Ermitage hotel in Beverly Hills. I've known Heavy for a long time and he's a very interesting man. He's also a well-liked and respected personality in the hip-hop community. He asked me, as a personal favor, to meet with a good friend of his named Lewis Tucker.

Lewis is in his early forties and he grew up with Heavy in Mount Vernon, New York. Lewis played basketball at the Tuskegee Institute in Alabama. He was president of Bad Boy Records, Sean "Diddy" Combs's record company, for five years and now he was dabbling in sports through a start-up agency in New York called Essential Sports. With his music connections, Lewis signed five very good young players—Jarvis Hayes, Charlie Villanueva, Ben Gordon, Daniel Gibson, and Antoine Wright. That's an impressive lineup for an agency just coming out of the blocks. His partner was a young man named Billy Ceisler. After the fifth or sixth client, Billy decided they needed to get divorced and split up the business. Both of them probably thought they would keep all the clients. Heavy wanted me to advise Lewis about the business. Heavy had a personal interest in Ben Gordon, who also had grown up in Mount Vernon, the small town north of Manhattan that for decades has been a hotbed of basketball talent. Gus and Ray Williams, Rodney McCray, Earl Tatum, Rudy Hackett, and a lot of other talented players who played in the NBA grew up in Mount Vernon.

Lewis wanted to keep Ben as a client. His idea was to partner with me to negotiate Ben's new contract. Lewis wasn't even a registered basketball agent. Billy was the registered agent for their company, with Lewis handling the marketing. Now that they were getting divorced, Ben was trying to decide which parent he wanted to live with, or whether he wanted to live with someone else entirely.

I hadn't signed a top rookie since Elton Brand in 1999 and had barely spent any time trying to, so interacting with Ben was fun for me. At this point in my life, whether I sign a player or not is not going to make a material difference in my lifestyle or track record. So I wanted to get to know Ben to decide if I would be motivated to represent him. As it turned out, I really liked him. He is a very serious, hardworking, and likable young man.

The process was completely different than the usual agent-client recruiting game. I was completely blunt with him from the start and maybe even a little irreverent. I think it stunned him. He had never really talked to anyone in my position who wasn't trying to stroke him, recruit him, or tell him how great he was. He seemed to like the fact I was candid, though it was difficult for him to process. At times he would laugh out loud. At others he would look at me as if I were an alien. Lewis was very confident that once Ben developed a comfort level with me (which he already enjoyed with Lewis), he would decide to go with us.

Our meetings continued for months into the late spring of 2007. I couldn't believe Ben hadn't made a decision. I had business in Chicago and went to see the Bulls play in March of that year. After the game Ben and several of his friends joined me for dinner at a place Ben picked called SushiSamba. It was a combination of Mardi Gras and salsa and it was amazingly loud.

Between the dancing and the music it was virtually impossible to have a conversation. At one point I asked Ben, "Do you think if we had a meeting in the middle of the runway at O'Hare it could be any noisier?"

Several days before our dinner, I had received a call from a very good friend, affectionately known as "Worldwide" Wes. He asked me if I was trying to sign Ben Gordon. I told him I had visited with Ben at Heavy's request but that I was simply trying to help Lewis keep him.

"I'm just trying to get a comfort level with him," I told Wes, "to determine if the relationship will work."

"He's talking to the Raymond brothers. If you want, I could help you," Wes replied.

I had never heard of the Raymond brothers. I knew the Goodwin brothers, who were twins, and the Posten brothers, who also were twins. So that night I told Ben I heard he was meeting with the Raymond brothers.

"David, it's not the Raymond brothers," Ben responded. "It's just one person, Raymond Brothers."

I had clarified that fact earlier in the day, but I was trying to jibe Ben just the same. During our time together, Ben developed a passion for collecting watches. I have been collecting watches for years. It got to the point that before Ben would shake my hand he'd lift up my sleeve to see what kind of watch I was wearing.

"If you can't tell the difference between Raymond Brothers and me, it would be like walking into Cellini's in New York and not knowing whether you like a Timex or a Rolex."

He thought that was hilarious. As someone who loves analogies, I admit I found it amusing as well. But when the laughter subsided, and thank God so did the music and dancing, I knew it was time to get serious.

"I want you to know that I really like you and I have enjoyed getting to know you. I would truly love to help you. You are a very serious young man with enormous talent and there are a lot of things I could share with you both about competing on the court and about business off the court. But I want you to understand that at this point in my life, I don't *have* to be representing players. I'm doing it because I want to, because I love to. You have taken seven months agonizing over your decisions. I just want to make it easy for you. You need me to help you a lot more than I need you to let me help you."

He didn't react at that moment. After the fact, it turned out that those words destroyed seven months of relationship building. My bluntness really affected him. It actually offended him. Ultimately he decided to sign with Raymond Brothers.

When Lewis informed me of Ben's decision his disappointment was palpable. Of all his clients, Lewis felt closest to Ben because they came from the same hometown. So he was more than a little upset that I had been so blunt. Maybe blunt wasn't so beautiful in this case. So I called Ben.

"First, I want you to know I'm disappointed you chose not to stay with Lewis. Second, I want you to know that if I offended you by what I said, I want to apologize. I was not trying to be arrogant, or to offend you. Having said that, I'll just tell you it's time for you to grow up. You are not coming out of high school getting recruited by colleges that are all going to tell you how great you are. You are now a professional. The impact on you of not making a good decision regarding a professional representative is something you *cannot* afford. The impact on me of you not selecting me as your agent is something I *can* afford. I didn't intend to make that point in a way that is offensive to you. But I do intend to encourage you to grow up, make good decisions, and to become a better businessman.

"If you are playing poorly, do you want the coach to tell you that you are playing great? Or do you want the coach to tell you the truth? How do you get better if people aren't honest with you? I wasn't trying to big-time it with you or be arrogant. I was trying to shock you into making a decision, to change the inertia."

Ben listened, then he responded.

"Look, I like you a lot. But why do you think money is the only thing that's important?"

"I *don't* think money is the only important issue," I said. "But I do think that when you are a professional athlete, you have a limited amount of time to make the most money you can, to create lifetime security. In any walk of life, you want to be paid what you are worth. If you choose to donate the money to charity, to build a community center in Mount Vernon, to give it to your church, or to hand it out to homeless people, that's your prerogative. But you always should be paid what you are worth. As an athlete, how else do you measure the job your agent is doing for you other than by how much money he gets you? That's the barometer of success."

Ironically, the very concept I wanted to direct his attention to—the idea of eliminating emotion and making sound business decisions—was the very factor that derailed the opportunity. In retrospect, I should have been more patient. I am disappointed in myself that my attempt to be candid backfired on Ben. I think he made a mistake and as a result he has been living with that mistake. Clearly, I made a mistake in judgment approaching him with the same candor I employ when dealing with my clients. As a result, he was upset and made an emotional decision. I believe his decision will turn out to be a mistake.

To appreciate the state of the NBA in 2007 and 2008 and Ben's place in the market, you first have to understand Ben the player. Chicago selected him with the third pick in the 2004 NBA draft. Ben is a six-foot-two shooting guard. His ability to create instant offense reminds me of Detroit's Vinny "The Microwave" Johnson. But at six-foot-two, Ben is undersized for his position. He is a very specialized talent.

Following the 2007 season, Ben's third in the league, he was eligible for a contract extension that would commence with the 2008–2009 season, at the conclusion of his initial four-year contract. If the Bulls failed to finalize an extension after his third year, he would become a restricted free agent after his fourth season. As a restricted free agent, the Bulls could still retain his services by matching any offer Ben might receive in the open market. The ability of a team to match free agent offers received by its players following the fourth year means there is absolutely no risk to the team of losing players. In the worst case, the team matches a higher offer.

So why would a team elect to sign a third-year player to an extension? If the team thought it could sign that player for a discount on his eventual market price in exchange for the player receiving the security of a long-term deal a year early, then both sides should agree to a new contract. If the team is not able to negotiate a discount, then it has nothing to lose by not extending the deal after year three. Once again it can simply match any offer after the fourth year and retain the player long term. That's one aspect of the business I wanted to teach Ben.

Regardless of what Ben was worth in the summer of 2007, the Chicago Bulls had no financial incentive to sign him to a long-term extension unless it received a reasonable discount.

But there were at least three important market dynamics relevant to Ben's situation. First, there was a virtual saturation of the salary cap. When Ben could become a restricted free agent in the summer of 2008, there would be only two or three teams with enough cap room to sign him for the amount of money he was seeking.

The second dynamic was the pecking order of the pool of free agents who would be available in the summer of 2008. Gilbert Arenas, Elton Brand, and Shawn Marion had clauses that gave them the right to opt out of the final year of their contracts (2008–2009). Emeka Okafor, Ben's teammate at Connecticut; Luol Deng, Ben's teammate on the Bulls; and Andre Iguodala were all third-year players considered more valuable than Ben. As a result, Ben wasn't likely to be one of the available players. There might have been as many as ten players ahead of him but only two or three teams capable of signing *any* player.

Finally, Ben is a six-foot-two shooting guard. He is an extremely talented offensive machine, but he needed to find a team that wanted or could afford to have a shooting guard that is six-foot-two rather than six-foot-six or six-foot-seven. As a result, Ben's market was more limited than his talent would indicate.

When you sit down with a player, it is imperative to explain every one of these market dynamics. For example, John Lucas III is a terrific player. But he's also an inch or two short of being six feet tall. If he were six-foot-two, he would have been a lottery pick. Can he play any less effectively being three or four inches short of six-foot-two? No. But the perception is that he's small. John has to overcome that perception to have a consistent NBA career. Ben has to overcome the prevailing bias among most general managers that shooting guards need to be bigger than he is.

As Ben's advisor, my job would have been to tell him that it doesn't matter what he is worth if no team can afford to pay him. If you are a Ferrari dealer in the inner city of Detroit, there's a good chance you aren't going to sell many cars. It's not because a Ferrari isn't worth $250,000. It's because the vast majority of people who live there can't afford to buy a car at that price. Similarly, if you are a very good player and there are ten other very good players on the market and only three teams with any available money, it's not an insult to your ability. It's just a reality that it's a buyer's market.

Ben needed someone honest enough to tell him, "Based on your talent and performance, you might be worth one amount, but the issue is whether or not you can *command* that amount of money in the marketplace."

What happened instead? Ben turned down a five-year, $50 million deal from the Bulls and returned for his fourth season without long-term security. Because he is so serious and sensitive, Ben didn't play well at all. The lingering effect of not having security apparently bothered him to the point that it negatively affected his performance. If he didn't understand the dynamics of the marketplace when he turned down the Bulls' offer, then the agent he chose instead of me did him a serious disservice. Perhaps the agent didn't even understand the prevailing dynamics himself. Or maybe the agent felt so much pressure to make his client "happy" that he didn't allow himself to tell Ben what I told him.

Ben is a perfect example of why it's important to be candid and frank with clients. If you distort expectations then you risk negatively affecting the player's ability to perform within the ebb and flow of his professional life.

Still, it's ironic that he asked me, "Why do you make money the most important thing?"

My response is that if money isn't the most important element, then why turn down the extension the Bulls offered? I'm not saying I think he should have taken the money, but if money isn't of primary importance, then why not take the deal? He's in a great city, with some of the greatest fans in the NBA filling up the building every night, and he's playing with some very good young players. If he makes an extra $1 million a year somewhere else, is it really going to change his life? If money really isn't that important, then why not make the deal?

It was a great lesson for me. Maybe I needed to develop a stronger foundation in the relationship before I was so blunt, because Ben wasn't willing to accept that approach. It's as if I had great credentials but couldn't get into the school because I said something really dumb in the entrance interview.

You can't always throw the same pitch, literally and figuratively, to every batter. It was a good learning experience for me because it also taught me that younger players have more people stroking them than ever. In hindsight, had I waited another two or three months and allowed the process to evolve on Ben's timetable, perhaps at that point I could have been more blunt with him.

My experience with Jeff Green has been the converse of my experience with Ben. John Thompson III, the current Georgetown coach, invited me to meet with Jeff after his junior season at Georgetown in 2007. Both of John's talented juniors—Jeff Green, who was the Big East player of the year, and Roy Hibbert—submitted their names for the 2007 NBA draft. Hibbert eventually pulled himself out and returned to Georgetown for his senior season. I had spoken to John, whom I represent, and told him I wanted to discuss the pros and cons of leaving school early with the players because I had so much experience with those decisions.

I've known John for more than twenty years, but he's not John Thompson, Jr. He's got his own personality. I didn't have any preconceived notion about whether he'd even allow me to speak with the players. Then one day John called: "Jeff is starting to speak with potential agents. If you would like to come and meet him, then you need to be here on Friday."

"Gosh, I've been waiting all spring for this call. But I'm going to be away with my family at my beach house. Can I do it on Monday?"

"No, you can't," John said. "If you want to meet him, you have to be here Friday."

So I flew up from vacation to meet with Jeff and his parents. This was immediately after the NBA draft lottery in May 2007. In one of the most bizarre lotteries since it was instituted in 1985, none of the three worst teams ended up with the top three picks. The odds of that happening are astronomically low.

I sat down with Jeff, a mature and understated young man.

"My advice to you is to not pick an agent," I said.

Right away I knew what he was thinking: David is going to try to convince me to go back to school. I don't know if he's trying it to impress Coach Thompson or what.

I wasn't trying to impress anyone. I was just suggesting to Jeff that he needed to keep his options open and get a better sense of what was going to unfold before he lost the ability to go back to school. If he was going to be drafted No. 20, did it really make sense to skip his senior year? I explained in great detail the risks, most of which had very little to do with his talent.

There were a lot of young forwards coming out in the 2007 draft. Al Horford and Joakim Noah were from national champion Florida, Julian Wright from Kansas, Al Thornton from Florida State, Brandan Wright from North Carolina, as well as Corey Brewer from Florida, who could play small forward for some teams. So there were a lot of players at Jeff's position in the 2007 draft. I wanted him to have the proper intelligence report before he committed. Because he's such a low-key individual, I couldn't get a read as to whether he thought it was a good idea or a horrible idea. I started to think that maybe the environment really had changed.

In the old days, a player or his parents might have thanked me for recommending a concept contrary to my own interests. I was one of three people invited by Coach Thompson to make a pitch. Then I effectively took myself out of the game because I wanted what was best for Jeff. To my pleasant surprise, he and his parents liked the presentation and Jeff chose me. Because he hadn't officially signed with an agent, Jeff couldn't have the teams pay for him to attend workouts in other cities. So we arranged all the workouts at Georgetown so he could finish the school year without disrupting his studies with travel.

As a result, a limited number of teams came to Georgetown to work him out. Finally, right before the deadline, and on John's behalf as his lawyer, I called the interested teams so John would have the necessary information to advise Jeff. At that point we were pretty confident he would be drafted between the fifth and seventh picks. In the end, Seattle made him the No. 5 pick.

When I look at the two situations—Jeff's and Ben's—I took a pretty similar approach. I told both of them something they didn't want to hear. One accepted the advice, the other one did not. It worked great for the one that did. Ben spent the summer without a contract, then came into the season in a little bit of a funk. He didn't play particularly well and the team played terribly. Not only did Ben not maintain his market value, it might have slipped a bit. I think we both made a mistake.

A more tragic example of this concept is Jason Williams, the former Duke All-America guard who was drafted No. 2 by the Chicago Bulls in 2003. Once again I was on vacation when Coach K called, this time to tell me Jason was interviewing agents. I had spoken to Jason after a few games during the season and he always asked, "Are you going to take care of [my teammate] Shane Battier?" I always responded, "I don't know, but I hope you let me take care of you."

In the meeting, I asked Jason how he was going to decide on which agent to choose.

"David, I've never made a decision in my life. My parents are going to make the decision for me."

Jason's parents were similar to Grant Hill's. His mother is an educator. His father is a successful businessman. They are comfortable financially and very bright. Like Grant, Jason is an only child and the family is extremely close. They had invited me to dinner a couple of times during Jason's last season at Duke to pick my brain about the draft process and the league itself.

Jason and his parents eventually chose another agent, Bill Duffy. Normally when you meet with a player and his family and they decide to go with someone else, you get a letter or a phone call. In this case, a screening committee, which didn't include Coach K, ran the process. In the end, no one from the family or the school ever contacted me following the initial meeting.

In fact, that was the last I heard of Jason until I bumped into him at the 2004 All-Star Game.

"I want you to know you are the first player in my entire career that didn't have the courtesy of saying thank you for coming to the meeting," I said.

"I picked someone else," Jason responded.

"I'm not mad you didn't pick me. I'm just disappointed no one took the time to tell me."

"Didn't my parents contact you?"

He apologized and explained the family decision. "Bill Duffy told my parents he would be a mentor to me. He played basketball at the University of Minnesota and said we would have a very close personal relationship. That was very appealing."

I understood.

Players in most sports, particularly the NBA, are prohibited from engaging in what are known as "ultrahazardous" activities such as hang gliding, contact sports like football or boxing, and snow skiing. Aside from the obvious potential for injury, ultimately the reason those activities are prohibited is financial. Player contracts are guaranteed in the NBA and teams buy insurance against them in the event a player becomes injured and is no longer able to perform. The policies do not cover players injured while participating in "ultrahazardous" activities.

Jason was involved in a serious motorcycle accident during the summer following his first professional season and for all intents and purposes it ended his professional playing career. To say the least, I felt terrible for him. But it was so poignant to me because I never had a client who didn't know exactly what he could and could not do relative to his playing contract. That's part of the education you provide rookies.

Virtually all of our players were high draft picks with a pile of guaranteed money from the minute they stepped onto the court as professionals. I explained to them that there is an even bigger pile of money for them out there in the future. The only way to forfeit that money is to engage in one of these activities, become seriously injured playing the game, rob a bank, or do drugs. Other than that, the money's as good as in the bank. It's not complicated. Yet the reason Jason selected his agent was that that person promised to be a mentor to him.

His career ended and a large amount of money was lost because he rode a motorcycle. None of those things should have happened to a person like Jason Williams. It's incomprehensible to me that someone of his background, who graduated from Duke in three years, could wind up making that kind of mistake.

A couple of years later, I bumped into Jason at Coach K's sixtieth birthday party. We must have talked for three hours out in a hallway after the celebration. He was crying. I had tears in my own eyes. He knew he had made a terrible mistake and he wanted to know if I could help him. As much as I wanted to help Jason, there wasn't much I could do for him at that point. I left that night with all the same questions. How could this fate befall *this* young man? He came out of Duke. He had great parents. He had a wonderful relationship with Coach K. Nothing of the kind ever should have happened to Jason Williams.

Short-term Pain Often Translates Into a Long-term Gain

The concept—the customer's not always right—applies to anyone in a position of authority, particularly those responsible for the long-term well-being of individuals they manage or represent. With few exceptions, the downside risk associated with being brutally honest pales in comparison to the price to be paid for bad decisions.

The whole concept of lying in a judicial inquiry, or at any time for that matter, is an example of the customer not being right.

Chris Webber lied to a grand jury and was caught. Michael Vick lied and wound up in jail. Barry Bonds was indicted for his questionable testimony before a grand jury. The FBI started investigating Roger Clemens just two weeks after he testified in February 2008 to determine whether he lied to Congress under oath.

Lying, whether they each did so or not, is never a reasonable option. But was anyone there to tell them that? And were they even capable of accepting the message if it was delivered?

Alonzo Mourning wasn't right when he wanted to stay in Charlotte in the summer of 1995. The team offered him the first $100 million contract in the history of professional sports. I advised him to turn it down.

At Charlotte's request, we entered into contract negotiations to extend Alonzo's contract at the end of his third year. We had been engaged in extensive negotiations when the team offered Alonzo a nine-year extension for $99 million. Added to the three remaining years on his existing contract, it would have produced a twelve-year contract for nearly $115 million. Alonzo thought it was a great deal. I was far less enthused. Of the $11 million a year they were offering, only $8 million was in cash and $3 million was deferred income. I never liked deferred income because it lowers the true cash value of the contract. Also, I didn't want the extension to start after what would have been Alonzo's sixth NBA season. We had the right to opt out of the first contract after four years and I wanted the new deal to start after Zo's fourth season. So from my perspective there were substantive structural problems.

Initially Alonzo reacted with absolute shock. Despite whatever criticisms I had as to the components of the deal, $100 million is still $100 million. When you grow up a ward of the state, as Alonzo did, that's an awful lot of money. I remember saying to Alonzo, "The only way I can prove to you that I truly believe you would be making a terrible mistake accepting this offer is by refusing to sign the agent certification to the contract. So you can fire me and it will cost me four million dollars in fees, but I do not want you to accept this contract." Alonzo is an incredibly passionate man, a true warrior, and that really got his attention.

But he genuinely wanted to stay in Charlotte. He loved the city, loved the environment, and considered Charlotte a great place to raise his family. Acknowledging my limitations, I wasn't sure I had the clout to convince Alonzo to turn down the offer and allow himself the opportunity to test his value as a free agent with a team that would pay a lot more money. So I set up a meeting with John Thompson, Alonzo, and myself in Washington, D.C.

In the fall of 1995, Alonzo and I met with John and his colleague Mary Fenlon, an academic advisor at Georgetown. John asked me to explain the lay of the land. I talked about the money involved and the structure of the offer. In the end, I explained why I thought Alonzo should turn it down. It wasn't just the mechanics of the deal that presented a problem. He was on the cusp of becoming a free agent in the summer of 1996. I had a strong belief that the players would finally win unrestricted free agency for the first time. I knew his value in the open market would command a significantly higher offer. When I finished, John asked Alonzo to share his thoughts.

"Coach, I really love Charlotte. It's a great environment for my kids. I like the weather. We have great fans. I like my teammates. I really like everything about it."

John, in his own inimitable style, thought about it for a minute, King Solomon–like. Then he asked, "Do you really like Charlotte that much?"

"Yes sir, I do."

"Then I think you should visit there in the off-season."

That was the end of the discussion. Alonzo's instincts were right. Charlotte is a great place to live and a wonderful place to raise a family. But in the world of professional athletics, players have a limited window. In Alonzo's case his career was nearly ended by a rare kidney ailment. Had that happened early in his career it could have had a major impact on his ability to fund the kind of charitable work he likes to do, and his ability to provide financially for his children. It was truly a case of the customer not being right. But I definitely had to know my limitations. On my own, as much as I think Alonzo respected me, I don't think I had the clout to persuade him not to stay.

In the end, he and the Miami Heat came to terms on the first $100 million contact in the history of sports: seven years for $105 million with no deferred money.

Alonzo's fellow Georgetown alum, Patrick Ewing, is one of the people I most admire and like. He is a true gentleman, one of the most gentle, caring, respectful, pleasant people I have ever been around.

In the spring of 2000, Patrick was nearly thirty-seven years old. Though he had taken the Knicks to the NBA finals twice, Patrick never was able to get them over the top to a championship. The first time against Houston, John Starks went 2 for 17 in the deciding game. The second time against San Antonio, Patrick had a very serious injury and missed the play-offs.

By 2000, there was a certain level of dissatisfaction with Patrick among the New York players. Off the record and anonymously, players were quoted as saying that Patrick clogged up the middle.

In any organization, it's very difficult when you have an extremely valuable employee who has provided great service for a long period of time and he starts to age. Perhaps his contribution isn't as great as it was earlier, but you have a long memory and you know he has stood strong through tough times. How do you deal with that employee when his productivity starts to decline? It's a very difficult issue. Should you move him out and make way for a younger employee who might eventually do a better job? Do you keep him around out of loyalty to his past accomplishments? There's no easy answer.

The Knicks faced that question with Patrick. He wasn't the player in 2000 that he was in 1990. At the same time he was the backbone of the franchise and still highly productive—15 points and 9.7 rebounds per game—as one of the top centers in the league. There was no other player the team could get who would do a better job at that position. But these undercurrents began surfacing in local newspapers. Patrick heard all the criticism and he's a sensitive person.

It was a challenging situation for management to handle. Do you tell the players, "Hey, I don't want to hear this criticism. Patrick Ewing is an icon, the greatest player in the history of the

franchise"? Do you tell Patrick, "Hey, we've got to cut your minutes because you are slowing down"? Being sensitive to all the
facts, there was no easy solution. Eventually management felt the
team was better without Patrick.

And I think Patrick got to the point where he was really fed up
with the criticism. It wasn't fun for him and Patrick has a great
passion for the game. No one forced a trade but both sides instinctively felt they would be better off with a change of scenery. I
didn't agree. I felt Patrick had tremendous equity in New York.
Whatever lack of love he was experiencing, he was near the end of
his career. With the tremendous character and work ethic he had
displayed and the great years he brought to the franchise, the
business community would embrace him through the transition
into eventual retirement. I didn't want to see him lose that equity
by leaving at the end of his career.

We had lengthy discussions about this. I told him, "Look, you
are a very intelligent man. You can handle the criticism." Clearly
he knew he could. It wasn't the criticisms that bothered him as
much as the fact that the job was no longer fun.

One day he asked me, "Why did you decide in 1992 to stop
working with Donald Dell?"

"Because I didn't think he was fair to me. As a result I wasn't
having fun."

"Then you understand why I want to leave New York," Patrick
said.

"I'm not Patrick Ewing," I responded. "I'm not one of the
world's great athletes. I have a lot more time in my career to cover
up any mistake I might make. It doesn't matter as much where I

work. There isn't much time left in your career and you have tremendous equity where you work in New York."

His question had a great impact on me because I realized how deeply he had analyzed the problem. He was being driven by his unhappiness, not his ego. Is the customer always right? Should the customer be happy? Are you going to make him happy in the short term when you know there is a price to be paid over the longer term? In any event, over my dissent, Patrick and the Knicks agreed it would be best to have a change of scenery.

When you are one of the highest-paid players in the history of the league, getting traded is not an easy exercise. I worked with Knicks president Dave Checketts to find a solution. Eventually we worked out a trade that took Patrick to the Seattle SuperSonics in a complicated four-team deal.

Patrick played a year in Seattle. It didn't work out to his expectations, so he went to Orlando where he played his final season. In hindsight, I don't think the Knicks franchise has ever been the same since Patrick left. The players they acquired for Patrick changed the chemistry. Then they brought in Isiah Thomas and it went from bad to worse.

In sports, precedent is revered. In fact, there is such a tendency to compare current players to previous players that a pundit once noted that the official religion in sports must be Hinduism because every player comes back reincarnated as someone else. I think the same thing holds true with the way teams are managed. There are certain axioms or methods that teams invariably employ in professional sports. Since the advent of the salary cap, for example, when teams sign a player to a long-term guaranteed contract and it doesn't work out well, there is an adage that says you always trade long for short. In other words, you try to trade a player with multiple years left on his contract for players with one or two years remaining on their contracts to create future relief under the salary cap when the shorter contracts expire.

In the five or six years through 2008, there are very few axioms that have been more universally followed in the NBA than trading long for short, with the singular exception of the New York Knicks under the management of Isiah Thomas. He did exactly the opposite. He traded short-term players such as Dikembe Mutombo, Keith Van Horn, and Nazr Mohammed for players such as Malik Rose who had six years remaining. Rose is a good player, though probably a little overpaid. Once he arrived in New York with a long-term contract it became impossible to move him to another team. If the salary cap is roughly $55 million, you are talking about committing nearly 12 percent to a player who is not among your top nine or ten players. That is unthinkable. Thomas did the same thing by signing Jerome James as a free agent and bringing in Jared Jeffries as a free agent. Each of these players at $6 million a year is making more than 10 percent of the salary cap. None of them were among the top seven or eight players in the Knicks rotation.

For contrast, consider the Utah Jazz, which has a very modest payroll. Under the leadership of general manager Kevin O'Connor and the coaching of Jerry Sloan, who I think is one of the top two or three coaches in the league, the Jazz have been able to obtain top players in one of the smallest markets in all of professional sports. They acquired Deron Williams and Andrei Kirilenko in the draft, traded for all-star Carlos Boozer, and signed Mehmet Okur as a free agent. Just through sheer ability to draft and trade for quality players, the Jazz have been able to maintain a relatively low payroll and continue to win. They acquired Kyle Korver, who is one of the league's best pure shooters, for a player that is out of the league. I've never been one to let precedent bear me down. At the same time, if you are going to buck the trend and choose a different path, as Isiah did, then you had better be sure the road you select is going to lead to a good result.

There are those who would argue that ascribing the blame to Isiah is unfair because when Larry Brown was the coach he asked Isiah to bring in more talented players. Isiah responded by bringing in players such as Steve Francis, who is on a maximum contract, and Jalen Rose, who was at the end of a maximum contract. If you are the president of the team and your coach asks for players you think are categorically inimical to the long-term success of the team, you simply say no. It would be like a parent blaming a child for getting sick because the child asked for ice cream at two o'clock in the morning. If you are the parent your job is to say, "I'm sorry but we don't serve anything at two o'clock in the morning." Every coach puts pressure on the general manager to acquire players. The reason he's called the general manager is that his job is to manage the general, which is the coach. It's a very weak argument to suggest Isiah was merely accommodating the coach. I guess they didn't accommodate Larry Brown when they fired him.

When I look back, I believe today exactly what I believed before the Ewing trade. Both sides would have been better off by working it out. The Knicks could have kept Patrick another year and he would have become a free agent, perhaps retiring as a

Knick. The team would have realized tremendous cap relief. Patrick would have been one of the few players to play his entire career in one place. When the fans saw Patrick in absentia for the first time, they realized what he had brought to the table. They developed a much greater appreciation for him as a player and as a personality when he was gone compared to when he was there and unable to leap over the last hurdle to a championship.

When New York retired Patrick's jersey I talked to Dave Checketts about the trade. I said the same things then that I said when the deal was made: "The Knicks made a mistake trading Patrick and Patrick made a mistake leaving New York." Patrick, as he always does, dealt with the aftermath with dignity. Not surprisingly, the New York fans have embraced him.

It was one of the few times in my career when I wasn't able to persuade a player to make what appeared to me to be the obvious right decision. I don't think it was as catastrophic for Patrick as it turned out to be for the franchise, but it was one of those situations where both sides were wrong.

Truth or Consequences

That brings us to perhaps the most interesting issue in sports, one that connects to the world at large. It's nothing more complicated than simply telling the truth. We have come to idolize our heroes to the degree that they sometimes don't appreciate the idea of being held accountable for their actions. Several obvious examples come to mind, perhaps none more interesting or revealing than that of Chris Webber.

In the late 1990s, the University of Michigan was investigated for the improper activities of a booster during the "Fab Five" era. Webber, the star of the 1992 and 1993 Michigan teams that went to the NCAA championship game, was called before a federal grand jury in August 2000. This was a year before he signed a seven-year, $127 million contract with the Sacramento Kings. Webber was asked if he had accepted improper gifts from the booster, Ed Martin. The evidence indicated that he had. All Webber had to do was say, "Yes. I was nineteen years old. My father was working several jobs. Money was tight. I made an error in judgment. I took something I shouldn't have taken. I regret it."

There is nothing illegal about a player taking money from a booster. It is illegal, under NCAA rules, for the school to allow a booster to provide gifts of any kind to players. Webber had absolutely no reason to lie. Yet he lied to the grand jury, a fact that was later confirmed.

In September 2002, Webber was indicted for lying to the grand jury and obstruction of justice. He had just finished the best season of his professional career, leading the Kings to a franchise-best 61-21 record and to within a game of the NBA finals. In July 2003, he was found guilty of one count of criminal contempt for denying he received as much as $280,000 from Martin, some of it going all the way back to eighth grade.

Michigan was placed on probation and all results from the "Fab Five" era were expunged from the record books along with all of Webber's college statistics. The 1992 and 1993 Final Four banners were removed from Crisler Arena and the Michigan State High School Athletic Association even suggested that all of Webber's high school feats, including three state championships, be erased, an idea resisted by Detroit Country Day School, where Webber attended high school.

The entire episode was the culmination of a series of instances where the customer, Webber, was wrong.

On Mother's Day in 1993, we were invited to Michigan to meet with Chris, his parents, and others. It was clear he would be the first player selected in the draft. The word on the street was that Webber wanted an African American representative. Fred Whitfield, who is now president of the Charlotte Bobcats, was working for me at the time. I intentionally didn't bring Fred, an African American, because I always found it offensive to try to display your racial sensitivity by making an overt show of the fact that you had people of color working for you. So Curtis Polk, my partner, and I went out to Michigan. Chris's parents are lovely people. We met Charlene Johnson, Chris's aunt, and her boyfriend, Fallasha Erwin. The Michigan coach at the time, Steve Fisher, and the dean of the University of Michigan Law School also attended the meeting. The only person who didn't come to the meeting was Chris Webber.

There were four groups in the running to represent Chris and we were the last one to present. It was a funny situation because we had signed Shawn Bradley that year even though we had never met him. Shawn was on a Mormon mission in Australia. He decided to leave school after what would have been his junior year. He had played one year of ball at Brigham Young and then went on a two-year mission. The head of the mission had the view that it would be impossible to interview agents with Shawn in Australia. So he called a number of owners in the Western Conference of the NBA and asked each of them the same question: If Shawn were your son, who would you pick to represent him? All of them said they would choose David Falk. He chose us sight unseen. I thought that was a great comment on our track record.

At the time of our meeting with Chris, there had been a story in a New York newspaper joking that I was going to get Shawn Bradley more money at No. 2 than Chris Webber was going to make at No. 1. This is before Webber had even chosen an agent. It was against that backdrop that we went out to meet with his representatives. We faced two obstacles. One we knew about: the fact that we had signed Shawn Bradley and he was going to be the No. 2 pick in the draft. The question was which player we would push to be the No. 1 pick if we represented Shawn and Chris. The second obstacle, which I didn't know about, was that this newspaper item had apparently really affected the parents.

I tried to explain the value of the two top players being with the same agent by asking them why Chris, Jalen Rose, Juwan Howard, Ray Jackson, and Jimmy King—five great high school players—all decided to play at Michigan together.

The answer was that when you put all that talent together, you get a team that goes to the NCAA finals two years in a row as freshmen and sophomores. Most often, great players go to the school where they can be "the man" rather than part of a team full of men. In America there are anti-monopoly laws to prevent the conglomeration of power at the top because the prevailing wisdom in economic circles is that if you put a lot of very valuable assets together and they're controlled by one entity, it wields an unreasonably strong level of economic power. If in theory, every year in the draft prior to the wage scale, the top five players all got together in a hotel room and all chose the same agent, all five would probably make more money than if all five chose a separate agent because that agent would be able to wield monopoly power for the entire draft.

That is definitely true. Unfortunately, the three people who preceded us had told the Webbers, "Whoever you hire, don't hire David because he represents Bradley."

I could look at their faces and know they weren't buying what I was telling them about monopoly theory. Then the question became "Are you going to be able to give my son more attention, make him the number one dog in the pound?"

I knew after about an hour that we were going nowhere. It was Mother's Day and I wanted to get home to my wife.

"Today is May 10, 1993. The draft is going to be in approximately seven weeks. On draft day, your son Chris will be drafted number one and Shawn Bradley will be drafted number two. When I get Shawn Bradley more money than Chris makes, I want you to know that every person who came in here before us looked you in the eye and lied to your faces." Then I got up and left.

Draft day came. Chris had initially chosen the Goodwin brothers to represent him. They had actually sat at his table at the draft. Eventually Fallasha Erwin came to represent Chris and Bill Strickland, an agent I had hired at ProServ, became a consultant. We signed first, Shawn getting an eight-year contract for $44.35 million. Anfernee "Penny" Hardaway, the No. 3 pick, and Chris signed very long contracts, Chris for fifteen years and Hardaway for thirteen. They both had outs, which they exercised. But Webber and Hardaway signed rookie contracts that in the first eight years *combined* paid them less money than Shawn made in his first eight years.

The following year the NBA All-Star Game was in Minnesota. Mayce Webber, Chris's father, approached me.

"I want you to know that I can remember our meeting in Michigan like it was yesterday. I thought you were the most cocky, arrogant individual I had ever met in my life. But everything you said came true. So if you need a recommendation for any player in America coming out of the draft this year it would be my pleasure to recommend you."

I was blown away by his candor.

"First of all, I can't thank you enough for your candor. And I want you to know I am not by nature arrogant or cocky. But everyone else you talked to fed you pabulum. I realized as time went by I wasn't getting through. I tried to shock you into reality by what I said. I wasn't trying to offend you. The truth is that the players would all be better off if they got together and chose one agent. Maybe you don't set the market with the number one player. Maybe the team at number three is in a more dire situation, or has more cap room."

As it turned out, Golden State, the team that drafted Chris, had salary cap issues, so he got a terrible contract. At the end of the first year Chris opted out and he signed a one-year contract with Golden State for $2 million. He was traded to Washington during his second season and at the end of that year, in 1995, Webber signed a six-year contract with the Wizards for $57 million, or $9.5 million a year. At the time it was the highest contract ever for a forward.

One year later I negotiated a deal that paid Juwan Howard $15 million per year from the same team, the Washington Wizards. The agent business is incredibly competitive. When I signed Patrick Ewing to the largest contract in NBA history, everyone said, "Well, he's a center and centers make the most money. And besides, New York pays more money." Other agents always find a rationalization to compare contracts.

However, Webber versus Juwan is probably the closest comparison in the history of professional basketball. You had two players who were exactly the same age, had gone to the same university, played the exact same position, and signed contracts with the same professional team within twelve months of each other. However, one made close to 60 percent more than the other.

If, when Webber and Juwan were freshmen, you told anyone in Michigan that six years down the road they would end up on the same team but one of them would earn $5.5 million a year more than the other, everyone would have said that player would be Chris. Why? Because Chris was the man at Michigan and Chris had been the man everywhere he played.

I love Juwan Howard. He is a salt-of-the-earth kind of person. We have had a tremendous relationship since 1994 and he is truly one of the most caring, honest people I have ever represented. So I was thrilled we were able to do a great job for him.

Chris needed someone outside his family to tell him the customer isn't always right. He came from a two-parent family, attended a prestigious private school, and is talented, attractive, well spoken, and intelligent. So those very serious but easily avoidable judgment errors should not have happened. He probably never became the dominant player he should have been. Consider the position he played. Chris Webber and Alonzo Mourning are exactly the same size. One played center his entire career, the other played power forward but wanted to play small forward. What's the difference?

Alonzo is the ultimate warrior. He played out of position his entire career with an intensity and passion that allowed him to realize every ounce of his potential. Chris never demonstrated that kind of commitment and heart, particularly when it mattered most.

Everyone remembers his technical in the 1993 NCAA title game against North Carolina, which sealed a second straight defeat for Michigan in the finals. Years later, in the NBA Western Conference finals in 2002, Sacramento took the defending champion Los Angeles Lakers into overtime. In the final 29 minutes of the biggest professional game of his career, Webber was 2 for 9 from the field with a technical foul. He disappeared and so did the Kings, despite an incredible performance by Mike Bibby.

But Webber is not alone when it comes to questionable testimony in front of a grand jury. Barry Bonds, who commanded our attention over the last several years as much because of steroids as home runs, is perhaps the most obvious case of a player seemingly incapable of taking responsibility. The best player of his generation was asked by a grand jury if he had ever knowingly used steroids. At the time, steroids were not illegal in baseball. Like Webber, all Bonds had to do was tell the truth. If he had, the San Francisco Giants might not have felt compelled to disassociate themselves from Bonds after the 2007 season. He wouldn't have been indicted for perjury. Rather than harming his public image, Bonds might even have improved it.

All he had to do was to express a level of humility and simply tell the truth. He might have said, "I took steroids because it was common knowledge among players, management, and the leadership of baseball that many players were using performance-enhancing drugs. While they might not have been explicitly allowed, they were implicitly allowed as evidenced in their use by other players. I simply wanted to keep the playing field level."

I think the public would have understood. They would have been disappointed, but if Bonds is convicted of perjury charges, the penalty for lying, which could include jail time, will do far more harm.

Michael Vick is another player who seemed incapable of accepting responsibility for his actions and as a result ended up in jail. There was overwhelming evidence Vick had been involved in dog fighting and cruelty to animals. Had he come right out and said, "I made a terrible mistake. I allowed my associates to run this operation on property I own. I am embarrassed about my role in these activities," there is a very good chance the penalty would have been probation rather than jail.

Instead, he lied to the NFL commissioner; he lied to Arthur Blank, the Atlanta owner who supported him; and he lied to the authorities. As a result, he served time in jail, a terrible penalty to pay for the temporary embarrassment of being humble and admitting a mistake.

Has our societal idolatry of these people gotten to the point where they are no longer able to maintain a sense of reality when they strike out, fumble, or shoot an air ball? Do they have the humanity and humility to admit they might be wrong? Do they have the emotional maturity to listen to anyone who doesn't tell them exactly what they want to hear? Or is there no one around them sounding the alarm?

I remember a time in Michael Jordan's career when he was invited by his good friend, Al Wood, to play golf with some shady characters. Al did a terrible job of screening these people. There were allegations Michael was involved in criminal activity and the story of him playing with these people went national. After the first game following the newspaper reports, I watched Michael walk up to the interview stand wearing sunglasses. Michael is one of the greatest interviewees in the history of sports. He's bright, personal, witty, and humble. Behind the sunglasses he looked as if he was hiding something.

I flew out to Chicago the next morning and we sat down. It was another one of those situations where the customer wasn't right. Michael had come out with a quote saying, "I have the right to associate with whomever I want to associate with." Jesse Jackson had called Michael and reinforced that feeling. Jesse told him, "You are Michael Jordan. It's none of anyone's business who you hang out with."

On the trip to Chicago I thought about the interview the night before and how I would address him. I knew Michael was going through a great deal of pain. I wanted to be supportive. But at the same time, I knew without a doubt that the customer wasn't right.

As we sat down to talk I said, "Here's how I look at the situation. You didn't rob a bank. You didn't commit a murder. But you made a mistake. You associated with people you shouldn't associate with. And yes, you do have every right to associate with whomever you want. But when you are representing Nike, Gatorade, and Wheaties, these bedrock American companies, and when kids are looking up to you as a result and you associate with these kinds of people, then you are misrepresenting these companies.

"So if your desire is to hang out with whomever you want, God bless you. I will cancel all the contracts and you will have no responsibilities. You will have total freedom to hang out with whomever you want. But if you want to be a spokesperson and role model nationally and internationally, then you have to acknowledge that you made a mistake. I think when you acknowledge you did, because you are Michael Jordan and you have an absolute clean record, they will support and forgive you."

Michael got really angry with me.

"I knew you would take that position. You never support me. You always support the companies."

"I *am* supporting you. I am not telling you what you want to hear, but I am supporting you. This is the correct analysis and approach. You have to pick your poison. If you want to be a role model and receive the benefits of all these corporate associations, then there's a certain level of responsibility they expect from you and you have let them down. You have let your parents down. You've let your teammates down. This is nothing heinous. It's just a mistake. You are Michael Jordan. Even though no one treats you like you are human, you are human. All you have to do is say you are sorry. I respect Jesse, but screw Jesse Jackson. He doesn't have to live with this. We have to live with this. So I am beseeching you to trust me. I have been a good advisor to you all these years. All I'm asking you to do is think about it and apologize."

The meeting did not end well. Michael was fried. It was the only time in my career that I thought there was a good chance he would fire me. I was upset that someone as intelligent as he is would allow people to stroke him. Then to see the sunglasses, which was completely out of character and at odds with everything he had been taught by his parents, was troubling. I went to the game that night and I didn't know if I should fly home or wait for a letter to be released announcing Michael's decision to fire me.

After the game, I went to the locker room to see him. I couldn't get within twenty feet of Michael. There were what seemed like fifty reporters and camera crews. Very calmly, Michael apologized to his parents, to the fans, to the Bulls.

"I know I've made a mistake in judgment. I embarrassed people who rely on me. I am sorry."

It all went away in two days. To his credit, because he is such an intelligent person with such a level head, once Michael stepped away and thought about it, it was obvious what he had to do. It bothered me greatly that everyone supported the wrong approach. "You're Michael Jordan. Do whatever you want." We all have responsibilities. If you want to be totally independent of responsibilities, then you can't ask to wear the mantle of a role model.

The corollary to the story is that all of these individuals—Vick, Webber, and Bonds—needed to understand that their actions were going to be magnified and have ramifications precisely because of who they are. The people around them have to be aware of that fact, even if the player is not. We have a penchant in our society to take down our heroes. We idolize them to a certain point and then, as if to confirm their godlike pedestal, we search for flaws.

In each of these cases, the people around the athlete didn't do a very good job of protecting them. Al Wood, who was a client of mine and has since become a minister, had no business whatsoever inviting Michael to play golf with people he knew or should have known were unsavory. That was an absolute breach of responsibility and fidelity to a friend. Al should have known they weren't the type of people to bring to play golf with Michael because the spotlight is on him at all times, and it was particularly bright then.

People around Michael Vick should have said, "You like dogs? Great. When you retire, if you want to take the risk of doing this, wonderful. But when you are at the height of your career, when you have $100 million on the line and all these endorsements, what do you like better, football or dog fighting? If you want to do dog fighting, then quit football and enjoy dog fighting full-time."

The customer is not always right. The question, then, is who is denominated to *tell* the customer when he is not right. Very few people, even when they know the customer is not right, want to deliver the message. It's unpopular. It can have consequences. While on the surface the customer may think the messenger is not an ally, the truth is that the person who has the courage to deliver a message that needs to be delivered is the ultimate ally because that person is risking the relationship to protect the customer.

Because the money has become so great, so too has the responsibility of an advisor or manager. Ultimately, the client has to determine which advice he is going to follow. Barry Bonds would have suffered a temporary setback by admitting he took steroids because they were not illegal at the time. He wouldn't have been outside baseball looking in when spring training started in 2008. Dave Roberts, the Baltimore second baseman, was implicated in the Mitchell Report in 2007 and the Chicago Cubs were talking about trading for him a month later.

The public loves their heroes and they want to forgive them for their trespasses. But when heroes lie, they have breached the public trust and that is a sin fans do not want to forget.

It works the same way in politics. The Scooter Libby case is an excellent example. There was an allegation that the Bush administration revealed the name of a CIA operative, Valerie Plame, because her husband, Joseph Wilson, had criticized the administration for alleging that Saddam Hussein had attempted to import uranium from Nigeria. Patrick Fitzgerald, an incredibly sharp United States attorney from Chicago, was hired to investigate. Libby was ultimately convicted of lying to the grand jury. Had he admitted, "Yes, we were really upset over Wilson's article and perhaps we overreacted," it's questionable whether he could have been convicted for revealing the name. Once he lied, it was easier to convict him of perjury because the stream of testimony didn't appear to make sense. Here is a man of high standing in the White House: chief of staff to the vice president of the United States. What did he get in trouble for? Did he get in trouble for his actions? No. He got in trouble for lying about what he did.

While it's true that the customer isn't always right, it's also true that I was wrong when I played the role of customer with Ben

Gordon. That was a failure. None of us can afford to be actively engaged in behavior that dooms relationships because of mistakes we make up front.

In the end, being mindful of the long horse race helps the customer avoid making short-term mistakes.

FALK'S FUNDAMENTALS

Don't be afraid to let a customer know when he's wrong.

In an age of increasing specialization, customers look to their dealers, brokers, and advisors for specialized advice. Often the customer has strong opinions about his purchasing options and just as frequently these opinions are based on a faulty set of assumptions. Never let your desire to please the customer interfere with your responsibility to give him candid advice about his decisions. Otherwise his next purchase will be his last purchase.

Short-term pain often translates into a long-term gain.

Most individuals steer a wide path to avoid confrontation. But a trusted business advisor is like a personal trainer; sometimes where there's no pain there's no gain. In order to avoid a result that would ultimately constitute an unacceptable level of risk or damage to the client, the advisor must be willing to deliver the hard facts up front.

Truth or consequences.

While experience is sometimes the best teacher, there are situations when a bad experience can be fatal. An individual facing such a critical decision must be informed in the strongest terms that a wrong turn will lead him right over the cliff.

EIGHT

Know When to Hold 'Em,
Know When to Fold 'Em

Rule No. 1 in negotiations is that you can never make a good deal unless you are willing to walk away. If you asked a twenty-four-year-old basketball player who never went to college if he can afford to walk away from basketball, the answer would be no. Where else is he going to make $15 million a year? If you are Howard Schultz, however, and you started Starbucks, then bought the Seattle SuperSonics before deciding you weren't so fond of the sport; or Paul Allen, cofounder of Microsoft and owner of the Portland Trail Blazers, can you afford to walk away? Any day of the week.

In the collective bargaining process between a group of unionized professional athletes and management, the playing field is not equal because the players don't have the ability to walk away.

Why? Because there is nowhere for them to walk away *to*, especially as a group. I'm not saying Patrick Ewing couldn't have walked away, or that Michael Jordan couldn't have walked away, or that LeBron James wouldn't be able to walk away after playing six years in the league. There may be a handful of players who have made enough money to walk away, but they are not representative of the players' union as a group. And as a group they will never have the ability to walk away.

In business it's as critical to know when you can walk away and when you have to hold your position. In the business of sports, particularly in the course of collective bargaining over work rules, knowing when to fold 'em is even more critical because the field isn't close to being level. And both sides know that fact before the process commences.

Nowhere has that been more apparent than in the NBA. In fact, no union in the three major sports has violated, as a group, virtually every principle discussed in this book to the extent the National Basketball Players Association has.

In both 1995 and 1998, the NBPA became embroiled in a controversial negotiation with the league over a new collective bargaining agreement. In 1998, the impasse led the league to lock out the players, who lost nearly 40 percent of the season and hundreds of millions of dollars they never recouped, all because the players had absolutely no understanding of an essential concept in negotiations: You've got to know when to fold 'em.

Remember the Golden Rule: He Who Has the Gold Rules

I remember some players being apathetic. They didn't pay attention to the nuances of the negotiations or understand the essence of the disagreement between the union and management. For many players, the entire experience was polarizing. Conservative players such as John Stockton, for whom I have the utmost respect, didn't appreciate the long-term impact of management's proposals. John is one of the most humble, down-to-earth individuals I have ever met. I represented John for seven years and he was completely committed to the purity of the game. He didn't want endorsements or outside commitments interfering with his schedule because he was so focused on basketball and his family. John is just a wholesome, first-class individual. But he's also very conservative. He didn't understand why I, as his former representative, felt so strongly about the position I was taking regarding the impact the proposal put forth by the league would have on the business structure of the game.

In 1995, the league wanted to create a wage scale for rookie contracts, eliminating negotiations that had led Glenn Robinson, the No. 1 draft pick in 1994, to ask for a $100 million contract from the Milwaukee Bucks. Their owner, Senator Herb Kohl, calmly responded, "You give me $100 million, and you can have my entire franchise." The proposed wage scale was for a period of three years, after which rookies would become unrestricted free agents.

"John, if the union allows rookies to become unrestricted free agents after three years, the rookies will suck all the money out of the system from the veterans."

"How do you know, David? We have never had this system before."

"You are one of the greatest point guards in the history of basketball and you're driving down the court. How do you know whether to pull up for a jumper, pass to a player cutting in from the wing, or drive to the basket? Do you call a time-out and huddle with your coach? Do you consult the game plan and figure out, given the time on the clock and the nuances of the defensive player in front of you, that a pass is the right move?"

He laughed.

"David, I've been doing this my whole life. It's instinctive. It gets to the point where you just know. If you are good at what you do, you are going to make some mistakes and have a turnover, but ninety percent of the time I'm going to make the correct decision because I've trained my entire life to execute correctly in that moment."

"Exactly. That's why I know what the impact of these proposals will be. I'm on the three-on-one fast break and I'm John Stockton. My job is to know whether I pull up for the jumper, drop it off for one of my teammates, or take it to the hole. In business, that instinctive ability to make instantaneous decisions that will have a lasting impact is absolutely crucial. There are no hard-and-fast rules. There are no guides. It's not like you are in Las Vegas playing blackjack and you ask the dealer, 'What are the odds if I take another card?' and he tells you 62.7 percent of the time you should take the card. These are situations where you know all the factors and you have to instantly balance them in your mind and know what to do."

I've always felt that this moment of truth, if you will, is best reflected by the lines in the Kenny Rogers song, "The Gambler": "You've got to know when to hold 'em, know when to fold 'em, know when to walk away."

Negotiations and making deals is a function of knowing when you have the leverage, when you can push the envelope a little, and when you don't have the leverage and so have to perhaps take less than you'd like to achieve and graciously walk away knowing you did the best job you could under the circumstances. In 1998, the players had virtually no leverage as a result of their decisions in previous collective bargaining processes. It's a classic example of violating virtually every principle in this book, of being completely ignorant of their lack of leverage. They didn't have a clue as to when it was time to fold.

Billy Hunter was named executive director of the NBPA in 1996. Billy went to my alma mater, Syracuse University, and later was a running back in the National Football League for the Washington Redskins and the Miami Dolphins. He became a federal prosecutor on his way to the NBPA.

I went to see him his first week on the job. I wanted to explain the history of the union to that point, particularly recent history. Larry Fleisher founded the NBPA in 1965 and served as its executive director until 1988. In the 1980s there was a growing jealousy of Larry among agents because Larry was not only the executive director of the union, he was also probably the most powerful player agent. He represented most of the executive board of the union, players such as Bill Bradley, Oscar Robertson, Bob Lanier, and Junior Bridgeman. There was a growing movement to force Fleisher to pick whether he wanted to be executive director or an agent. The irony of the situation is that he wasn't charging the players a dollar to be the executive director whereas today Billy Hunter is making $4 million a year in the same role.

Nevertheless, as the criticism grew, Fleisher stepped down. While there were provisions in the union constitution for succession, Isiah Thomas basically arranged for the assistant executive director, Charlie Grantham, to be named executive director. I'd known Charlie when he was the associate dean of admissions at the Wharton School at the University of Pennsylvania. He is a very bright man, but the way he was elected undermined his authority, though not necessarily his competence. Because he didn't receive a vote of confidence from all the players, just a vote among fifteen or so on the executive committee, I believe Charlie began with a weak power base. Isiah was a very active and opinionated president. He frequently cautioned the young players about nefarious agents who would try to steal their money and do them harm. I think he effectively separated the star players from the rank and file, the black players from the white players, and the players from the agents. From the early 1990s on, the union went from being a strong, unified group with strong player management to a splintered group with most players apathetic about the activities of the union, which led to a small group making decisions for the masses.

Since Fleisher stepped down, the NBPA has never had a labor lawyer running the union, which is ironic since that is the primary qualification for the job.

Isiah fired his first agents, Charles Tucker and George Andrews, after they had negotiated long-term contracts that not only kept him off the open market, but included substantial deferred money. He had been the second pick in the 1981 draft. Mark Aguirre was selected first by Dallas; and Buck Williams, my client, was the third pick. Buck ended up making significantly more money than either Thomas or Aguirre.

When Isiah became president of the NBPA, his own experiences with agents had been so negative that he projected those feelings to the players. Now, I don't necessarily disagree with him. I think there are a lot of agents who are weak and not particularly honest. But agents are partners in the union. We represent the players in individual contract negotiations based on the rules that are negotiated by the NBPA in collective bargaining negotiations. When you create a rift between the agents and the union, and you publicize that rift, you have seriously weakened the organization in the eyes of the league. The whole concept of separation between agents as individual contract negotiators and the union as collective negotiators is destructive because there are only two sides. There is the union on one side and management on the other. There are not three sides.

If the union implements strong pro-player rules, the agents flourish. If the players are not able to negotiate good rules for themselves, or they create rules that are restrictive, then the ability of the agents to do their jobs on behalf of the players is dramatically diminished. So there is complete symmetry of interest between the union and the agents. The agents want a strong union that makes great rules and the union wants good agents who negotiate great contracts with the rules the union created. To suggest that they are not in lockstep is patently absurd, but because of Isiah's mind-set, the power and prestige of the union had been diminished.

Ironically, I agreed with him that agents, as a group, should be a lot better. But the union certifies and polices the agents. If the union doesn't like the group, then do a better job of approving them. Increase and improve the requirements to be an NBA agent, demand more experience, raise the dues. Do something, don't just complain about the agents. In theory the union, as the official bargaining agent of the players, has the right to negotiate all player contracts. But the union delegates those rights to the agents, whom they license based on a series of requirements. The players could agree tomorrow not to license agents and they might get sued, but under labor law the union has that right. There doesn't have to be individual player negotiations just as there aren't individually negotiated deals for carpenters, auto workers, and electricians. That's how labor law works in the United States. So when the union under Isiah's leadership criticized the conduct and the quality of the agents, it was really criticizing itself because it is responsible for regulating agents.

As a result, since 1988 there has been a serious level of distrust, animosity, and lack of solidarity between the agents, as a group, and the union. As president of the NBPA, Isiah created and left that legacy, which was in place when Billy Hunter became the executive director. I explained that history to Billy, along with the fact that ten agents represented 80 to 90 percent of all the players in the league.

"All you have to do, Billy, is get those agents in a room, and have an internal boxing match so when everyone emerges from that room there is consensus in support of the union's agenda."

To my profound disappointment, Billy never seemed to recognize the need to have the agents and players on the same page. The league is keenly aware of that divide and the owners continue to exploit it to the detriment of the union and its players.

When Billy came on board, I knew he was bright and I felt he would be independent. As the senior agent with the best players, I wanted not only to support Billy, but to embrace him. Though Billy was polite, he consistently distanced himself from me. So one day I called him up.

"Billy, I'm missing something. Why are we having this disconnect? I truly believe you could use my help. I speak for a lot of very powerful voices in your union including the best player in the history of the game. I am their representative and I'm going to have influence in shaping their opinions of the agenda you are creating. Why aren't we on the same page?"

Sadly, he said, "David, you don't understand. I am a black man trying to seek my identity in this sport. I cannot have a white lawyer as my advisor. It's going to undermine my authority."

I listened.

"What kind of pile of crap is that? I represent Michael Jordan. I represent Patrick Ewing. I represent John Thompson. I represent some of the most powerful African American figures in sports. And none of those players are even remotely concerned that my involvement is going to undermine their credibility in the black community or the community at large. If that is your reason, then that is the most woeful excuse I have ever heard."

It bothered me to the quick that he could make such an uneducated statement. I like Billy. We've been able to maintain a cordial relationship over the years. But during the course of the 1998 collective bargaining process I did what Larry Fleisher, the greatest NBA union director ever, had done many years before. I got smart. Patrick Ewing became president of the union. Dikembe Mutombo became vice president, and another client, Juwan Howard, became involved in the leadership. These players were making $15 million or more and I told them they had to take some control over their destiny.

"Jump in there, roll up your sleeves, and go to work, or these kinds of contracts are going to go away."

In July 1998, in the midst of the collective bargaining process and facing a potential lockout by management, the players scheduled a meeting in Las Vegas and invited the agents. As you would expect when all these agents are thrown into a room, the tendency is for some of them to show off, or try to one-up one another. After the union made its presentation, I made a statement that I repeated throughout the collective bargaining process.

"Let me try to frame this. [NBA Commissioner] David Stern is the undisputed heavyweight champion of the world. If you go up to him and flick his nose, he says, 'Okay, let's get in the ring and go fifteen rounds.' You climb into the ring with him and after three rounds your ribs are broken, your nose is broken, your eyes are swollen closed, and you tell David that you've had enough. He's going to say, 'Oh no. Stand up. We've got twelve more rounds. I want to finish.' The point of the story is that you don't flick the nose of the heavyweight champion if you aren't prepared to go fifteen rounds in the ring."

One of the agents asked what that meant in the context of the 1998 collective bargaining negotiations.

"What it means is that you have a window of opportunity to make a deal. If you pass, they close the window and lock you out. If that happens, assume you will be out for the year. Either make the best deal you can now, or be prepared to sit the year out."

Another agent, Dan Fegan, who is a cocky guy, said, "Oh really, David? So are you prepared to sit out the year?"

We had sold FAME a month earlier and I made a lot of money. "As a matter of fact I am. I have $100 million in the bank. How about you?"

He asked me why I was being so arrogant. I asked him why he was being so stupid.

"This is not a game. This is a high-stakes process with a lot of money at stake. Management has the wherewithal to lock out the players not just for one year. These owners—some of whom are billionaires—can afford to lock you out for three years. They could shut it down until you come back on your knees. Why can't we figure out a way to be realistic and make the best deal we can? Besides, all of you proved your true colors in 1995 when you talked tough in the summer and then, when the heat turned up, you folded the tent. I have no confidence that if we take a tough position any of you will follow through."

What happened? They took the tough position, got locked out, and then folded the tent in January 1999. The players lost 40 percent of the money with no chance of ever getting it back. I never would have allowed myself to get locked out. I would have made a deal. But if you are going to allow yourself to be locked out, then once that line has been crossed you have to show the owners that you are in it for the long term.

Marvin Miller, the legendary union representative for Major League Baseball players, was probably the greatest players union representative ever, with Larry Fleisher a notch below. Miller was a labor lawyer for the United Steelworkers union. I always told my players that while I liked Billy Hunter and considered him a very intelligent man, his background is as a federal prosecutor. It would be like a team needing a rebounder and me trying to sell them on John Stockton. They might agree that Stockton is a great player, but the fact is that the team needs a rebounder. What the players need is a labor lawyer with collective bargaining experience.

"David Stern is a very smart guy and he knows there are rifts in the union," I told Billy. "We have to show complete solidarity. There will come a time, mark my words, where David Stern will come out publicly and ask, 'Who is running the union? Is it Billy Hunter or is David Falk pulling all the strings behind the scenes?' Now when he does that, you have to realize it's nothing more than a fan taunting you from the cheap seats. You have to ignore him. You know who's running the union. I know who's running the union. I don't want your job. I have no desire to have your job. All I want to do is support your efforts to get the players the best deal possible."

Sure enough, the very first time Stern pulled that chain publicly, Billy went crazy. He came out and said, "No, I want to make it perfectly clear. David Falk is not running the union."

I immediately called Billy.

"Relax. I prepared you for this. Just say, 'Of course I am taking

David Falk's advice into consideration. The guy has thirty years of experience and he represents some of our most prominent players. I'd be a fool not to take his advice. I'm making the decisions.' But relax and don't be so defensive."

Stern understood exactly what would happen when he sent that shot over the bow and Billy reacted exactly as Stern expected. The result was that Stern had effectively taken the agents, me in particular, out of the equation and turned the game into a one-on-one match between himself and Billy Hunter. Billy is not going to win that game and no one understood that better than Stern. I'm not sure there is anyone on the players' side who could win that game.

I think most players are reasonably intelligent. But they are not experienced in collective bargaining. Asking them to do a job for which they have questionable qualifications and a definite lack of experience is setting them up for failure. It would be like the players having me suit up for the deciding game in the NBA finals because I'm a reasonably intelligent guy. I'm not qualified to be on the floor.

David Stern might be the best there has ever been in any sport in serving his constituency. The truth is that while players make the final decisions, they are not qualified to go onto the collective bargaining floor with David Stern.

The players need somebody who's as talented in collective bargaining as they are at playing. Should they be involved? Absolutely. I think they should be more involved. Should they make the decisions? Yes. But to flatter their egos by convincing themselves they are qualified to go back and forth with David Stern in collective bargaining is absurd.

After the agents had their meeting in Las Vegas, the players had a meeting of their own. Led by Karl Malone, the players did not want agents in their meeting. They concluded it was not an appropriate place to discuss the rules by which the best players are going to be paid their individual contracts. So, twenty of the most experienced agents met. We had invited Donald Fehr, the executive director of the Major League Baseball Players Association, to address our group. I happened to be sitting next to Don. He finished talking and asked if we had any questions.

"What role do the agents play in the baseball union's collective bargaining process?" I asked.

"That's easy. I have a board of advisors comprised of the five seniormost agents—Arn Tellem, Randy Hendricks, Scott Boras, Ron Shapiro, and Tom Reich. Those men each have twenty-five years or more of experience and they have great relationships with a lot of the owners, so there are times when I will have them call an owner and feel that owner out on a particular issue. Or I'll call the agents in as a group and try to get some feedback on our position or proposals. I think it's a great resource to have all these agents with all this experience and they are respected by the owners."

Not a word at the table.

"That's very interesting," I responded. "In our group, if someone suggested we had an executive board, or a sounding board comprised of the five agents with the most experience, nobody would support the idea because they would consider the designation an unfair recruiting advantage for the five agents on the sounding board."

Now you would think, after what we had just heard from Fehr, that somebody in that room would have said, "Now David, that's absurd. Of course we want the most experienced agents helping the players secure the kinds of rules that will help the agents negotiate better contracts."

Not a peep. They would rather have lousy collective bargaining rules in exchange for the perception that the playing field was level when it came to recruiting clients. Nobody wanted to recognize there are levels to the game we agents play, just as there are levels to the players in the union. Not all of them are created equal. Yet no one would recognize what was obvious.

Do the players have equal bargaining power with the league? Of course they don't. Could I outlift Arnold Schwarzenegger in his prime? We're both men about the same age. Why couldn't I outlift Arnold? Simple answer: he's a professional and I'm an amateur.

It's short-term self-interest—a complete inability to acknowledge the long horse race—that blinds the union and the agents from taking the necessary steps to achieve long-term gains. That's why it really amused me when Bryant Gumbel made disparaging comments about Gene Upshaw, the former head of the NFL players union. I thought his comment about Upshaw being a pawn of the owners and not doing his job on behalf of the players was not only wrong but demeaning. If you have to fight for show, that's sad. Upshaw was confident enough in his abilities that I don't believe he fought for show. Also, compare Upshaw to Billy Hunter. There were a lot of similarities: they both ran unions representing professional athletes, both were former athletes, both were African Americans, and they were about the same age. But one union works better than the other. No one ever said Gene Upshaw wasn't a tough guy. I'm not saying he was perfect when it came to being a labor leader, but it took a wise man to recognize when he had to fight and when he didn't.

When you get into a discussion about the relative strengths of the three major unions—basketball, baseball, and football—people usually point to the fact that basketball contracts are virtually 100 percent guaranteed, and football contracts are largely not guaranteed. In actuality over the last ten years, the amount of guaranteed money in football contracts has grown significantly. It's paid in the form of a signing bonus. The signing bonus may be as much as two-thirds of a rookie's entire contract and it is guaranteed. By contrast, NBA rookie contracts are less guaranteed than they were ten years ago. In 1995, when the rookie wage scale was first implemented, the contracts were for three years and fully guaranteed. Today rookie contracts are for four years and only the first two are guaranteed. The third year is an option that cannot be exercised until the end of the first year and there is a fourth-year option that can't be exercised until the end of the second year. While veteran contracts still remain dramatically more guaranteed in basketball compared to football, the rookie contracts guarantee provisions are going in opposite directions.

Prior to 1987 the NFL Players Association (NFLPA) was almost dysfunctional. It had an extremely contentious relationship with the league, as evidenced by the 1987 strike. At the same time, the NBA was enjoying unprecedented success and the labor-management dynamic worked a lot better even though there were a number of antitrust lawsuits—the Junior Bridgeman case, the Oscar Robertson case, and the Bob Lanier case—that improved the rules. Larry Fleisher knew the sport was neither strong enough nor popular enough to sustain a strike or a lockout. While a lot of rhetoric flowed on the front pages, there was a lot of give-and-take between Fleisher and Stern in the back room. Since Fleisher's death in 1988, the tracks of the two unions have gone in opposite directions. The NFLPA has developed a better working relationship with the league and the income that has flowed from sponsorships, television, and marketing is enormous. No one has wanted to kill the goose laying the golden eggs. The last twenty years in professional football has produced an era of good feelings between players and management and the players are making dramatically more money. Ironically, it's because the NFLPA has worked so smoothly that Upshaw's critics considered him to be too close to management.

By contrast, the relationship between the NBPA and the league is dramatically more contentious. At one point the league offered to increase the number of games in the first round of the playoffs and the players initially opposed it even though the majority of additional income from those games would have gone directly to the players. They have opposed a variety of proactive measures designed to increase revenues even though they get 55 percent of increased revenues. There is such distrust between the two sides that it has been difficult for the union to accept new proposals even when they are in the players' interest.

When NBA players are making nearly 60 percent of the revenues there isn't much to fight about. I'm not suggesting 60 percent is the absolute ceiling, but it's awfully close. Once you get above fifty-fifty, I think you're on thin ice.

What it boils down to is the issue of credit: being concerned with how it all looks. The union is more concerned about being perceived as tough despite the fact that David Stern has man-handled it. The very fact that there is not a strong relationship between the union and the agents—a fact that is transparent to the league—dooms the collective bargaining process before it starts. The league knows there is no solidarity between the agents and the union, between the stars and the rank and file, between black players and white players, between old players and young players. It's almost an oxymoron to call it a union. I don't blame all of that on Billy Hunter. That's what he inherited. And that reality will be one of Isiah Thomas's growing list of dubious busi-ness legacies.

In 1998, the players had no money. There was no strike fund. There was no planning. And they took on an opponent they abso-lutely could not beat. A bunch of locker-room lawyers thought they could take their game to David Stern's court and they dra-matically overestimated their ability. Stern did what he is great at doing. I have no problem with what David Stern did on behalf of the owners. That was his job. I am very fond of David Stern and I have tremendous respect for his abilities. Look what happened in hockey when the players played the same hand. It was beyond ir-responsible. They lost all the money. And what happened in hockey? The director of the NHL players union was fired. What happened to the director of the NBA players union? Billy Hunter got a raise.

Incredibly, at the end of the negotiating period, Leonard Armato had proposed rules designed to protect his only client, Shaquille O'Neal, from new restrictions that imposed maximum salaries on all of the players. His efforts might have applied to other players, but he was essentially interested in rules that protected O'Neal. I don't fault Armato for trying to protect his client. That's his job, even though O'Neal subsequently fired him.

But where did Billy have the final meeting with David Stern to resolve the conflict? Right inside Leonard Armato's office. Did Billy invite Patrick Ewing, the president of the union, to that meeting? No. As a result, Patrick was outraged. He had spent a lot of time and effort working on behalf of the union and as the highest-paid player in the league, Patrick lost more money than anyone during the lockout, almost $6 million. Truly incredible.

Know When to Hold

Early in my career I experienced a painful lesson when I probably should have known it was time to fold rather than hold. At that time, I was closer to Adrian Dantley than any client I had ever represented. My first daughter, Daina, was born in 1983 and as a reflection of our personal relationship, I asked Adrian and his wife, Dinitri, to be the godparents. Adrian grew up in the Washington, D.C., area. He was a star at DeMatha Catholic High School, then later at Notre Dame, where he was a member of the team that broke UCLA's eighty-eight-game winning streak during the Bill Walton era. He was the sixth pick in the 1976 draft and rookie of the year in 1977. He led the league in scoring several times and was probably the most productive player, pound for pound, in the history of the league. He was about six-foot-four-and-a-half, played inside, and had better post-up moves than 90 percent of the centers who have played in the NBA over the last twenty-five years.

Adrian was traded several times and in 1979 ended up in Utah, where he played for seven seasons. Then, in August 1986, he was traded to the Detroit Pistons for Kelly Tripucka and Kent Benson. Adrian had three great seasons with the Pistons. As Detroit started gelling into a championship team, and right before the trade deadline in the 1988–89 season, he was traded to the Dallas Mavericks for Mark Aguirre.

Many people have long surmised that Isiah Thomas engineered the trade because of his childhood friendship with Aguirre and the rivalry Thomas had with Adrian, who was an extremely confident, strong-willed person. Adrian would run through a wall if you told him there was a championship on the other side. He was extremely goal oriented, highly motivated, and dedicated. He wasn't the type of individual to become a sycophant of Isiah, who was the leader of the team. In fact, Adrian was extremely close to Joe Dumars because they were two private people of high integrity.

Initially we tried to block the trade. Adrian had sacrificed to fit in with the Pistons. He went from being a scoring champion averaging thirty points a game to a twenty-point scorer with Detroit. Dallas was a recent expansion team. They had drafted Roy Tarpley, who was having serious drug problems. We implored the owner, Donald Carter, not to make the trade. But the trade was made and in 1990 we approached Carter with the possibility of terminating the last year of Adrian's contract. He had one year left at over $1 million, which was big money back then. Adrian was very unhappy and wanted to go to a playoff team. Carter graciously gave me his permission to talk to four or five teams, which I did. Every team I spoke with had a high regard for Adrian. No one committed to definitely signing him, but each said that if Adrian were a free agent they would have a very high level of interest.

I was in my late thirties at the time and had a deep personal interest in the situation because of my relationship with Adrian. I wanted in the worst way to put him in a better situation because I knew he had worked so hard. We had a discussion and I told him that based on my due diligence, there was a very high level of interest in him shown by Boston, Denver, and Indiana.

Adrian wanted out of the Dallas situation so badly that he asked me to negotiate what was probably one of the first early terminations of a contract. It's certainly not something I would ever brag about, though, because it didn't have a happy ending.

The deal was done in early January. We signed the papers and the early termination of the contract was going to take effect at the end of the 1989–90 season. Just subsequent to the signing of the contract, in which Dallas agreed to put him on waivers at the end of the season, Adrian broke his leg. When the season ended, all the teams that had previously expressed interest were circumspect because of his leg. For one reason or another Adrian wasn't able to sign a contract for the 1990–91 season until April. He signed with Milwaukee and played the last ten games of the season and never played again in the NBA.

In 1991, $1 million a year was probably as much as Adrian made in his first five seasons combined. To put that into perspective, the second player selected in the 1976 draft, Scott May, signed a rookie contract for $100,000 a year.

In hindsight, it was a disastrous decision. Never again in my career did I ever recommend that a player terminate existing years on a contract without having an ironclad commitment for a new deal in place.

Because Adrian made the decision based on my advice, and my due diligence, I felt an overwhelming level of responsibility. It wasn't my fault that he broke his leg. It wasn't anticipated he would break his leg. The experience literally brought me to tears—many times. The following year, we would sit down and discuss the situation and I would break down and cry. I was embarrassed, humiliated, and disappointed beyond description. The worst part is that Adrian didn't trust many people but he trusted me completely. I knew that while my intentions were impeccable and my due diligence was thorough, there are no ties in basketball. You either win the game, or you lose the game. Based on this decision, we lost the game and Adrian lost a significant amount of money. It's not the way a future Hall of Fame player should end his career.

It was the beginning of a rift in our relationship that wasn't resolved until the last couple of years. As much as any player I have ever worked with, this was a case where Adrian was making a career decision. I totally believed in Adrian and I believed in the information I got from the five teams. I knew there was an element of risk but I thought that based on his stature, ability, and the feedback, it was an acceptable risk. If he hadn't opted out of the contract he would have had the security of another year at more than $1 million. And having the contract with Dallas would have provided him a platform upon which he would play leading up to free agency. Not having the money or a place to play at his age and at that point in his career created a perfect storm.

The experience scarred me to the point that when other players subsequently approached me about being unhappy with their situation I didn't allow them to get the fifth word out of their mouths before I said no. I told them I'd resign before I'd allow them to terminate existing years on a contract for a change of scenery. I could never live through that again.

In 2002, at the end of his third year, Elton Brand was eligible for an extension from the Los Angeles Clippers. To that point he had averaged twenty points and more than ten rebounds in three seasons since the Chicago Bulls made him the No. 1 pick in the 1999 draft. Given his work ethic, personality, and maturity, Elton was a little like Tim Duncan, almost too good to be true.

When the Clippers asked what we were looking for in terms of an extension, I told them Elton deserved to be paid what was termed a "max contract." If anyone deserved the max, Elton did. It would have paid him $72 million for six years. The Clippers countered with a six-year offer for $60 million, which was certainly a lot of money. But a contract extension wouldn't kick in for one year, at the end of Elton's fourth season.

Elton is a product of the Dunbar housing projects in Peekskill, New York, an underprivileged area with high unemployment. His mother, Daisy, is one of the strongest people I have ever met.

She did an amazing job of raising Elton, often working two or three jobs around the clock. Elton is polite and very intelligent.

I advised him to turn down the offer. I really felt he was worth the max. Elton had to go home and tell Daisy I advised him to turn down $60 million. Not surprisingly, she was very upset. I was telling a mother who had worked tirelessly to raise her child in a very difficult environment to turn down $60 million, which was more money than either of them had ever dreamed about. It represented instant security and solved any and all of the family's financial problems. She was irate. I love Daisy. She has been a wonderful supporter of mine. She's the kind of lady who lets you know exactly where you stand. In that sense Daisy is the epitome of John Thompson's idea about having a good enemy rather than a neutral friend. Daisy is never neutral.

I told Elton I was sensitive to how Daisy felt. The extension wouldn't have gone into effect for another year anyway, so regardless of whether he accepted the deal, Elton was going to make the same money in the 2002–2003 season. Finally I prevailed upon him to turn down the deal. He completed his fourth year and became a restricted free agent; the Clippers could match an offer he received from any other team and retain his services. Any other team could offer him a six-year contract for approximately $82 million. When free agency starts, it's like a game of musical chairs. There are usually a number of good players, but only a few teams with enough cap room to sign them. In some years there are no teams with the cap room to sign even one player. In 2003, there were two teams, Utah and Miami, with enough room to sign a player to a "max" contract. At midnight on July 1, the musical chairs started.

One second after midnight I was on the phone with Utah's

Kevin O'Connor and he offered Elton the max, $82 million for six years. I told him I really appreciated the offer and would get back to him after discussing it with Elton. At 12:10 A.M. the Clippers called. They offered Elton a five-year deal in the mid–$60 million range. I told them we weren't interested in anything other than a max contract.

The Clippers were astounded to learn we already had one offer at the max and that I expected to get another. Elton was very serious about Utah. I happen to consider Jerry Sloan one of the top two or three coaches in the NBA. In an era of prima donna players, Sloan runs the ship and gets players to play the right way. I have great admiration for him because of that. As it turned out we got an unlikely assist in the process from another agent, Bill Duffy. Bill had a client named Anthony Carter, who played for the Miami Heat. Carter had an option to extend his contract for the 2003–2004 season for $4 million. Duffy missed the deadline for exercising the option, which gave Miami another $4 million in cap room. We quickly got into a discussion with Coach Pat Riley about Elton going to the Heat.

Elton preferred to be in the East rather than the West. It was a tough choice to decide whether you wanted to play for Jerry Sloan or Pat Riley, two Hall of Fame coaches. But Florida is a tax-free state and it's in the East. We signed an offer sheet with the Heat and in an effort to maximize their financial position, they agreed to pay Elton 70 percent of his annual salary—the maximum allowable—up front. The change increased the value of the contract from $82 million to $86 million in addition to the fact there would be no state income tax.

I tried to dissuade Los Angeles from matching, out of respect to

Pat Riley for extending the offer, but the Clippers immediately matched the contract. Eventually, everything worked out well.

Had we succumbed to the natural pressures from the family and taken the $60 million the Clippers initially offered, it would have cost Elton $26 million. By holding rather than folding, Elton made approximately 40 percent more. In no way did I fail to understand where Daisy was coming from, but in a business with limited earning years it is incumbent to maximize your income in every available year.

Like the famous Yogi Berra quote, it was "déjà vu all over again" in the summer of 2008. Elton's six-year contract with the Clippers gave him the right to terminate after five years. He had to notify the Clippers before June 30, 2008, of his decision to exercise this Early Termination Option.

But in August 2007, while practicing with his teammate Chris Kaman, Elton ruptured his Achilles tendon. The injury caused him to miss all but eight games of the 2007–2008 season. Dr. Craig Morgan, one of the most prominent orthopedic surgeons in America, performed the surgery to repair Elton's Achilles.

When Dominique Wilkins was a client in the early 1990s, he suffered a similar injury, and the surgeon not only repaired the rupture but braided the damaged tendon with a donor tendon making it stronger than a normal human Achilles. I asked Dr. Morgan if a donor tendon would be appropriate in Elton's case. Initially he said it wasn't necessary but ultimately decided it would provide additional stability both structurally and psychologically. Elton jokingly asked Dr. Morgan if he could find a donor whose tendon would increase his vertical leap.

After months of rigorous rehabilitation that began each morning at the crack of dawn, Elton returned to the Clippers with eight games left in the season. Incredibly, he averaged 17.6 points and eight rebounds in thirty-four minutes of play. Throughout the year, Elton and I had spent hours discussing whether he should opt out of the final year of his contract.

I had recommended that he not opt out for three reasons. First, there would be only one or two teams, at most, that would have sufficient room under the salary cap to offer him a free agent contract at "the max," such as the one he had received from Miami in 2003. Second, there would be legitimate concern for the condition of his Achilles in the face of our demand for a $100 million contract. And finally, if Elton opted out, the first year of a new contract at the max would pay him virtually the same salary for the 2008–2009 season that he would have earned under his existing contract if he hadn't opted out. So there was no financial inducement to do so.

I spent the weekend prior to the June 30 opt-out deadline in Los Angeles. Elton and I had dinner Saturday and Sunday night, and he reconfirmed his intention not to opt out of the final year of his contract. On Monday, June 30, the day of the deadline, Elton came to my room at the L' Ermitage Hotel in Beverly Hills and told me that he'd had a change of heart. His beautiful wife, Shahara, was expecting their first child in October, and Elton wanted the security of a long-term contract now. He also did not want to be a "lame duck" with the Clippers in the final year of his contract. To say the least, I was flabbergasted. After planning for almost a year to not opt out, we had to suddenly pull a one-eighty.

During May and June, I'd had countless discussions with Mike Dunleavy, the Clippers coach and de facto general manager, about Elton's contractual situation. Mike had explained that the owner was reluctant to pay Elton his market value until Elton had demonstrated on the court that he was fully recovered and playing at the same level as he had before the injury. This was not an unreasonable position; however, under the collective bargaining agreement, Elton was eligible for a max contract valued at $125 million in the summer of 2008. But one year later, as a ten-year veteran, he would be eligible for a max contract in excess of $151 million. We knew that even if Elton stayed and demonstrated to Clippers management that he had returned to his rock-solid level of play that had defined his career up to that point, there was absolutely no way the owner would feel comfortable paying him $151 million in the summer of 2009.

We were in a veritable catch-22. Mike indicated to me that the owner was comfortable offering Elton a five-year contract for $60 million if he opted out early. However, Elton was scheduled to earn $16.44 million in the final year of his current contract, which meant that the additional four years the Clippers were offering averaged less than $11 million.

This represented approximately 50 percent of the max contract that a player of Elton's stature would expect to receive. Mike said he didn't want to take the risk that Elton would play out the final year of his contract, become an unrestricted free agent in the summer of 2009, and sign with a new team, leaving the Clippers without any compensation. He said he would prefer to trade Elton and obtain a player or players of comparable value. We discussed a number of possible trade scenarios.

Unbeknownst to me, while I was working to promote Elton's position with Mike, Mike and Elton were having private discussions about his future. Elton knew that Mike was scrutinizing his workouts so he would be able to evaluate the risk associated with signing Elton to a long-term contract. And while Elton and his doctor felt that he had recovered 100 percent from his injury, Elton suspected that Mike still had doubts.

Unfortunately, I was not aware that Mike and Elton were discussing his contract. During all of my discussions with Mike about a max contract, he never once revealed that he was having private conversations with Elton. I had always considered Mike a good friend. He had often invited me to play golf at Bel-Air Country Club and we met regularly for drinks and dinner during my trips to Los Angeles. I believed that our relationship had transcended the boundaries of the basketball court.

On Monday, June 30, Elton signed the paperwork to exercise his Early Termination Option. The Clippers offered him a five-year contract for $70 million. The four "new" years after the 2008–2009 season averaged $13.39 million. I told Mike this was unacceptable. He responded that the owner, Donald Sterling, was uncomfortable negotiating an extension until he saw a 100 percent healthy Elton Brand on the court. In fact, Mike explained that he had pushed Donald to the wall to get this offer, and that because he was uncomfortable, the owner hoped that Elton would turn it down.

I told him I wanted to speak directly to Donald, but I was informed that Donald was not available that day, and would not be available to discuss the contract, and that this was the Clippers' best offer: take it or leave it.

In a period of approximately two hours, Elton had taken a U-turn on his decision to opt out, and the team had given its franchise player an ultimatum on a contract worth almost the identical amount he had turned down as a restricted free agent in 2003.

To put the entire matter in perspective, from the day Mike took the job as coach of the Clippers in the summer of 2003 until the day Elton opted out in the summer of 2008, I traveled to Los Angeles almost once a month to visit with Elton and watch him play. Donald Sterling and Andy Roeser, the Clippers president, had been gracious hosts. My relationship with the team, which had been very strained early in my career, had greatly improved. I had fully expected Elton to finish his career with the Clippers and I even announced that publicly on June 30.

The Clippers eventually signed Baron Davis for $65 million. They had enough cap room to sign Davis and still pay Elton $100 million. This still would have been $25 million less than the max for Elton in 2008, but he would have gladly made the sacrifice in order to return to Los Angeles, play with Davis and obtain the security for his growing family. But at $70 million, the Clippers were essentially asking Elton to sacrifice an additional $30 million. In thirty-five years of representing superstars, I've never known or heard of a player potentially worth $125 million who was willing to sacrifice $55 million over five years to play for a team that made the playoffs once in the last decade.

Elton signed as a free agent with the Philadelphia 76ers for just under $80 million for five years. The 76ers had to trade three players to create enough cap room to make this offer. If Philadelphia had waived any more players, it would have damaged their potential as a serious playoff contender in the East. I coined the phrase the "Philly Max" to describe the amount of money Philadelphia could offer Elton and still be a viable playoff contender.

The important thing was that Elton knew Philadelphia offered him every available dollar to persuade him to come. The Clippers had $100 million at their disposal, but only offered $70 million. I totally understand and appreciate Donald Sterling's concern about paying $100 million to Elton coming off surgery from a serious injury. But I'm not certain the team understood the psychology of it: Elton wanted to feel that the Clippers "maxed out" for a player that had given them maximum performance for seven years.

In the aftermath of the announcement that Elton signed with Philadelphia, I became the target of a barrage of negative press. While Elton and I both knew that I was an innocent bystander in the cross fire caused by Mike and Elton's secret dealings, it was my responsibility to protect my client.

I am thrilled Elton is with the 76ers, back East near his home of Peekskill, New York, and on a team that should seriously contend for the Eastern Conference title. At the same time, I regret that Elton left the Clippers under those circumstances. As bright as he is, I think Elton learned that "a lawyer who represents himself has a fool for a client."

I've tried very hard to not be intimidated by the profile of my clients, whether it's people as strong as John Thompson or Coach K, or someone as famous as Michael Jordan, because if you believe in the long horse race and you want the relationship to last and stand the test of time, you have to get over these challenges. You have to prove yourself through the courage of your convictions. If you truly believe, then you have to be willing to risk temporary anger, disappointment, frustration, or all of the above. I believe blunt is beautiful and while it's not fun having to tell Elton Brand to turn down $60 million or Alonzo Mourning to turn down $100 million when there is no absolute guarantee that they are going to make more, you have to be a caring and courageous advocate to say what you really feel. If you are able to back it up, you cement the relationship forever.

Know When to Fold

Countless other players have failed to recognize the importance of knowing when to fold. The Clippers made Michael Olowokandi the No. 1 pick in the 1998 draft. He was very athletic for a center and he had some terrific games against Shaquille O'Neal, his crosstown rival with the Lakers. At the end of the 2001–2002 season, which was Olowokandi's fourth year in the league, he became a restricted free agent. It was common knowledge that year that no team had sufficient room under the cap to sign a free agent for more than the midlevel exception. The new rules provided a number of exceptions that allowed teams to exceed the salary cap for various reasons. One was the disabled player exception, which allowed a team to sign another player to replace a disabled player. Another one was the veteran player exception, which became known as the Bird exception, which allowed a team to exceed the cap to sign its own free agent. Another exception, called the midlevel exception, allowed a team over the cap to sign an additional player once a year. The first year of that player's contract could not be higher than the average salary in the league, which at that time would have been between $4 million and $4.5 million, and it could only increase 20 percent off that number each year of a multiyear contract so that a six-year contract would translate into roughly $33 million. That was the maximum any team could pay a free agent that year.

Olowokandi wasn't a highly motivated player. He was very talented and a nice guy but he didn't really love to play. The Clippers offered him a five-year deal at $9 million a year plus incentives. Incredibly, he asked for more. The Clippers knew it was a one-horse race because no other team could offer to pay him as much as the Clippers could. At the end of the negotiating period, Olowokandi declined the offer and accepted a qualifying offer under which he played the next season for about $5 million. He became an unrestricted free agent the following summer (2003) after playing only thirty-six games due to an injury. He ended up signing a three-year deal with Minnesota for $5 million a year.

The irony is twofold. Everyone knew it was a buyer's market in the summer of 2002. To turn down that kind of money when everyone knew Olowokandi had serious motivation questions was unimaginable. He probably ended up with less than half of what the Clippers had put on the table.

By contrast, that same summer, faced with the landscape of no teams having any room, we were trying to negotiate an extension for Mike Bibby at Sacramento. We came up with a compromise. If we agreed to take the qualifying offer for one year, would Sacramento stipulate that Mike would get the max for the next six years? They agreed and we ended up signing Mike, who was the No. 2 pick behind Olowokandi in 1998, to a deal that paid him $80.5 million.

It was an absolute no-brainer. Neither side could bluff because both sides knew there were no other buyers. The Clippers called Olowokandi's bluff and he probably lost $25 million, which is irresponsible.

More recently, Latrell Sprewell was coming off a very lucrative contract that paid him $14.5 million a year. Minnesota tried to re-sign him even though there was a certain stigma around Sprewell for the choking incident involving his coach at Golden State, P.J. Carlesimo. Subsequent to being suspended, Sprewell had some solid years in New York and Minnesota. But he was getting on in age and it was reported Minnesota offered him a three-year deal worth $21 million. It's also suggested Sprewell wasn't offered anything at all. In that environment, closing in on the end of his career, Sprewell came out with a quote saying he couldn't afford to feed his family on $7 million a year. That didn't engender a lot of sympathy. Instead of securing an additional $21 million, his career ended. The epilogue: In January 2008, Citizens Bank filed for foreclosure on a $405,000 home Sprewell bought in a Milwaukee suburb in 1994. His yacht, on which he owed $1.3 million, had been auctioned off for $856,000 a month prior.

Know When to Walk Away

The J. Walter Thompson advertising agency wanted me to start a sports consulting business and we had a series of great meetings in

2007. I was really excited. Instead of selling the Gatorade marketing department on signing a particular player, Gatorade would
become a client. They would say, "Here's our budget, where do
you think we should spend it?"

It was going to cost approximately $1 million to start the busi-
ness. I felt the deal was just about done. Office space had been
defined, a couple of young executives were going to be hired, and
everyone seemed to be on the same page.

In the last meeting, they brought in the CFO, a typical bean
counter. He asked me how I saw the structure of the company.

"I think it should be a fifty-fifty joint venture, but you should
own fifty-one percent because I'm going to jump-start it. Eventually it's going to be yours when I retire. I'll own forty-nine percent
and you'll be the majority partner."

"How much do you expect to earn?"

"As a start-up business, I'd like to earn $25,000 a month."

They wanted me to work sixty days a year, which is basically a
quarter of the year.

"Okay, that seems reasonable. How much of the $1 million
start-up money do you want to invest?"

"As much as you want."

"I don't understand. What do you mean? Would you put up
the whole $1 million?"

"Sure. I'd be happy to put up the whole million."

"Then why wouldn't we ask for that?"

"Because then I'd ask you to pay me $2.5 million a year in sal-
ary for my time."

"We can't afford to pay you $2.5 million."

"I know you can't. That's why I'm asking you to pay me

$300,000. The difference—$2.2 million—is my capital contribution."

"So you are proposing to put up no money?"

"At $300,000 I'm proposing to put up no money. At $2.5 million I'll put it all up or we could have some kind of number in
between."

He was really troubled by this.

"Look, I have a much better idea," I said. "You should have
Citibank as your partner. They will put up fifty percent of the
capital and they will be a fifty-percent partner in the business."

"But they don't know anything about sports marketing."

"Oh, my expertise has a value in this deal? That wasn't apparent by the way you wanted to structure the company."

It was so pitiful that it was the last meeting we had and the deal
fell apart.

Rule No. 1 in negotiation never ceases to be critical to decision
making. You truly do need to know when to hold 'em and when
to fold 'em.

FALK'S FUNDAMENTALS

Remember the golden rule: He who has the gold rules.

Just as every athletic contest requires a game plan, every major business transaction requires an analysis of the strengths and weaknesses of each party's position. Your ability to reach a successful conclusion is a direct result of the amount of leverage you have and your ability to communicate that leverage.

Know when to hold.

In basketball, a great point guard knows never to give up his dribble. Control of the ball gives him control of the game. When you have the leverage you should never settle for second best.

Know when to fold.

Modern fighter jets cost upwards of $100 million. Their pilots are trained to control the aircraft under all types of adverse conditions. However, when certain indicator lights come on they are taught to press the ejection seat. The same is true in business.

Know when to walk away.

In Las Vegas, the house always wins. After a hot run, a savvy gambler will get up and leave before he gives back his winnings. When you've attained most of what you need to make a good deal, learn to walk away and be a good winner.

NINE

The Godfather Theory

I'd Like to Make You an Offer You Can't Refuse

There's a famous expression in the law: When the reason for a rule ceases to be a reason, then the rule should cease to be a rule. That is also true when it comes to negotiation. There are very few absolutes in life and even fewer in most negotiations. When arbitrary positions create boundaries that can't be crossed, the ability of either side to achieve its goal is diminished because the artificial constraints make it difficult to employ the necessary flexibility and creativity required to make a deal.

Think of a professional golfer. He prepares for tournaments by walking the course backward from green to tee. The player will start at the cup and figure out where he wants the ball to land on the green; then where he wants to hit his approach shot from; and finally where he wants to place the ball off the tee to be in the desired position for his approach. That's my philosophy in negotiations. I like to start where I want to end up. Why go through a mechanical game of Ping-Pong when both sides know where they want to end up? Why not just acknowledge what each side needs and proceed to figuring how to get there?

As I got older, I came to dislike the traditional approach to negotiation, where one side throws out a number, the other side throws one back, and the process continues back and forth. The reason I didn't like that approach is that it invariably brought all the elements of human nature into play—ego, pride, status—none of which are necessary to making a great deal.

If you study history and go back to the eighteenth century you'll find there was a reason the French Revolution happened. The average person didn't have enough food to eat, while the royalty built four-hundred-room châteaus in the country. In a system of disequilibrium, the forces of nature tend toward equilibrium. They stormed the Bastille, tore down the structure, and created a more democratic form of government. If you have to exert discipline by force, then there are going to be negative repercussions. A great leader doesn't need to use "the hammer" unless he is in war or a state of emergency. You can use the hammer over and over again but at some point in time either the person being hit is going to become numb to the blows or they are going to find a way to counter your moves. If you have to use the hammer, and sometimes you do, then you have to be prepared for what follows.

If You Have the Power You Don't Need to Use the Hammer

My reputation is probably 180 degrees from what I believe it should be based on how I conduct myself in business. Maybe it's because I did a very good job of accomplishing my own goals, or maybe it's because others had functional fixity and thought the hammer was the only way for a person to get what he wanted. I'd be the first to admit that as a younger man I probably went to the hammer far too often and as a result I wasn't a very good negotiator. Think of it in terms of baseball. Most young pitchers in the minors have a great fastball. In the majors, the best pitchers have great change-ups. No matter how fast a pitcher can throw the ball, he can't use the fastball 100 percent of the time because hitters become acclimated to the speed, which eventually has the effect of making the pitch appear slower.

When I was first starting out, I thought my role was to win. I thought negotiations were a zero-sum game with a clear winner and loser. As I got older, I realized that to make a great deal, both sides have to win. They may not win equally but they both have to win. I came to recognize the fact that it's a sign of weakness if you have to use the hammer. If you have a big hammer and your opponent knows you have a big hammer, you shouldn't have to pull it out and show it to him. He knows you have one. Your job is to make a deal without having to use it.

I think most people have a perception of agents as being greedy. As a lawyer, I resent the broad brush we are painted with. I believe in being firm, but I learned over time you don't have to be tough or abrasive to be effective.

Most agents have the perception that they have to be tough to be successful. I had the same mind-set into my early thirties. When I was twenty-eight, I probably wanted people to know I had the hammer because I hadn't developed a confidence in my ability to close deals without overstating the obvious. I eventually came to the realization that if I really was tough, I didn't have to put on a show to prove the point. I think of Charles Oakley. Every player in the league knew that Charles was tough. He didn't have to talk trash or throw people around to make his point. Since everyone knew he was tough, Charles could be a low-key guy. Players knew that if they got on the wrong side of Oakley, then Mr. Hyde was going to come out instead of Dr. Jekyll. I didn't want to be seen as a goon. I wanted to be known as an artist.

I think most people in business never come to that realization. They think that to do well they have to be tough, impersonal, and in constant battle mode. I think you have to be smart. A great NFL running back is not going to last very long if he tries running over people all the time rather than running around them most of the time. I would never say I didn't resort to the hammer, but I now know that doing so suggests a measure of weakness.

The Godfather is my all-time favorite movie. It opens with Marlon Brando holding court at his daughter's wedding. He's in his office with his consigliere. People are coming in to pay their respects. One of them tells the Godfather that his daughter has been abused, or roughed up. Brando, with the cotton in his mouth, says in a barely audible voice to one of his lieutenants, "Give this to Clemenza. I want reliable people."

He could talk with a soft voice because he was the Godfather. He barely had to whisper and people carried out his every command. As I got older, it occurred to me that there was almost an inverse relationship between people who really had the power—Bill Gates, Warren Buffett—and the volume of their speech. They have the juice. They don't have to yell and scream in order to get their way. They are never in a situation where the pecking order is in doubt.

I began to recognize that agents who constantly whine in the media about how one team or another isn't treating a client fairly do that because they don't have the juice. They vent their frustration over their own inability to accomplish what they want to accomplish because they lack the power to make it happen.

When I hit my forties, I thought to myself, I have one of the most elite clienteles in the world, certainly in professional basketball with Michael, Patrick, John Thompson, Alonzo, and Dominique Wilkins. I need to conduct myself in a manner consistent with that reality.

I reached the point where I no longer considered the traditional process of negotiating—offers back and forth from one side to the other—indicative of someone who really has the power. If I had the power and was considered an expert in the sport, then I should be able to shorten the game, so to speak. I shouldn't have to play the game by tossing different numbers back and forth when I know from the outset exactly where I need to be in the end. Instead, I should be able to say, "Here's how I see the deal evolving." If I am truly respected by the owners, who have more power than I do, then we should be able to abbreviate the process.

Around the same time, it should have been clear to anyone paying attention that the game was changing, not only on the court, but inside the executive suites. Washington's Abe Pollin was the senior owner and he was still running a mom-and-pop operation that was probably the principal source of his income. When John

Thompson started broadcasting for Turner, he was provided a summary of each team and its organizational personnel. If the Lakers had twenty pages of information, the Wizards had a third of that. The organizations were that much different. So when people such as Paul Allen, Mark Cuban, Howard Schultz, and Stan Kroenke started to buy teams, agents were dealing with an entirely different level of ownership than they had in the 1970s.

Bob Johnson bought the Charlotte Bobcats expansion franchise for $300 million in 2004. That was just the franchise fee. It didn't include any players, coaches, or administrative personnel. Bob was indicative of the kinds of owners coming into the NBA in the 1980s and 1990s. He had a master's degree in international affairs from the Woodrow Wilson School of Public and International Affairs at Princeton and founded Black Entertainment Television in 1979. Twenty years later, still holding 63 percent of the operation, he sold BET to Viacom for $3 billion. By comparison, Donald Carter, who owned a Rolls-Royce dealership among other business interests, invested $12 million to become principal owner of the Dallas franchise that came into the league in 1980. Even in 1995, when Vancouver and Toronto joined the NBA, the franchise fee was only $125 million.

It wasn't just that the owners were richer and much more sophisticated. It was my own evolution as well. How did I want to conduct myself? I'm not saying I never lost my temper. I wasn't perfect. But I aspired to conduct myself consistent with a person who had a special clientele. There's an expression, "If you've got it, flaunt it." In business it's almost the opposite. If you've got it, then you don't have to flaunt it because everyone knows you have it. Gates and Buffett don't have to walk into a room and tell everyone they are the two richest men in America. Everyone knows that. And that fact has an impact on those present, whether it's advertised or not.

At the same time, you can't act like the Godfather if you are only a capo. When you whine to the press or complain during the course of a negotiation, it makes it clear to everyone that you are a capo and nothing more. That behavior reflects a lack of power.

Wally Walker was in my very first class of clients. The Portland Trail Blazers chose Wally with the fifth pick in the 1976 draft. Wally is an extremely bright man. But he didn't play very much during his first season and then played only sparingly during the 1977 NBA finals against Philadelphia. Following a dramatic Game 6 victory by Portland over Philadelphia to win the title, television announcer Brent Musburger went up to Wally in the locker room.

"You barely got off the bench in the final series," said Musburger. "Are you upset?"

"Well," said Wally, "Coach [Jack] Ramsay wanted to play Bobby Gross because he thought Bobby would be a stronger defensive presence against Dr. J."

"How did you feel about that?"

"I understood his thoughts, but I think I could have held Dr. J to thirty-five points a game myself."

Wally was traded to Seattle during the next season and played in three straight NBA finals, winning two championship rings. He ended up playing eight years, then went to Stanford Business School, earned an MBA, and went to work for Goldman Sachs.

Eventually Barry Ackerley, Seattle's owner at the time, asked Wally to come back and run the team. Wally was conflicted, but he loved basketball and returned to Seattle. He ended up putting together the group that, along with Starbucks founder Howard Schultz, bought the franchise.

Before becoming part of the ownership group, Wally negotiated player contracts as president of the team. In 1989, Shawn Kemp became one of only a handful of players to go directly from high school to the NBA and the first one to do so in twenty-four years, though he took a circuitous route. Kemp enrolled at the University of Kentucky, left school before the basketball season started, and then enrolled at Trinity Valley Junior College in Texas. Kemp had never played a college game when he made himself available for the 1989 draft. Darryl Dawkins and Bill Willoughby entered the league directly from high school in 1975. Moses Malone played in the American Basketball Association out of high school in 1974 and came into the NBA with the merger in 1976.

Shawn signed a six-year rookie contract. By his third season, Kemp was averaging 15.5 points and 10.4 rebounds a game while shooting better than 50 percent from the field. His agent, Tony Dutt, approached the team about renegotiating the original deal. Because Seattle was over the salary cap, the new contract couldn't start until the existing contract expired after Kemp's sixth NBA season. In other words, the new contract had to be an extension of the old deal, not a renegotiation of the remaining years. That new contract was for eight years and $25 million. In the first game of his fourth season, Kemp had 29 points and 20 rebounds. He made the NBA All-Star Team for the first time and was fast becoming one of the league's young stars. However, he had to play seasons four, five, and six under the terms of a rookie contract that was dramatically below his market value.

With the salary structure changing rapidly, by the time Kemp finished his fifth season of his rookie contract not even the eight-year extension was close to his market value. So Dutt went back to the SuperSonics and demanded they change the deal again. Once more, the team could only add years to what was already in place. In an attempt to bring the second contract up to the market value, Seattle agreed to add two more years, Shawn's fifteenth and sixteenth years, at an average of $20 million apiece. The net result of all this negotiating activity was that in an era where salaries were escalating rapidly, particularly for stars such as Kemp, he never came close to realizing his true value because he never came close to being a free agent.

I remember a conversation I had with Wally around that time.

"I'd love to have your job for one hour," I told him.

"What would you do?"

"I would call Shawn Kemp and his agent in my office. I'd say, 'Look, I know you guys are upset with the contract. Explain the problem to me.' Tony would say, 'Shawn has this eight-year contract and it's way below his market value. We want to adjust the contract.' I would say, 'Hey, I totally agree. I think the contract is dramatically below his value in the marketplace. Now, who is the dummy who negotiated this eight-year deal in the first place?' Tony would have to say it was him."

All of us have renegotiated contracts. We've missed the market and made mistakes. But when you have negotiated two contracts for a total of fourteen years, and you ask during year four of the first deal to negotiate a third one that won't start for ten more years, you have so totally missed the boat that you should be embarrassed even to walk into the room and ask for the meeting.

That's the Godfather theory backward. If you are young and you don't have the clout, you can't act like the Godfather. The louder you assert your claim that someone is being unfair, the more you advertise the fact you haven't done your job well. Your job is to make sure your client is never in that position.

Had I been his agent, I would have told Shawn Kemp that there are two roads you can take. The easy road in the short term is to renegotiate the deal, which will make the player feel as if he's getting a lot more money even though the new money doesn't start to flow for three or four more years. If you choose that road, then you had better know those additional years are going to stand the test of time in the market.

The tougher road is to be brutally honest.

"Shawn, you were the seventeenth pick in the draft. No one knew how good you would be. You were very raw. If you really want to break the bank, then play out the remaining years on the contract. No matter what you do you are going to make the same amount of money for the next three years whether you have an extension or you don't have an extension. Just play it out and when you get closer to the end, you will make a lot more money than you can make now on any additional years."

But most agents don't have the confidence to do what I did and tell Alonzo Mourning to turn down $113 million. From the agent's standpoint, he is putting out a fire by holding money in front of the player's nose even though the player won't get the money for three or four years. The agent has locked in his fee on the extension so even if he's fired, he still gets paid. Meanwhile the player got bad advice.

If you are in business long enough, you are going to fail and you are going to get hurt. Neither is worth the pain unless you gain a measure of insight from those experiences. You have to be aware of what happened so you can take something from failure to prevent it from reoccurring. In my experience, really successful people become stronger through failure. Life can be unfair, but do not be afraid to confront your failures.

(You) Control Your Own Destiny in a Negotiation

If someone asked me to define negotiation, I would say it's a process of finding a creative solution to a business problem. The word *creative* has a very important role. The way you reach a deal is not as important as getting a deal made.

What are the goals of a negotiation? Is the goal to make a great deal that stands the test of time? In sports we aren't negotiating international treaties that are going to last a century. I want to make a deal that accomplishes two things. It can be difficult to accomplish both, but I don't think the two things are mutually exclusive. I want to make a deal I feel good about for my client while maintaining a cordial relationship with the person on the other side. It's very difficult to make a good deal when the other side walks away with nothing. If the other side has a philosophy that demands victory, then you will never make a deal.

You have to understand the other person's position and know there are certain things he needs to achieve. It could be as simple as making the deal. After all, what is the purpose of the process? It's not to show off or entertain. Negotiation is all about finding creative solutions to issues keeping the two sides apart.

The most compelling aspect of negotiation for me is the fact that you can control your destiny. In an arbitration hearing, or a legal proceeding, your case is presented before a third party, either a judge or a jury. You can do all the homework and make the most persuasive argument possible, but the final decision is out of your hands. In negotiations, the rules you adopt should be designed to help you control your destiny.

Taking control means finding a solution that negates the need for a third party to make a decision. That solution prevents one side from suing the other and having an impartial judge determine the outcome; or, if you are negotiating with a team, it obviates the need to bring the commissioner or an arbiter into the equation. If you want to maintain control, then you have to be good at the process of negotiation. Think of it in terms of the differences between golf and basketball. There are no judges in golf. There are judges in basketball. Neither the coaches nor the players have total control on the basketball court. In golf, unless you violate a rule, the result is completely in your hands.

That's what I love about being a lawyer who negotiates deals rather than one who tries cases in front of a jury. There are a lot of similarities in terms of developing an argument and presenting a case. The difference is the presence, participation, and power of a third party in a court or an arbitration hearing.

In order to successfully maintain control there are rules—those outlined in this book for example—that must be followed. If you lose sight of any one of the rules, you might not be able to complete the process and you undoubtedly will lose control over the outcome. It might not even be a matter of whether you can make a good deal or a bad deal; you might not be able to make a deal at all. If an agent can't make a deal, then he is not controlling the destiny of his client and in the most basic terms, he has failed.

I've seen players negotiate themselves right out of deals. Michael Olowokandi turned down $45 million from the Los Angeles Clippers in 2002 because he believed his value was $12 million a year, despite the fact that every single team in the league was over the salary cap and thus no team could pay him more than what his own team offered. As a result, he ended up making $15 million in Minnesota. Latrell Sprewell didn't think $7 million a year was good enough for him either and he ended up out of a career.

In the NBA it's reasonable to ask whether a player can truly control his destiny in a salary-capped environment. But when you turn down the best offer from the only team that has the room to sign you, then you have given up any ability to control the situation.

Mike Bibby is a good example of how we were able to maintain control despite a very narrow market. In 2001, Sacramento had signed Chris Webber to a max contract worth $120 million over seven years. But Mike had really stepped it up in the 2002 play-offs, particularly in the deciding Game 7 of the Western Conference finals against the Lakers. He scored twenty-nine points and hit one big shot after another down the stretch while the highest paid player on the team, Webber, had a total of four points and a technical foul in the second half and overtime period.

After the game, I saw Kings assistant coach Pete Carril, who had spent a lot of time working with Mike. I thanked him for all he had done for Mike and told him it was too bad his franchise player didn't show up because Sacramento should have won the game with its eyes closed.

Pete said, "What game were you watching? My franchise player had twenty-nine points and made every big shot down the stretch."

He was talking about Mike, not Webber, which I found very interesting. Mike was a restricted free agent after the 2001–2002 season. Both sides had a choice. The Kings could make a one-year qualifying offer of roughly $5 million, which would entitle them to match any offer Mike received from another team. Mike could accept the offer, play another year, and then become an unrestricted free agent. Or we could try to negotiate an offer from another team. But in the summer of 2002, there wasn't a single team with enough cap room to make an offer that was significantly better than the Kings' mandatory qualifying offer. Both sides knew that fact. Accordingly, the Kings knew there was absolutely no risk that Mike could get a better offer that they would have to match.

We had asked the Kings for the max, which came out to seven years for a little over $90 million. Their first offer was for seven years in the mid-$60 millions. I didn't find myself in that position very often, but we were miles apart. To that point, I had never dealt with the Maloof brothers, the Kings owners, both of whom I came to love. They were obviously enamored of Webber's talent. I never considered Webber a big-game player. He was enormously talented but he couldn't win at the University of

Michigan on a team with three future NBA players, he never won
in the NBA, and, given the opportunity in Game 7 of the conference finals, he didn't show up in the second half. So we had a serious disconnect. Mike didn't want to take the qualifying offer,
which provided him no long-term security, and we knew we
couldn't get an offer from another team. The Kings didn't want us
to take the qualifying offer either because it would enable him to
become an unrestricted free agent in a year and leave the team
without compensation. They had given up their starting point
guard, Jason Williams, in the trade with Vancouver that brought
Bibby to Sacramento.

Together we came up with an effective solution. Because no
team had the cap room to make Mike an offer, the most Mike
could make in 2002–2003 was the Kings' qualifying offer of one
year for $5 million. We assumed for argument's sake that he ac-
cepted the qualifying offer and had a great year. At that point, he
could sign with another team for a max contract, which would be
six years for $75.5 million. The Kings could offer him seven years
for $91.7 million because the rules allowed a team to pay its own
player slightly more on a percentage basis than any other team.
(The rule was designed to keep stars in the city in which they
played.) So we constructed a deal we called the "outside max,"
which was equal to the Kings' qualifying offer plus the six-year
maximum contract another team could pay Mike if he became an
unrestricted free agent. The deal came to $80.5 million. Unless
the Kings were willing to give Mike a seven-year deal, the "outside max" was the absolute best deal he could make.

We accepted the deal because the concept was so logical. The only way Mike could have made more money in the summer of 2003 was if the Kings arbitrarily decided to pay him more. But they knew for certain no other team had cap room to pay him more. The irony is that because we had been so far apart, even after we shook hands on the deal the Maloofs thought I was upset or angry about the process. First of all, I try not to take deals personally. Second, I appreciated the fact that from their point of view, they traded for a player who had been averaging around thirteen points a game and suddenly had a breakout year. And we were asking them to make a huge commitment for the next seven years.

Mike didn't like to travel, particularly when the season was over. He lived in Phoenix and rather than fly he was going to drive to Sacramento for the press conference announcing the signing. The Maloofs own the Palms hotel and casino in Las Vegas and I suggested we have the press conference there. Right before it was to start they asked me how I wanted to proceed. I said, "Let's just be honest. Let's tell everyone it was a difficult negotiation because no team had cap room. Mike had a blowout year and it took a little longer to find a solution, but he's with the Kings for the next seven years and everyone is happy."

"Are you happy?" they asked.

They were stunned that I wasn't angry. I thought Geoff Petrie, the Kings president and general manager, and the owners had really stepped up. Would I have liked Mike to get the max? Yes, but it's hard to argue when the team is giving your player the most money he could possibly make under the circumstances.

They didn't believe you could disagree without being disagreeable. It was a new experience for them. I wasn't angry at their position because I understood their reluctance to make the kind of commitment we were asking for under the market circumstances. I also understood that they were apprehensive about another big contract after paying Webber and having a disappointing experience. But the concept reflected the realities of the marketplace and you could say the team paid Mike every penny he could have earned from any other team in the league over the seven years. It was simple but brilliant. And it was the concept that saved the deal.

On a scale of 1 to 10, I'd say we got to about 9.5. The Kings wanted to control their destiny, too. They had to be mindful that another team a year later might offer Mike a max contract and Sacramento could lose one of its two best players without getting anything in return. That's the kind of dynamic that exists when each side has done its homework both ways. At some point you have to figure out who has the edge. It's rare to have two exactly equal positions. One is always going to be stronger. The other party has to find a way to overcome that strength, though sometimes the stronger party doesn't even know the relative strength of its position.

Avoid Unnecessary Confrontations

Do I enjoy the art of negotiation? No. I enjoy results. Michael Lynn used to be the general manager of the Minnesota Vikings. I really liked Mike but I think he enjoyed the wrangling more than making the deal. I recognized that after dealing with Mike once or twice. When I went in to negotiate Chris Doleman's third contract, I was very prepared. Mike proceeded to tell me that Chris didn't cover the run, he can't do this or that, and the team has him rated the eighth-best player on the squad. He went on and on.

I listened to the whole show, then I said, "Mike, I'm only here for two hours, then I have to head to Los Angeles. We're never going to make a deal, so let's just forget about Chris and go out and have breakfast."

He was stunned that I didn't want to join the fight, because he was all revved up and ready to do battle. The idea that I just wanted to eat took the wind out of his sails and we made the deal in an hour. He wanted to fight because he felt that he was the toughest guy on the block. He wanted my best shot so he could knock me out. Then I came along and effectively said, "Make love, not war," and he was not prepared for that approach. That's what I had to learn about Mike Lynn. Did I want to outfight him, or did I want to make a deal?

I reached a point early in my career when I realized it was best to avoid confrontations. I'm not afraid of having them because you have to be willing to confront someone if the circumstances dictate that necessity. But if you are good at negotiations, then as a matter of course you don't have to end up in a confrontation. I always tried to find a way to make the deal. Nevertheless, sometimes a deal can't be made because the personalities or the dynamics of the situation don't allow the two sides to come together.

Both Sides Have to Win

I once asked Chicago Bulls owner Jerry Reinsdorf why he was so enamored of general manager Jerry Krause. Reinsdorf said, "David, he works long hours. He's tireless."

I said, "Let me ask you something. You had a wonderful assistant for twenty years named Sheri Berto and she was tremendous. She came in at nine and left at five but she got all her work done. Suppose the next person you hire came in at seven A.M. and worked until nine-thirty P.M. Are you going to pay the second person more money because she works longer? Or do you ask yourself, why does it take her longer to accomplish what Sheri can accomplish in an eight-hour day? The question shouldn't be which of the two is more dedicated. The real question is why did the second person have to work fourteen hours to accomplish what the first did in eight?"

As I've said, I am fascinated by human nature. In Krause's case, was he more dedicated, or less qualified? Is it better to drag out the deal-making process for six months, or is it preferable to make the same deal in six hours? The answer is neither. The best negotiation is one where you achieve a result that works for both parties. As I've said, both sides have to win.

In 1981, when I was first getting into football, we tried to sign a defensive end from the University of North Carolina named Donnell Thompson. Donnell really liked us because he was friendly with some of our basketball clients. But he wasn't sure we knew enough about football to represent him and so he selected another agent. As time went on we came to represent a number of NFL players and in 1984 I negotiated the largest deal to that point in the history of the NFL, for Green Bay wide receiver James Lofton.

Around that time, I bumped into Donnell and New York Giants great Lawrence Taylor at James Worthy's wedding. When we first met, Donnell kept asking me how much money I thought we could get him. I told him I really didn't know because it depended on where he was drafted. He told me to assume he went smack in the middle of the first round, No. 14 (there were twenty-eight teams at the time), and to give him a number.

"Can you get me $300,000?"

I told him there was no way I could get him that much money as the fourteenth pick. So he went with an agent named Marvin Demoff, whom I respect. Donnell ended up getting about $190,000.

The fact that he went with someone else always bothered me because Donnell was a bright guy and I knew he understood that I was telling him the truth. Sometimes players have an inability to separate their ego from reality. Then we ran into each other at Worthy's wedding and Donnell sat right next to me at the bar. I am an extremely competitive person and sometimes I am not very good at letting things go. No sooner did Donnell sit down than I asked him what happened the night he decided to go with another agent.

"David, I was just too immature to accept what you were saying."

Later on he fired Demoff and signed with us. By then he was playing for the Baltimore Colts, where Frank Kush was the head coach. Kush promised Donnell that the team would renegotiate his deal. Donnell went to minicamp expecting a new deal but it didn't happen. When it came time for training camp to start, Donnell decided he was going to show Baltimore he was upset by dogging it through drills. Kush knew Donnell well, and he figured Donnell would pull a stunt like that. So they had cameras watching his every move. They were taking notes. When camp ended, Donnell was suspended for "conduct detrimental to the team." At the grievance hearing, the team presented a mountain of evidence. Donnell ended up being suspended for four regular season games. When he returned from the suspension, he had to take a physical. The team doctor asked him how he was doing and Donnell said his shoulder was a little sore. The doctor asked him what he had been doing the last four weeks that made his shoulder sore.

"Playing a lot of golf," Donnell said.

I finally had to step in and tell Donnell to get back to work so I could do my job. We ended up getting him a very good deal despite his actions.

Consider what Drew Rosenhaus pulled with the Philadelphia Eagles. The team knew exactly what to expect when Terrell Owens fired his agent, Fred Joseph, and hired Drew Rosenhaus. Rosenhaus had a very simple—in every sense of the word—plan to pressure the franchise into renegotiating a contract Terrell had signed a year earlier despite being advised by the union to turn down the offer.

The backstory is that Terrell had a contract with the San Francisco 49ers that included an option to terminate the deal. When the termination window arrived, his agent missed the filing deadline. A hearing followed and Terrell emerged from it with his right to terminate the contract reinstated even though his agent had failed to file the proper papers. But the union advised him not to terminate the contract because he didn't have enough leverage to get a better deal. Terrell did it anyway and signed a long-term contract with the Eagles. One year into that new deal, he wanted another new deal. So he fired his agent and hired Rosenhaus.

Rosenhaus apparently had a plan to very publicly pressure the team. As with Donnell Thompson, the team was 100 percent prepared for what Rosenhaus had in mind. Management took notes and when it came time for a hearing on the matter, what happened? Philadelphia suspended Owens for "conduct detrimental to the team." That was as predictable as the sun rising in the morning. There is so much competition in the marketplace today that it sometimes forces agents to make promises that are unrealistic or unachievable. Owens was such a high-profile example of that reality that it was almost comical. I felt bad for him because he is a great player and someone should have sat him down and said, "Terrell, you made your bed and you are going to have to sleep in it."

I had to tell Michael Jordan exactly the same thing early in his career. Donald Dell negotiated Michael's first contract and it was a disaster, too many years for not enough money. After about three years, I told Michael that if he ever wanted to be paid what he was worth, he would have to play out the contract and become a free agent. We could renegotiate the current deal and get a better contract, but he would never be paid market value until he became a free agent. That's just the way it works. There is always a price for security.

I was giving a speech at the University of Tennessee when football player Maurice Clarett said he wanted to leave Ohio State after his freshman season. The purpose of his departure was to challenge NFL rules that prohibited players less than three years removed from the graduation of their high school class from entering the league. I was asked what I thought his chances were of overturning the rules. My answer was that a first-year law student would be able to tell you that any rules negotiated between the players and the league are immune to antitrust challenges. And that's exactly what happened. The rule that stipulates players cannot enter the draft until three years after their senior year in high school was collectively bargained between the league and the union. Collective bargaining is protected by federal preeminence, which says rules that might otherwise be illegal under antitrust laws are protected as long as they are collectively bargained between the certified bargaining unit of the players (the union) and the certified bargaining unit of management (the league).

I have great sympathy for players in these kinds of situations. They go into battle thinking they have hired a specialist and believing in their advice. As high-profile celebrities, the players are remembered for their successes and failures, but their advisors are quickly forgotten. And what happened to Clarett and Owens? One is out of the sport and the other is out a lot of money. I think Terrell Owens is an incredible talent and I believe he's a good guy. I just think somebody needs to look him in the eye and say, "If you want to make really big money, here's how you do it."

Here's the flip side to the Clarett case: there's been considerable discussion about the age limitation rule in the NBA, whereby an American player is restricted from being drafted until one year after his high school class has graduated. Ironically, until the early 1970s players could not be drafted until they finished their college eligibility. Then the league implemented what was known as the "Hardship Rule," which allowed players who had not yet completed their senior year in college to apply for the draft based on financial hardship. Like most licensing requirements, the hardship qualifications came to be abused and the league finally dropped the façade of economic hardship and simply allowed players to declare themselves available for the draft.

In 1995, Kevin Garnett became the first player since Bill Willoughby and Darryl Dawkins in 1975 to go directly to the NBA from high school. Garnett's decision set off a tidal wave of high school players declaring for the draft. The succession of these highly talented young players included Kobe Bryant, Tracy McGrady, Dwight Howard, LeBron James, and others. After several years, some of them were among the top twenty to twenty-five players in the league.

For me there are a number of very compelling reasons it is important to have an age limitation for players coming into the NBA. First and foremost, the NBPA is a union. The purpose of a union is to negotiate wages, hours, and terms of employment while providing job security. Now if a player at age seventeen or eighteen is talented but unskilled, much like an apprentice in a craft guild, then you send that worker or player elsewhere for seasoning so he can learn the skills of his job before he becomes a member of the union. If we were talking about someone in the electricians union or the carpenters union, a master craftsman who has been in the union for twenty-five years, the union would never allow a first-year worker, no matter how talented he might be, to take that master craftsman's job. Yet in basketball we've allowed young players who have tremendous upside potential but really don't have the skills to perform the job this year or perhaps for another two or three years to be drafted or signed and take jobs away from older, more skilled players.

Secondly, if you trace the history of basketball on television to 1979 when Michigan State played Indiana State in the NCAA championship game, Magic Johnson against Larry Bird, it kicked off a rivalry that lasted for more than a decade. Every year from 1980—when Magic led the Lakers to the NBA championship as a rookie—until 1989, either Bird or Magic, and sometimes both of them, were in the finals. During that period, virtually every major star in the NBA had played in the NCAA tournament, which is nationally televised over a three-week span, and miles of newsprint were generated that extolled the talent of these great college players. In the case of Grant Hill, who spent four years at Duke and went to three national championship games, or Patrick Ewing at Georgetown, fans knew everything about them by the time they entered the NBA. They became household names before they ever dribbled a ball professionally. That familiarity drove up television ratings. Today, by contrast, if Kevin Durant, who is a tremendous young talent and was rookie of the year during the 2007–2008 season, had gone directly to the NBA from high school rather than making a stop at the University of Texas, I bet less than 5 percent of America would have known who he was or what sport he played.

Under the new rules, instituted in 2005, Durant was forced to attend college for a year. He went to Texas and became the first freshman in history to be named college player of the year. At the end of his freshman year he entered the draft and was the second pick in 2007. As a result of the television exposure he had at Texas, Durant was a well-known national figure when he entered the NBA. Imagine if the old rules were in place and he had to come back to Texas for the next two seasons rather than enter the NBA. Every year the story line would develop further: could Durant use his extraordinary talents to lead Texas to the national championship over Ohio State and its two remarkable freshmen, Greg Oden and Mike Conley, Jr.? The rivalry between Texas and Ohio State might have taken on the magnitude of the Bird-Magic contests.

If all those players were forced to come into the NBA at the end of their junior seasons, they would absolutely be household names. The marketing around their jerseys, television ratings, and attendance would be enhanced by the additional notoriety. In the NBA, the players currently make roughly 55 percent of the revenues while the owners make roughly 45 percent. I question why the players as a group would reject an age limitation rule when they stand to make the most money as the revenue pie grows because of the increased name recognition and popularity of the players coming out of college. Why would they ask the owners, who already make less than the players, to pay something additional for something that is in the players' inherent economic interest? Conversely, why would the players, to spite the league, say, "Okay, we'd rather make less money on our fifty-five-percent share just to show you we don't want to give up any ground on the age limitation issue."

That's why, from a business standpoint, I think the union is making a drastic mistake in not supporting an age limitation rule to protect its veteran members and to enhance the income stream that would flow from greater recognition of the incoming players. It is the most illogical negotiating situation I have ever seen. It begs the question: Are you being smart at the table, or smart at the bank? When you are representing a client, sometimes giving things up is in your client's interest. You shouldn't be reluctant to concede points you know are in your client's long-term best interest even if it makes you look like you aren't being "tough."

By contrast to the NBA, the former head of the NFLPA, Gene Upshaw, was unequivocal in refusing to allow the aforementioned nineteen-year-old Maurice Clarett to take the job of one of its veteran players. Careers in sports are very short, Upshaw noted, and the union's job is to protect the veterans. How could two major sports with unions run by African American executives who were former players look at the same picture and see completely opposite images? One, Upshaw, believed his overriding compelling responsibility was to protect the jobs of his existing players and bar young players from joining the union. The other, Billy Hunter, feels it's not his place to bar the young players because it's a restriction on their personal freedom.

In the law, the famous Chicago Board of Trade case states a maxim that to bind or restrain is the essence of regulation, but the test is not whether a regulation restrains competition. The test is whether the regulation is reasonably formulated to promote competition. To a certain extent every rule restrains personal freedom. Is the fact that players have to attend practice a restriction of their personal freedom? It's one of the obligations that come with signing a professional contract. If a rule is promulgated that players cannot enter the draft until after their third college season because it enhances the ability of existing players to earn more money and at the same time grows the sport, then it's a good rule. If Dale Earnhardt, Jr., had a seven-year-old son who, because of the genes of his grandfather and father, was more skilled than 99 percent of all drivers in America, should he be allowed to get a license to drive at age seven? No, because while he might be skilled he doesn't have the experience or judgment to drive a car. So while there are players such as LeBron James, Kobe Bryant, and Kevin Garnett, for the most part, permitting high school players to enter the draft has not been a good rule for the league in terms of business.

Whatever restrictions are put on the personal freedom of high school players, those restrictions have been accepted for decades. There are restrictions on college players to maintain certain grade point averages. Is that un-American? No. It fosters their academic growth. To suggest that rules are unfair or un-American because they restrict a player's ability to earn a living is incorrect. An age limitation rule wouldn't restrict his ability to make a living, but it would restrict his ability to take the job of a more senior player. If you try to suggest that there is a racial component to age limitations, which I don't see at all, then what you are really saying is: Let's make it easier for African American players to avoid a college education so they can earn a living in professional basketball. I just don't understand that. When you consider how short careers are, I think it's essential to teach young players life skills so when sports end, or don't work out financially, they have a viable way to earn a living.

You Need a Game Plan for Success

What I really want to do in a negotiation is persuade the person I am negotiating with that we are talking about the right concept. If they believe in the concept, the money follows. I believe the best negotiations are based on the best concepts. In that way it's very similar to sports. A player can't score a lot of points until he embraces the concept behind the team's offense. Do you believe in the passing game, or do you believe in a half-court game? I think there is always a concept that needs to be embraced before I can make a deal.

Once I lock into the concept, I become passionate about my position. If a team says it wants to pay an amount of money that goes against the concept, I'm not as upset about the money as I am about the fact they failed to accept the foundation. What bothers me is that they either don't understand or choose not to embrace my concept.

I developed a very simple approach. As a result, I have been called a horizontal negotiator. Instead of going up and down, I worked to keep the numbers constant while moving side to side. I did a lot of research and I developed concepts designed specifically for the players I was representing in a particular negotiation. It would be like asking Phil Jackson why he didn't stop using the triangle offense after winning six championships. He totally believed that the triangle, the system, was creating victories. Jerry Krause, the Bulls general manager at the time, believed the organization was responsible for the team's success. While you can agree or disagree, Jackson got to the point where he was completely invested in the concept and felt that if the players could accept the triangle, success would flow accordingly. That's roughly the way I approached negotiations and I had no problem telling the other side exactly where I was coming from up front. If we could agree on the concept, then the math would flow. The concept didn't flow from the math.

I also tried to always look at the process from both sides. If I owned a team and an agent walked in and told me his client was worth $10 million a year, I'd want to know *why* he felt that way. If the agent didn't have a logical, rational concept to support that number, then there wasn't much to talk about. As the NBA changed and I was dealing with owners worth billions of dollars, I believed that if you provided them with a concept they could sink their teeth into, a concept that made sense, then the money would be easy. But they wanted to know why. They wanted to achieve a comfort level that what they were being asked to do was logical and made sense economically.

The first question I asked an owner or general manager was how they determined an appropriate position to take on a particular player and what the thought process was that led them there. A lot of times they would turn the question around because they really hadn't thought their position through. They asked me how I determined the position I was taking and I would tell them exactly how I did it. I would explain the concept.

The first Charlotte expansion team came into the league in 1988. We represented the very first player the team drafted, Rex Chapman, as well as the first player Charlotte selected in the expansion draft, Muggsy Bogues.

To avoid confusion and as an aside, let me offer a little background on the franchise. Owner George Shinn moved the original Charlotte team, the Hornets, to New Orleans in 2002.

In 2003, Bob Johnson, who created Black Entertainment Television among other highly successful entrepreneurial endeavors, bought a new Charlotte expansion franchise and named the team the Bobcats. The team's first NBA season was 2004–2005. Two years later, in 2006, Fred Whitfield, who worked for me at FAME, became president and chief operating officer of the Bobcats, and Michael Jordan became a part owner and managing member of basketball operations.

During its first incarnation in 1991, the Charlotte Hornets had the No. 1 pick and they were leaning toward selecting Larry Johnson, who had been a dominant player at the University of Nevada– Las Vegas, over Dikembe Mutombo, whom we represented.

We wanted Dikembe to go to the Denver Nuggets, which had the fourth pick. New Jersey had the second pick and Sacramento had the third pick. Neither team had its sights set on a big man. Indeed, the Nets eventually selected Kenny Anderson and the Kings took Billy Owens, both guards.

The night before the draft, Charlotte's head coach, Allan Bristow, asked if he could work out Dikembe. He wanted to be sure he wasn't making a mistake. Dikembe has always been a shot blocker and rebounder, certainly not a player known for his offense. Coach Thompson had his son, John Thompson III, on hand feeding the ball to Dikembe during the workout.

There was a popular Reebok commercial around that time about a guy named "Lamar Mundane" raining jumpers from all over the court. That night Dikembe was like Lamar Mundane. He was shooting jumpers from everywhere, making shots that he probably hasn't made since. Everything he put up was going in. At the end of the workout, Allan asked if he could play Dikembe one-on-one. Allan played ten years in the NBA as a six-foot-seven forward.

"Do not hold back," Coach Thompson told Dikembe.

If we had scripted the workout, we could not have asked for a better showing by Dikembe. It was the workout of a lifetime. The minute it was over, Allan looked at Coach Thompson and said, "Thanks, Coach. I'm definitely going to take Larry Johnson."

I was stunned.

"No problem, Coach," said Coach Thompson. "But please don't ever say I didn't give you the opportunity to avoid making the mistake you are about to make."

So Charlotte went ahead and drafted Johnson, who was a very talented player. The Hornets came to believe Johnson was as good as any player in the league and even equal to, if not better than Michael Jordan. He wasn't, however, good enough for the Hornets to avoid another trip to the lottery.

In 1992 Charlotte ended up with the second pick in the draft. This time the first two picks went as expected. Orlando took Shaquille O'Neal at No. 1 and the Hornets selected Alonzo Mourning from Georgetown.

Because of his dominant nature, Shaquille, in my view, represented a Patrick Ewing situation. He was going to receive a contract unique to his ability to become a dominant player capable of carrying an entire franchise. His contract, like Patrick's in 1985, wasn't going to have any relationship to the prevailing rookie salary structure. I concluded that it wouldn't be fair for us to follow the traditional route and negotiate a contract for Alonzo based on what O'Neal was likely to receive.

The first meeting with Charlotte took place in our offices in Washington, D.C., with team president Spencer Stolpen. Since I dealt with him for Rex and Muggsy, we had a good relationship. I wanted him to understand that we appreciated the significance of Shaquille relative to the rest of the market.

"There are two ways that we can evaluate Alonzo's market value to Charlotte," I said. "The traditional way is to say Shaquille O'Neal is the first pick in the draft, and we should base Alonzo's contract as a derivative of O'Neal's deal. But I don't think that's a realistic position for the team because O'Neal is an anomaly. He's a dominating franchise center. So my suggestion is, rather than look at Alonzo as the second pick, we should ignore Shaquille and deal with Alonzo as if he were the first pick. In other words, we should negotiate a contract absent the anomaly that is O'Neal."

In that first meeting, I proposed a six-year contract that averaged $4,250,000 a year and gave Alonzo the right to terminate the deal at the end of four years. Larry Johnson had signed one year earlier for an average of $3.1 million a year as the No. 1 pick. As a result, management had a very difficult time with the idea of paying Alonzo more than it paid Larry. Even though Johnson was only six-foot-six, they viewed him as the centerpiece of the franchise.

"No problem. If you don't want to ignore Shaquille and view Alonzo as the first pick, we are happy to do it the traditional way.

But O'Neal is going to make $5.5 million a year. If you wait for him to sign that kind of contract, then we are going to come back asking for $5 million for Alonzo."

At the close of the meeting, Spencer said, "If we accept your offer, would you agree that half of the sixth year wouldn't be guaranteed?"

Normally NBA contracts are 100 percent guaranteed. By 1992 it wasn't even a negotiating point, particularly for the second pick in the draft. But I never thought we'd get to the sixth year with Alonzo because he would exercise the early termination clause at the end of the fourth season.

"If that will close the deal, then yes, we would agree to it."

But it didn't close the deal. That meeting took place in early July, about two weeks after the draft. The entire summer went by and along the way Shaquille signed for around $5 million a year. Christian Laettner, who was the college player of the year from Duke and the third pick in the draft, signed a six-year contract worth $3.6 million a year with Minnesota.

Charlotte had neither the hammer, nor a concept. The Hornets came back offering Alonzo the same deal Laettner received.

"Alonzo Mourning isn't Christian Laettner. We aren't interested in what the third pick received."

This went on for months. Alonzo eventually missed the entire preseason and the first four games of the regular season before Charlotte came back around to the first offer we made back in July. Alonzo signed a six-year contract for $4.2 million a year with an out after the fourth season. But this time the sixth year was fully guaranteed. In the end we gave up $50,000 a year for six years, a total of $300,000, in exchange for Charlotte guaranteeing the entire sixth year for an additional $3 million.

By not having a concept, or even an idea from which to negotiate, it took the Hornets more than three months to agree to a deal that was worse for them than our first offer.

How Do You Spell Success?

Business negotiations are generally about trying to place a value on something, whether it's a service or a commodity. If I had arbitrarily picked numbers out of thin air, then the process was likely to become personal because the negotiation would come down to what one person believed versus the other. Conversely, if the two sides open the discussions by explaining how they determine value, then both participants can agree upon a concept to determine that value. Imagine you are sitting at a racetrack and two cars go by. I ask you which car you thought went faster. You said the Pontiac went faster and I tell you I think the Chevy was faster. We then get into an argument about something without any real basis in fact. Now if you take out a radar gun and determine the speeds at which the two cars were moving, then we have a platform from which we can discuss the facts and reach an agreement. You have to have some tool to measure value or else negotiations can become a completely arbitrary argument.

In 1985 that concept is what led to the largest contract in the history of the NBA. Patrick Ewing, the "Hoya Destroya," was the first overall pick in the draft by the New York Knicks. One approach would have been to pay Patrick Ewing like a typical rookie based on what the player selected in the same spot a year earlier had been paid. That's how most agents would have approached Patrick's first deal and the team would have been comfortable with that concept. But by embracing that mechanism, you were trapped by what another agent had done before you. It's similar to the question of precedent. I can argue a case in front of the U.S. Supreme Court, but if there are seventeen cases similar to mine with a series of outcomes contrary to what I hoped to achieve, then I'm out of luck. The court is bound by precedent and it doesn't matter how persuasively I present my case.

In Patrick's case, I acknowledged what happened before but I opted to put that off to the side and examine a new concept. Precedent can trap people who are trying to change the world. Change comes from making new rules, new precedents. All the modern advances, the truly breakthrough achievements have not been built on precedent. They have been initiated by creative people who thought differently, or ignored the evidence supporting the way things had always been done. I never set out to change the world, but my approach to negotiation, particularly when I was younger and less confident, meant I needed to know my position was grounded and logical. I felt people would respect an argument that made sense. They might not agree with you, but the first step is to let the other side know you are presenting a thoughtful, logical position.

I was the consummate sports junkie when I joined ProServ in 1974. I knew every player's batting average, all the Heisman Trophy winners, the shooting percentages of virtually every NBA player, and I thought knowing these facts would help me in the sports business. One day someone said, "David, do you think you are going to walk into Red Auerbach's office and wow him with statistics? He's not going to give a damn whether or not you know the shooting percentage of every player in the history of basketball. He's going to tell you that's great, now here's what *I* think your player is worth."

I realized very quickly that I was never going to know as much as Pat Riley or Jerry West, much less Red Auerbach. Even if I did know as much about the game as they did, they weren't going to acknowledge that I did.

If the process came down to them dictating terms based on a superior knowledge of talent evaluation, then the player really didn't need me. I realized that I could not wage battle against their strength. I was a lawyer and I needed to approach the process from *my* strength. I constructed economic arguments to support my client's value. I couldn't argue talent. That variable had been stipulated by the team's decision to select the player at a specific spot in the draft or in a trade. I wanted to discuss all the other factors. I wanted to be as strong an arbiter of economic value as Red Auerbach was of talent. In time, that's what I became. I was able to understand the system by understanding where the salary structure was going based on economic value, not ability.

It was a very simple process of analysis initially because I had no standing to debate talent with experts. It was like going in front of a bunch of scientists and debating the theory of relativity. I always found it interesting listening to different agents discuss what they thought their clients were worth. It got to the point before the inception of the rookie wage scale that agents used every justification imaginable to support their contention that a player deserved a particular salary. Ray Patterson, who was a long-time executive with the Houston Rockets, told me that an agent named Lance Luchnick, who later was decertified by the union, walked in with a second-round pick and told Ray that Houston had to pay the player like a first-round pick because the agent had promised the kid's mother he would go in the first round. Now, could you possibly think of a worse argument?

I realized that whatever I knew about basketball represented a losing hand at the negotiating table. It is like what I told the players twenty years later during collective bargaining negotiations. They were not going to step onto David Stern's court and beat him any more than he could beat them in a game of one-on-one. At a minimum, they had to find a level playing field, a middle ground from which to negotiate. In the beginning I wasn't trying to become anything more than someone who was effective at his job. My thought process evolved into what I thought was a logical approach to business. There's an expression that says, "It's not about the money, but it's just about the money." Even though I didn't set out to redefine or change the market, in the end my approach did change the market because I evolved as the market evolved.

When it came time to negotiate Patrick Ewing's last contract with the Knicks in 1997, New York was way over the cap, as it had been for a long time. When a team is over the cap, under what came to be known as "the Larry Bird exception," it can still sign and pay its own free agents any amount. If it fails to sign its own free agent, a team over the cap can only replace the lost player with another player making the minimum salary.

We entered into an interesting negotiation because I knew Patrick was irreplaceable to the Knicks. He was still their best player even though he was thirty-four years old. And if they didn't sign him, they would have to replace their best player with a minimum salary player, who is barely qualified to be in the league. Not only that, but Patrick was a center, arguably the most important position on the team.

On the other hand, the Knicks knew that no other team had enough salary cap room to pay Patrick more than $10 million a year. So the question became, Who had more to lose? Did Patrick have more to lose by accepting $10 million a year versus whatever the Knicks might offer, or did we have more leverage because New York could only replace their best player with a highly inferior alternative? The Knicks were going to have an enormous payroll no matter which direction they chose, but without Patrick the team wasn't going to be competitive.

Both sides were in the position of having perfect knowledge. We asked for $20 million a year because Patrick wanted a five-year deal for $100 million. We ended up signing a four-year deal for $68 million, or $17 million a year. I knew we probably could have gotten closer to $20 million, but it would have been "blood money."

In that situation the question was whether I wanted to drop the anvil. I never really wanted to do that unless I thought somebody wasn't dealing in good faith. The Knicks had always paid Patrick well. In 1991, we had gone to arbitration to have Patrick declared a free agent based on his opt-out clause and lost. Even after we lost, the team gave Patrick a two-year extension at $11 million a year that made him the highest paid player in the league. Since the Knicks had always recognized Patrick's importance to the team, and rewarded him fairly, if not generously, I felt $17 million for four years at age thirty-four was an incredible contract. Whether we could have gotten them to pay $18 million or $19 million a year at that point was really just rubbing their nose in it. And given the relationship, it would not have been appropriate, so we accepted the deal.

It really came down to a simple concept. Was Patrick, who had probably made more than $60 million playing basketball at the time, better positioned to take $10 million somewhere else rather than the $15 million the Knicks offered to pay him? Or were the Knicks in greater jeopardy of not retaining their captain and leader on a team totally dependent on his output in an environment in which the franchise was still going to have an enormous payroll? I felt they had more to lose and eventually the team agreed.

The fact that Patrick was irreplaceable established his value. The $100 million number was a milestone Patrick wanted to achieve but it went against the grain of how I approached negotiations. It was an emotional number rather than a number based on financial analysis. We had made deals that paid Alonzo Mourning and Juwan Howard $15 million a year. Patrick was definitely a higher-profile player, particularly playing in the league's largest market. That's why he ended up making $17 million.

I didn't need the hammer to make my point. The concept, as is often the case when it is well thought out, won the day. If you have to go to the hammer, then you don't have the strength to make a fair deal. And if you have to scream and yell to get yourself heard, then everyone knows you don't have the juice to be a Godfather.

FALK'S FUNDAMENTALS

If you have the power you don't need to use the hammer.
In fashion it is said, "If you've got it flaunt it." But in business if you've really got it, then everyone knows you've got it and there is no need to flaunt it.

(You) Control your own destiny in a negotiation.
Almost every variable in a negotiation—where you meet, how you dress, how many people are in the meeting—has an impact on the final result. Take control of the variables and you will take control of the deal.

Avoid unnecessary confrontations.
Really successful negotiators show how *smart* they are, not how tough they are.

Both sides have to win.
Boxing matches are frequently judged on a "must" scoring system where the loser of the round still receives points. There are no shutouts. In business, even if you win the fight, it is important that your opponent wins some points in order for him to accept the deal.

You need a game plan for success.
In sports, a coach devises a game plan to exploit his team's strengths and attack the other team's weaknesses. A success-

ful negotiation depends on a well thought out game plan that conceptualizes the path to a deal.

How do you spell success?

The last player in major league baseball to hit .400 was Ted Williams more than sixty years ago. In other words, Williams failed to get a hit in 60 percent of his plate appearances. Nevertheless, hitting .400 is considered an iconic achievement in baseball. Learn to define what success means in your business.

TEN

Get Out Ahead of the Curve

The first time Enzo Ferrari sat behind the wheel of a car he had conceived, created, and built, he knew something wasn't quite right. The leather was beautiful, the seat was perfectly positioned and comfortable, the engine was an engineering marvel. But something was out of place. He could *feel* it. After several minutes, Enzo Ferrari reached up toward the windshield and ripped off the rearview mirror.

"When you are driving a Ferrari," he said, "there is no need to look behind."

Business is no different. If you are constantly looking behind, then it's impossible to lead. I always wanted to be mindful of the past, but I never want to be locked into paradigms created by others. Like Enzo Ferrari, I didn't want my clients to be limited because I wasn't able to see future opportunity even when most of my competitors were looking in the rearview mirror and worrying about past precedents.

The difference between seeing the whole court and getting out ahead of the curve is the difference between executing today and determining how to navigate in the future. Successfully executing today requires you to be mindful of every option and to select the right one. Getting out ahead of the curve requires you to envision options that don't even exist today and to create strategies to manage them. It is, therefore, more about seismic shifts in the landscape, paradigm-changing movements that often appear to be obstacles when viewed through conventional wisdom.

It's not that highly successful people don't see obstacles. Enzo Ferrari no doubt encountered difficult moments and momentum-stopping problems en route to creating the world's most famous sports car. It's not that he didn't see the obstacles. It's *how* he saw them. For highly successful people, a large barrier simply represents a higher degree of difficulty. That's why successful people often appear to be fearless. They know that virtually every barrier or obstruction is most often nothing more than a near-term impediment they must navigate on the way to the top.

Consider an Olympic-caliber diver. The average person might be afraid even to climb the ladder to the highest platform. The idea of standing on the balls of your feet with your back to the water before jumping off a platform nearly thirty-three feet above the surface and contorting your body in a way that it enters the water perfectly and avoids injury would paralyze most people. They might be able to traverse an initial fear of heights, or even find the strength to stand on the lip of the platform. However, as the degree of difficulty increases, the ability to execute declines.

You have to force yourself to be bold. There was a book in the 1970s titled *Dare to be Great*. Really successful people act differently when all the financial and economic analysis doesn't close the gap between where they are and where they want to go. Those people take a leap of faith and jump across the gap without absolute knowledge of whether they are going to make it to the other side. Most people stay on the safe side because they don't have enough information. The lack of a guaranteed outcome becomes prohibitive. They can't make the leap.

Conventional Wisdom
Is Just an Element of the Status Quo

To get out ahead of the curve you have to see conventional wisdom, or any obstacle for what it is—nothing more than an element of the status quo. I never believed there was anything static about the status quo in sports. Rules changes produced intended and unintended consequences that led to a constantly shifting landscape. I never wanted my clients to be held to a salary or marketing structure established by someone else.

That approach was confirmed yet again in February 2008. The release of Air Jordan 23 produced all-night lines at specially selected retail outlets twenty-three years after the first shoe was released and more than five years after Michael played his last NBA game.

Tinker Hatfield, the principal designer of the Air Jordan shoes, indicated that when the first shoe was introduced in 1985 it established an entirely new paradigm. For the first time in basketball, a player promoted his own product rather than endorsing an existing one. In 1984, when I negotiated the original deal for Michael with Nike, the conventional wisdom was that basketball, like football and baseball, was a team sport. The idea was famously expressed in the phrase "There is no *I* in team." It was considered neither possible nor appropriate to separate and market an individual player apart from the team.

In the late 1970s and throughout much of the 1980s, two teams dominated the NBA: the Celtics and the Lakers. While they ultimately came to be defined by individuals—Larry Bird in Boston and Magic Johnson in Los Angeles—each of those two men was surrounded by four or five other great players. Bird had three Hall of Fame players in Kevin McHale, Robert Parish, and Bill Walton. Magic had Kareem Abdul-Jabbar, James Worthy, and at one point Bob McAdoo, all Hall of Fame players.

Boston also had other well-known players such as Dennis Johnson, Cedric "Cornbread" Maxwell, and Danny Ainge. The Lakers had Byron Scott, Michael Cooper, and others. Bird and Magic were great players but their individual talents were blended into the fabrics of two championship teams.

When Michael arrived in Chicago, the franchise was on its way to hitting rock bottom despite the presence of some highly skilled players. The Bulls were the opposite of those Lakers and Celtics teams. They were even different from the Detroit teams of Isiah Thomas, Bill Laimbeer, and Joe Dumars. In the nineteen years Michael played, including his two-year stint in Washington, he had only one teammate, Scottie Pippen, who even had a shot of making the Hall of Fame.

Under the circumstances, and given what I had done with James Worthy and New Balance, it was easy for me to get out ahead of the curve when Michael came into the league.

To appreciate the Nike deal, you first have to understand the prevailing landscape in 1979 and what we did to invert the market on the court and off in the years leading up to 1984.

Magic Johnson came out of Michigan State as a sophomore after beating Larry Bird's Indiana State team in the 1979 NCAA finals. That game was the highest-rated basketball game, professional or college, in history. Magic was an instant superstar, being named rookie of the year and then most valuable player in the 1980 NBA finals, heroically playing center for an injured Abdul-Jabbar in the deciding game against Julius Erving's Philadelphia 76ers. He had characteristics similar to Michael—the smile, a great nickname, a winning pedigree—but in 1979 Magic's management team couldn't foresee the opportunity that Michael would ultimately create in 1984. All of the elements were in place with Magic but nobody realized that they added up to something different from the existing paradigm. (That Michael invented a whole new universe of opportunities in the year "1984" was itself a delicious irony.)

As a result, the real precursor to Michael was his North Carolina teammate, James Worthy. James left North Carolina as a junior in 1982 and was the first (and only) player ever drafted No. 1 by the defending NBA champion.

Midway through the 1979–80 season, the Lakers sent Don Ford

and a 1980 first-round draft pick to Cleveland for Butch Lee and the Cavaliers' 1982 first-round pick. For the second time in three years, the Lakers, against staggering odds, ended up with the No. 1 pick when Cleveland finished the 1981–82 season with the East's worst record. In those days, the worst team from each conference flipped a coin to determine the first pick in the draft. The Lakers won the flip once again.

Three years earlier, the Lakers had allowed Gail Goodrich to join the New Orleans (now Utah) Jazz as a free agent following the 1976–77 season. At that time, by signing a veteran free agent the Jazz had to compensate the Lakers, which it did with three draft picks, including New Orleans' first-round pick in 1979. Ironically, the Bulls lost the coin flip in 1979 that resulted in Magic going to Los Angeles and UCLA's David Greenwood landing in Chicago.

When Worthy arrived in the NBA in 1982, the shoe industry was just starting to achieve momentum. Nike was beginning to make itself felt as a fledgling force against Converse and the international giant, Adidas. In James's case, the fact that he went to a championship team in the entertainment capital led me to believe that he had the potential to make a unique impact. If that wasn't enough, James was coming off North Carolina's 1982 NCAA championship victory over Georgetown, which the Tar Heels won on Michael's game-winning shot.

We inverted the market twice with James, once on the court and once off the court. His playing contract had no relationship to the existing salary structure for rookies while his shoe deal with New Balance was the largest in NBA history. As with Michael two years later, I refused to accept the conventional wisdom that a rookie effectively had to serve an apprenticeship. Worthy's entry into the league was unprecedented in a way that was the exact opposite of Michael joining the Bulls in 1984 or Grant Hill going to Detroit in 1994. In fact, in the twenty-six years since drafting Worthy, including the 2008 NBA draft, the Lakers have never had a pick higher than No. 10 overall.

As a person trained in economics, I recognized the value of an event not likely to be repeated. The Lakers were getting an individual who not only fit into their style of play, but also had the perfect personality for a team with two superstars. James grew up in Gastonia, North Carolina, just outside Charlotte, in a very strong family led by a very strong father. As a result, James had an unnatural maturity level even as a freshman at North Carolina. You could see he had a supreme confidence and maturity that didn't require him to show he was the man. He just *was* the man. There have been very few eighteen-year-olds in any sport with that kind of presence. When James got to the Lakers, that mindset and maturity were as important as his talent. He was comfortable deferring to Kareem and Magic. He didn't feel the need to prove he belonged. He knew he belonged.

In time, while Magic and Kareem received a greater share of the publicity and kudos, James came to be known as "Big Game James" because of his ability to elevate his performance in the playoffs. He stayed in the shadows and did what he needed to do during the regular season, but in the playoffs, when there was tremendous pressure and double-teaming of Magic and Kareem, James took his game to another level. And it really wasn't a surprise, because he had that kind of talent. His mental toughness, maturity, and confidence enabled James to play a role that very few great players would have been comfortable with.

When it came time to negotiate Worthy's first contract, we blew it out relative to the prevailing market. The previous year, Dallas had selected Mark Aguirre with the No. 1 pick in the 1981 draft. The Mavericks signed Aguirre to a contract with a present value of approximately $250,000 because a significant amount of the money was deferred. The present value of James's contract was probably triple that of Aguirre, and was more than a lot of veteran all-star players were making, including Magic, because a large portion of his contract also included deferred money. It was an interesting window in time because Magic had just finished his third season in the NBA. He had signed a historic twenty-five-year, $25 million contract that not only didn't kick in until the 1984–85 season—by which time he had been a four-time all-star—but also proved to be wildly below market value before it ever went into effect.

I was still the junior partner to Donald Dell in terms of the negotiating team at ProServ. Donald had known Jerry Buss, the Lakers owner, extremely well. Jerry owned four of the ten teams in the World Team Tennis league. He's known as Dr. Buss because Jerry has a Ph.D. in chemistry. He also is a genius in what is known as present value. It's a financial term used to describe the process of evaluating a future stream of payments in terms of current dollars. One of Donald's weaknesses was math. He wasn't instinctive when it came to numbers and he had very little feel for present value or its calculation. It got to a point where Jerry asked his lawyer, Jerry Fine, and Donald to leave the room so he and I could work out the contract. Dr. Buss had some very interesting concepts with regard to how he wanted James's deal to work. It all boiled down to looking at Magic's deal a little bit and considering present value with the salary cap coming in. It was typical Jerry Buss. The contract was very complex. I was only thirty-one years old and it was nice to get that kind of respect from someone as intelligent and creative as Dr. Buss.

Worthy was part of two seminal events—inverting the rookie salary structure and forever changing the economics of shoe endorsements. Bird was the savior of the Celtics after he arrived in 1979 and he inverted the market at that time because of the unique circumstances surrounding his arrival. James was the first player to invert the market to a degree that he made more as a rookie than established all-stars.

The salary cap went into effect in 1982 but in its first year it only applied to six teams, one of whom was the Lakers. Kareem was making $2 million a year and Magic had signed his new twenty-five-year deal right around that time. In an interview with Turner Broadcasting, I was asked if Magic's deal would revolutionize the sports landscape. I replied that Magic would be crying before the deal even kicked in in 1984–85.

As we saw earlier, that deal would turn out to be horrible for Magic. But it satisfied Magic from a cosmetic standpoint because even though he had to wait two more years, he became a $1 million a year player.

We didn't set out to get James more money than Magic, or anyone else for that matter. We were trying to get an amount of money that reflected the fact that the Lakers had essentially won the lottery, though the actual NBA draft lottery didn't even exist at the time. It was not predictable that the reigning champion could draft a player of James's talent, maturity, and pedigree with the No. 1 pick ever again. That gave the No. 1 pick, whoever it turned out to be, a unique bargaining chip. As it turned out, there were three great players in the 1982 draft—James, Terry Cummings from DePaul, and Dominique Wilkins from Georgia. While all three turned out to be all-star players, for style reasons I think it's extremely unlikely the other two would have been able to make the kind of impact James made. Dominique had the talent and flair, as well as the ability to run with the Showtime Lakers. But it's questionable whether he would have been able to defer and be the third player on a great team. For every reason under the sun, Worthy was the perfect pick.

We changed the existing paradigm of the entire salary structure with James. Between 1982 and 1995, when the rookie wage scale came into effect, rookies, not veterans, set the market for NBA salaries. But more than his playing contract, James's New Balance shoe deal changed that market forever. James made roughly 50 percent more than any player had ever made on a shoe deal to that point, and his contract with New Balance was truly the precursor to Michael's Air Jordan off the court.

In 1984, I certainly didn't know that Michael would become the greatest player of all time. I don't believe there is a human being alive, including his parents, who could have predicted Michael would achieve what he did during his career. It was, however, easy to see that he would be an exciting, electric player who could make a unique impact on a bad team.

In Chicago, as loyal to its sports heroes as any city in America, it wasn't hard to see that Michael would be popular. Whether it would work on a national level, no one knew. Few professional athletes and even fewer NBA players had a national following in 1984. The fact that the Bulls didn't have any other star players, combined with Michael's personality, led me to believe that regardless of his on-court success, he would have a level of popularity disproportionate to how he played. That notion by itself was revolutionary because the expectation at that time was that rookies came into the league and served what amounted to an apprenticeship. He would pay his dues, defer to the older, more established players, then after five or six years of strong performances he would *become* one of the more established players.

In Michael's case, the wake-up call for me was the 1984 Olympics in Los Angeles. He separated himself from the field in a way that made him the star of stars in the glitter capital of the world. In international competition against professional players from Spain, Italy, and other countries from around the world, and even with a team that included Patrick Ewing, Chris Mullin, and Sam Perkins, all playing for a coaching legend, Bobby Knight, Michael distanced himself to a degree beyond what he had done at North Carolina. He was a man among boys in Los Angeles, a fact Knight endorsed. I had no idea he would achieve what he did later on, but his excitement level was off the charts. Accordingly, in round one what I promoted was not the idea that he was going to be the greatest player of all time. Rather, I sold Michael's unique ability to generate a level of excitement in the third-largest market in the heartland of America.

In hindsight, and I've said this many times, if you reverse-engineered Michael Jordan down to the shot he hit to win the

NCAA title as a freshman at North Carolina, being named player of the year in college basketball, his great parents, all the success in the Olympics, his work ethic, smile, and intelligence, it would still take a spark of lightning to ignite the mixture. The mixture alone wasn't enough.

That's why in the twenty-five years between 1984 and 2009, every entity—from the NBA marketing department to the shoe companies to Madison Avenue—has been like Ponce de León searching for the fountain of youth. Only in this case everyone has been looking for the next Jordan.

The first contract with Nike was ahead of the curve for a number of reasons. First, by insisting on a very strong promotional commitment from Nike, I jump-started the entire Jordan marketing process not just with Nike, but across the board. The very first Nike poster—Michael dunking the ball with the Chicago skyline in the background—turned into the icon, or "Jumpman" logo, for Brand Jordan. For better and for worse it also became the prototype for every other player who tried to form a shoe line. From Shaquille O'Neal to Dwyane Wade, virtually everything that followed was a bastardized version of the original. Shaq had the "Dunkman," which, like the rest of them, was a very poor imitation of an iconic trademark.

The deal included royalty payments, a structure I was very familiar with. I had experience monitoring contracts Arthur Ashe had with Head for signature tennis racquets, and with Adidas for shoes. I oversaw Stan Smith's shoe deal with Adidas, which is still one of the most successful shoe relationships in sports history, as well as Stan's racquet contract with Wilson Sporting Goods.

A year earlier, in 1983, Ralph Sampson had a deal with Puma

for his own shoe. It turned out to be an abject failure. As a result, no one felt the model could work in basketball as it had worked in tennis and golf. Once more, the prevailing wisdom was that basketball was far too much a team sport to create the kind of individual success that players in tennis and golf had with their own lines of apparel, racquets, clubs, and shoes.

I remember telling Michael, who was twenty-one years old at the time, that I had a dream.

"My dream is that one day you will become very successful, get married, have children, and your son will walk into Foot Locker and be able to buy a pair of Air Jordan shoes."

Twenty-three years later, Jeffrey and Marcus Jordan don't have to buy their Air Jordans at Foot Locker, but millions of others buy them all over the world.

The fact that Air Jordan has stood the test of time is a tremendous accomplishment for Michael. It's probably the single most successful affiliation in the history of marketing, not just sports marketing. That's something I am singularly proud of because it clearly established a paradigm and was far ahead of the curve. Today it is de rigueur that when a top young player comes into the NBA he signs a deal and gets his own shoe. There have been several generations since 1984, and shoe companies have invested literally hundreds of millions of dollars trying to find, or create, the next Michael Jordan. Brand Jordan not only stands alone, but it is close to becoming a $1 billion a year business.

A year later, in 1985, Patrick Ewing became the first pick in the first ever NBA draft lottery and landed in New York. Patrick's situation was Worthy's magnified. Patrick wasn't just a very good player going to a great team. He was the very best player on a poor team that averaged twenty-three wins over the previous two seasons in the country's largest media market.

It had been my experience that rookie contracts continually fell behind the expanding salary structure. The most vivid—and painful—example wasn't even Magic. It was the seven-year rookie contract Donald Dell single-handedly negotiated for Michael Jordan with the Bulls in 1984. Although it would be the last contract Donald ever negotiated for Michael, its length was so damaging that it was not until 1996 that I was able to finally negotiate a playing contract for Michael that accurately reflected his unique value and that properly distanced him from the pack.

As a result, as much as I was concerned about the compensation provisions of Patrick's contract, I was more concerned with its structure and especially its length.

I ignored the prevailing market for rookie contracts despite the fact that the Houston Rockets had just used their back-to-back No. 1 picks to draft franchise centers Ralph Sampson (1983) and Hakeem Olajuwon (1984). When the negotiations were finalized, Patrick received 50 percent more than the highest-paid player in the history of the NBA, Kareem Abdul-Jabbar, was being paid. Patrick's contract was thus by far the largest contract to date. With the sole exception of Magic Johnson's twenty-five-year extension that had just kicked in during the 1984–85 season, it was also the longest. But I had experienced how quickly previous contracts for top rookies proved to be out of step with market value. Despite the presence of the salary cap, salaries were growing very quickly and making long-term contracts particularly risky. For that reason I negotiated the first early termination clause into Patrick's contract. His rookie contract was fully guaranteed for ten years but Patrick had the option to terminate the deal at the end of his sixth year if he wasn't one of the top four highest-salaried players in the league. The Knicks readily agreed to the provision because they couldn't imagine three other players getting close to Patrick's salary.

Today the early termination option has become a standard tool in every sport. It was a practical solution to my fear that no matter how well I did for our clients, the market was likely to be even higher a few years down the road. In 1991, even after losing an arbitration case in which we fought to prove that Patrick was not among the four highest-salaried players in the league, his second contract averaged more than $11 million a year.

Not only was Patrick's contract dramatically ahead of the curve because of his salary, but its length provided an unprecedented level of security and the early termination option gave him a level of flexibility that was truly unique. What happened between 1982 and 1985 with James, Michael, and Patrick established the standard that has not changed in more than a quarter century. Every great player—Kobe Bryant, LeBron James, D. Wade—gets his own shoe. They get a soft drink deal. They get either McDonald's or Burger King. It's like a multiple-choice test now. Everyone knows what's on the menu. The only question is whether you want item A or B. Prior to 1984, those choices didn't exist. Now they all want long-term contracts with the right to terminate because they want the long-term security with short-term flexibility. That option didn't exist until 1985.

In 1989, I represented Danny Ferry, who also was the player of the year in college basketball. He was drafted No. 2 and went to Italy for a year before we signed him to the highest contract in league history. I wanted to break the $4 million-a-year barrier, but Danny wouldn't allow me to do that. So he signed a ten-year contract that averaged $3.75 million with an out after seven years. Over a very short period of time, 1982 to 1990, we had completely inverted the market and changed the economic dynamics between young players and management.

You Must Know the Difference Between Talent and Value

We didn't wait for the rookies to become apprentices, then skilled craftsmen. As a former player, a very bright man, and a traditional coach, John Thompson found the idea of paying rookies so much money difficult to embrace. But we weren't negotiating talent. We were negotiating value. A team's experts determined talent. When a team selected Danny Ferry at No. 2, their experts proclaimed Danny the second most talented player in the country.

My job was to translate their determination of talent into dollars. In other words, what did that talent mean to that specific team in that particular year? The analysis had very little to do with basketball from my perspective. It had everything to do with economic impact and value. In Patrick's case, the lottery changed the odds of a team getting the No. 1 pick from 50-50 in the case of Magic Johnson going to the Lakers to a 1-in-7 chance. By 2008 it had become a 1-in-14 chance. As a result, the value of the first pick in the lottery increased dramatically because the likelihood of getting that pick dropped from 50 percent to 14 percent and then to 7 percent.

It's also important to understand the negotiating environment at the time. Teams had the upper hand in contract negotiations because in the NBA in the 1970s and early 1980s the teams had all the information. You might think a player is making $2 million and during the course of the negotiations find he was only making $1.3 million. Only one side—the teams—had accurate information, which made the entire process that much more difficult.

Also, I recognized very early that teams had no respect for an agent's evaluation of his client's talent. As a result you were coming in at a competitive disadvantage on almost every level.

James Worthy was going to be drafted No. 1 because he was the best player in the country. At worst, he was going to be drafted No. 3. My job was to make sure he was the No. 1 pick. Once he was drafted No. 1, I had to give him an edge in contract negotiations. I couldn't do that trying to argue basketball skills with Jerry West.

Two things were obvious to me. One: If I was going to bring a level of expertise to the table, it couldn't be based on the player's talent. Two: We negotiate within the parameters of a very simple economic model based on supply and demand. In 1982, could anyone imagine that there would come a time when we would walk into a supermarket and pay three dollars for a twelve-ounce bottle of water, something you could essentially get for free at home? Would it have been conceivable that ten or fifteen years down the road, we would pay two dollars for a cup of coffee that costs five cents to make? Smart people like Howard Schultz created value out of something—coffee—that was widely considered a commodity.

In every aspect of our lives smart people have sought to establish value by being selective at the upper end. Air Jordan has stood the test of time because Phil Knight had the insight and vision to limit production of the shoe. He probably could have sold 10 million pairs rather than a million pairs in the early years.

In my line of work, it was almost out of a competitive necessity that I tried to take a different look. Agents argued talent and allowed other agents to set the market by slotting their clients in a preestablished salary structure. In either of those cases, I really wouldn't be supplying a service to my clients. I gravitated to an understanding that at the upper end there was a dramatic difference between talent and value.

Today I think it's almost backward. Very few teams grasp the concept, as evidenced by the fact that they pay disproportionate amounts of money to very average players they could replace for half to a third of what they are being paid. You can't replace LeBron James or Kobe Bryant because they are virtually irreplaceable. As a result, they are probably underpaid almost no matter what they make.

If a team ends up with four or five players at what is termed "the midlevel exception"—$6.7 million a year in 2008—then they are making an inordinate investment in totally fungible players. Instead, they should make a larger investment in two irreplaceable players. No structure should allow premium prices to be paid for fungible products. The only time that happens is when there is a market aberration—the oil embargo in 1973, or the price of water prior to and sometimes after a natural disaster. Why does the price of water increase the day before a hurricane? Because the storm changes the value of that water. The very same product that cost two dollars a week earlier, in the same packaging and in the same size, will increase in price if people believe the supply is or is going to be limited.

Artificial Constraints Don't Work

So we had these three aberrational contracts—James Worthy in 1982, Patrick Ewing in 1985, and Danny Ferry in 1990. Then, in 1992, Shaquille O'Neal became another aberration. In a salary cap environment, the veterans had a logical argument: If an untested rookie is worth that much, then how much am I worth? Unfortunately, the argument didn't have as much power as logic might suggest because each team only had so much space under the salary cap and rookies were taking a disproportionate amount of that space.

Around the same time, we started to value contracts not on the total dollars paid, but on the average per year. When Magic signed a $25 million contract for twenty-five years, people were amazed by the size of that deal. At that time, if I had signed James Worthy to a six-year contract for $18 million, the perception among my peers would have been that Magic had the better deal because he was guaranteed an additional $7 million. In fact, Worthy would have been making $3 million a year while Magic was making only

$1 million. Worthy's contract would have been dramatically bet-
ter. The length of Magic's contract effectively capped his career
earnings while Worthy would become a free agent in his prime in
a rapidly escalating salary environment.

Alonzo Mourning was the No. 2 pick in 1992 and he was paid
substantially more than the No. 1 pick in 1991, Larry Johnson,
who happened to be on the same team. Then in 1993, in the next-
to-last year before the rookie wage scale came into effect, we signed
Shawn Bradley, who was the second pick in the draft, to a contract
that paid him more money in his first eight years than the No. 1
pick, Chris Webber, and the No. 3 pick, Anfernee Hardaway,
made *combined* in their rookie contracts.

The competitive pressure on agents to match these average salaries in a capped environment became so great that Webber signed
a fifteen-year deal and Hardaway signed a thirteen-year deal.
Though the average salary was low, the total dollars committed
started to become significant. In an attempt to keep up with the
average salaries, players were committing themselves to longer
and longer deals with no outs in some cases and only limited flexibility in others. It got to the point in 1994 that Glenn Robinson,
the No. 1 pick, locked himself into a ten-year contract with no
ability to get out. Jason Kidd signed a nine-year contract with no
out and Grant Hill signed a nine-year deal with an out after six
years. These players were kept away from free agency for six to ten
years, which should have been a dream situation for owners.

Instead, owners overreacted to the total dollars committed in
these long-term deals. The perception that rookie salaries had
gotten out of hand was fueled by the succession of deals we made

from Worthy to Bradley. As a result, the rookie wage scale was implemented in 1995. Owners wanted a mechanism that protected them from committing long-term dollars to unproven players. The system initially allowed players to become unrestricted free agents after their third season. So instead of having a ten-year period to evaluate Glenn Robinson, or nine years to evaluate Jason Kidd, a team could lose those kinds of players with no compensation after three years.

What happened? Teams were forced to give players a maximum contract after their second season. In the 1996 draft, we had four of the top twelve players selected—Allen Iverson, No. 1; Antoine Walker, No. 6; Kerry Kittles, No. 8; and Vitaly Potapenko, No. 12. Iverson and Walker received maximum extensions after their second years. Kittles signed a long-term contract for roughly $9 million a year after his second season. In 1997 we had Keith Van Horn, the No. 2 pick. He also received a maximum extension after his second year.

The irony is that our inverting the market led to rules changes that ended up allowing young players to be paid even more money. The idea of looking out and trying to be ahead of the curve changed the way rookies were paid and eventually led to a revolutionary change in the form of a rookie wage scale.

When an artificial constraint is introduced into a closed economic system like the NBA, the result is akin to pumping forty pounds of pressure into a tire that is only supposed to have thirty pounds of pressure. What happens? Does the tire inflate uniformly? No. A bubble forms. There is a bottleneck in one part of the system that makes it impossible for the air to be uniformly dispersed. Since the system is accustomed to self-correcting in the presence of a bubble, the tire explodes. In the NBA, the salary structure exploded every time an artificial constraint was implemented to avert the very problem the previous constraint created.

The outcome of the rookie wage scale is materially interesting to me. I argued against the wage scale with Buck Williams, who was my client and president of the Players Association at the time. The union and management believed rookie contracts had grown disproportionately large and thus were sucking too much money from the veterans. The response, agreed to by both sides, was to create a rookie wage scale that they believed would reduce the length and size of the rookie contracts. In practice they exacerbated the problem. The rookie wage scale, in its original version, forced rookies to sign three-year contracts. At the end of the third year, they became unrestricted free agents. As a result, teams ended up with a shorter period of time to evaluate draft picks. If the player was a high pick and performed as expected, then teams had to pay huge amounts of money after the player's second season to keep him from entering the free agent market after the third and final year.

There was hysteria within the ownership ranks that rookie contracts were out of control. Together with the players, the owners created a system that guaranteed the rookies even more money and it only took the players an extra two years to make it all. Rookies ended up making dramatically more than they ever could have earned in a traditional rookie contract prior to the rookie wage scale. Suddenly players with two years of experience were being paid "max" contracts worth $10 million to $14 million a year. As a result, a lot of mistakes were made. Teams ended up paying max contracts to players who otherwise would never have come close to making that kind of money based on their ability.

From my perspective, it was not difficult to get out ahead of the curve and take advantage of the new rules. We anticipated the change and worked to create a situation where virtually all of our high-profile clients' contracts expired in the summer of 1996.

The contracts of Michael Jordan, Alonzo Mourning, Dikembe Mutombo, Juwan Howard, Armon Gilliam, Kenny Anderson, and Chris Gatling all expired that summer. In what I called "Seven Days in July," once more we completely remade the NBA salary structure. At that time Patrick Ewing, another one of our clients, was making $11.2 million a year as the highest-paid player in the league. By the end of the seventh day, Juwan Howard and Alonzo Mourning signed $105 million contracts that paid them $15 million a year. Dikembe made about $12 million a year; Kenny Anderson, who most people expected to make a total of $25 million, signed for $50 million. Then Michael established the highest salary ever paid in professional team sports in America by signing a one-year contract for $30 million.

———

While all this was going on, the cast of characters began to change. In the 1970s and 1980s, Larry Fleisher, an agent, was the head of the Players Association. Larry, Bob Woolf, me, and Lee Fentress from Advantage, which was an offshoot of ProServ, were the most successful agents in the business. Most of the top college programs in the country would invite us to make a presentation when a player was leaving school for the NBA. That continued into the early 1990s. As we got into the mid-1990s some of the younger agents, who weren't at all established, started to sign players capable of becoming first-round draft picks. There were already indications of financial inducements floating around when this new group of agents started making serious inroads, signing some of the highest-profile rookies.

We looked at the landscape. FAME was doing very well financially. The company represented roughly forty clients. These were elite players, many of whom had been top-five draft picks. We literally saw the winds of change starting to blow. The collective bargaining process changed, the union was being increasingly weakened, and the agents were changing. I could no longer rely on quality people such as Larry Fleisher and Bob Woolf to maintain the integrity of the marketplace.

At the same time, it never occurred to me that you could sell a personal services business. We didn't have any hard assets or inventory. Essentially all we had to sell were contracts and expertise. Since it was critical to the players that individual agents service those contracts, it seemed impossible to believe someone would buy an asset that was so personally tied to one or two individuals. But I was wrong. We received feelers from a couple of large multinational corporations in the financial services sector. We received strong feelers from a billionaire who owns part of one of the largest retail chains in the world. Then, in early 1997, I received a call from a gentleman named Bob Gutkowski, formerly the president of Madison Square Garden.

Bob had left MSG and formed a business that rolled up some

small sports agencies into a company called the Marquee Group. Among the companies Marquee purchased was ProServ, which ran into serious financial difficulties following my departure in 1992. Bob came to Washington and approached me about purchasing FAME. I was intrigued but I knew Marquee owned ProServ and after working with Donald for seventeen years, I had no desire to be in business with him again.

We did a little more research and learned that Robert F.X. Sillerman, who had rolled up radio station properties into a company called SFX Broadcasting, was funding Marquee's purchases. Sillerman had sold SFX to Hicks Muse, a private equity firm, for $2.1 billion in 1998. He retained the SFX imprimatur and started buying all the mom-and-pop concert promotion companies across the United States. There were no economies of scale when music groups toured because promoters operated independently. Bob felt that if he created a unified national network, it would create much greater efficiencies, which it did. Eventually he sold SFX Entertainment to Clear Channel Communications in 2000 for $4.4 billion. Sillerman is a true business genius, one of the smartest men I have ever met. He gained a measure of notoriety in 2005 when he paid $100 million for the name and image rights to Elvis Presley, which included Graceland. That same year he also purchased the *American Idol* franchise for $161.3 million.

Eventually we acknowledged an interest in discussing a sale, but I did not want FAME to become part of Marquee. We would only talk to the parent company, SFX Entertainment.

We met Bob Sillerman in New York and I was immediately impressed with his mind. He's a very creative deal maker and great with numbers. I really didn't want to sell. If I had an interest in selling, it had more to do with this growing feeling that the industry landscape was changing right under our noses.

The union hadn't been diligent in enforcing the rules against agents engaging in illegal inducements. It was becoming more difficult to compete with some of the younger agents because we didn't break the rules. I also was concerned about the next round of collective bargaining in 1998. We had tried to organize the agents in 1995 to induce their clients to decertify the union in an effort to get better rules for all players. Almost to a man the agents ran for cover. So we had no confidence the agents and players would form a cohesive unit to negotiate a new deal with David Stern after the 1997–98 season.

Curtis Polk, my partner and FAME's president, is financially astute and he has a great mind. Rather than discuss a potential sale ourselves, Curtis suggested we do what our clients did—hire an expert.

"Even though we do this for a living, let's not make the same mistake you made all those years with Donald Dell," Curtis said. "Let's go out and hire a real high-powered financial services company to be our advisor."

We hired Goldman Sachs. Since we weren't Bank of America or Rolls-Royce, we didn't get Hank Paulson, currently Secretary of the Treasury, who was chairman of the company at the time. But we got a very nice junior analyst. He checked out the numbers and said the company was worth about $70 million, which was a lot more money than I would have dreamed the company could be worth. But at that level, I had no desire to sell, primarily because

I didn't want to work for someone else. I was making good money. I was happy. I liked the idea of controlling my own destiny and I liked walking in every morning and seeing my name on the door. While I was intrigued with the idea that our little company was worth that kind of money, I had no desire to sell at that number.

Bob did his own analysis and came back with similar numbers that valued FAME somewhere between $70 million and $80 million. At one point Curtis asked me to give him a number at which I would be comfortable selling.

"You always need a walk-away number in negotiation."

"Because of the aggravation of working for someone else, I wouldn't sell for less than $100 million."

Curtis tried to explain the fact there is no practical difference between $100 million or $90 million. But it wasn't necessarily about the number and it wasn't as simple as me being greedy or egotistical. I established a number that I felt represented the human cost of not controlling my own destiny. For me that number was $100 million. Along with our advisor at Goldman, Curtis explained to me that based on the discounted value of the cash flow of all the contracts, and all the other metrics, that if we could get $70 million or $80 million, we should do the deal. From my perspective, we had a $20 million to $30 million gap.

Even though I could tell that Sillerman was a very talented individual who was creating something that could be very exciting, I didn't want to take my name off the door. Eventually I was back meeting with Bob. Everyone was trying to explain what all the economic indicators were pointing to and I wasn't grasping the concept as fast as everyone wanted me to. I decided to

explain my position as best as I could absent the economic calculations.

"I have great respect for you, Bob, and what you have created
with both radio and concert promotions. And I do understand
what the indicators are pointing to. At the same time, if we are
going to get married, let's not say things to each other during the
courtship that will lead us to want a divorce before we complete
the vows. I'm not arguing what makes sense to you, but let me try
to explain what makes sense for me. Whether it's right or wrong,
consistent with the economic indicators or not, I am not going to
be comfortable selling the company for less than $100 million.
Based on what we bring to the table, if you don't feel the company
is worth $100 million, you aren't going to offend me. But please
understand that every year I stay on my own, I am going to be less
willing to sell. If it doesn't work this year and you come back to
me next year, my number will probably be $200 million."

Sillerman really wanted to buy FAME. He felt we were the
jewel among the companies he was buying because of the star
power of the players we represented. Eventually we structured a
deal that was intended to pay us $100 million—approximately
$83 million in cash and 1 million shares of stock, which was worth
$17 at the time. As it turned out, Bob did such an incredible job
of growing the company that the stock ran up to nearly $80 a
share. Right away, the deal was worth $150 million to $160 million. On top of that we had earn-outs, or financial targets we had
to hit to trigger additional payments. By the time we hit those
targets the deal was worth closer to $200 million.

We were excited to make the deal. It was not so much for the economic freedom it provided, since we were already doing very well financially. Rather, it gave us a different kind of freedom just as the industry was changing. We weren't beholden to a new environment that was being created against our will.

We could continue to be extremely selective with regard to the players we represented. There was no pressure to bend the rules or take on players that didn't fit with our brand. Of all the things I had been involved in to that point in my career, I never was further out ahead of the curve than when we sold the company.

And in one of the great ironies of my life, I became chairman of the entire sports operation and Donald Dell ended up working for me, which wasn't something either of us was thrilled about. While it was a very real example of the old saying "Turnabout is fair play," I had no desire to treat him as he treated me. At the same time, six years after I left ProServ, we sold FAME for more than fifteen times what Donald had received for ProServ.

We signed the papers on June 4, 1998, and at that time we were in the lead-up to what would become the lockout of 1998–99. We felt a very strong measure of financial independence, certainly more than I had ever felt in my life. I felt the same level of independence Michael felt when he left the NBA to play baseball. The economic success he had created to that point provided him the freedom to do whatever he wanted. In this case, I planned to continue in the industry. But for the first time, and after twenty-five years in the business, I really understood what freedom felt like. The book wasn't closed but it definitely was the end of a long chapter.

Preparation, Instinct, and Confidence
Are the Keys to Success

How do you get out ahead of the curve? The same way a running back surveys the field a split second before he breaks the play and goes right instead of left and scores a touchdown: preparation, instinct, and confidence. The running back practiced that play all week and every time he did, the play went to the left just as it was designed to do. But when the facts on the ground changed, he was able to make a split-second adjustment.

Highly successful people don't have a great deal more knowledge than the person who stays on the shore. The difference is that they instinctively know that they are going to land on their feet. If they don't make it to the other side, then they will have learned something that allows them to make another attempt. That's what it takes to get out ahead of the curve.

The inner confidence comes from doing your homework, and studying what is happening around you to develop confidence in your ability to see where things are going. After a while it becomes instinctive. As great as John Stockton was, he didn't always make the right pass. Once in a while he threw the ball away.

Peyton Manning and Tom Brady are two of the best quarterbacks of their generation. They study defenses. They study the playbook. They watch film all week before every game. If they throw five straight incomplete passes to start a game, does anyone really think Manning and Brady are wondering whether they can do it anymore?

They know that it's just as likely the next eight passes they throw will connect. A great shooter like Reggie Miller could start off missing shots he normally made but he never stopped shooting. All the preparation, all the prior experience allowed him to be supremely confident that the next eight shots would go in. Most athletes pull back when they reach that first threshold. They stop shooting. The great ones believe the next shot is going in the hole, the next pass is going to be a touchdown.

Take golf, for example. It's probably the most counterintuitive sport. If you want to hit the ball a long way, then you have to smooth out your swing. Swinging hard puts a lot of spin on the ball and that makes the ball come down faster. To be successful in golf, you really have to play the game backward. You have to figure out where you want to end up and what it's going to take within your skill set to get there. Tiger Woods can drive a ball three hundred yards over a lake. I'm going to hit one shot, lay up, and try to get a birdie by hitting a great second shot. Now I can try to emulate Tiger, but unless something dramatic happens I'm going to be in that lake every time. At some point, the pain of not being able to get on the green is going to induce me to realize I have to try a route different than the one Tiger is taking. Not everyone is going to reach the hole in the same way. The question is, Can you reach the hole in a way that allows you to still compete for the championship?

As you can see at the beginning of this book, one of my favorite quotes is from Sir Isaac Newton: "If I have seen further [than other men] it is by standing on the shoulders of giants." He did see further than other men. He was able to see ahead of the curve to develop advance thinking that no one in his generation was prepared to embrace. Why was the astronomer Copernicus able to prove that the earth wasn't the center of the universe when everyone at the time believed that it was? He was able to leap across the abyss by taking all the prevailing wisdom and throwing it out the window. As a result, he proved that in fact the sun was the center of the universe.

We can call it stubbornness, confidence, conviction, or drive, but to truly achieve you have to get to the point where the right decision stops being factual or evidentiary. You might not be able to prove it, but you know the right way to go because you can feel it. All the evidence takes you to the three-yard line. But the ability to get into the end zone comes from confidence.

In sports, periodically an innovative coach will create a new style. When it's successful, people will either try to emulate that new system or develop another system to stop the innovation from working. It is true in business, too.

Consider the music industry. Eventually the industry is going to have to acknowledge, as it has to some degree, that no one has been able to see out ahead of the curve. Music industry executives tried everything to save the traditional business model in the face of a rapidly changing technological and social landscape.

Advertising is another industry relying on a dinosaur model that is very quickly becoming extinct. It's as if the glaciers are melting, giant shelves breaking off into the ocean, yet people are still saying, "There's no such thing as global warming." Meanwhile, mile-long sections of ice continue to fall into the sea for the first time in hundreds of years.

We are in an era of narrowcasting. There are hundreds of channels, some of them of very narrow interest. The network model has been splintered because TiVo is changing the economic underpinnings of advertising on television right before our eyes. If you are Procter & Gamble and you want to bring attention to Nice 'n Easy, an advertising agency will tell you to advertise on *Desperate Housewives* on Sunday night because 61.3 percent of women between the ages of eighteen and thirty-four watch the show. Sounds great. That's the target audience. What's it going to cost? Somewhere in the neighborhood of $600,000 to run three thirty-second commercials. Sure enough, in the review meeting a few weeks later you find out that 61.3 percent of the women in the target age group were watching the show. The only problem is that 70 percent of them watched the show Monday morning, Tuesday night, or Wednesday afternoon without seeing a single commercial because they have TiVo.

You have all this information, but the new variable, TiVo, hasn't been plugged into the equation. We know TiVo has dramatically reduced the efficient delivery of commercials, so eventually the model must change to fill that vacuum. Sports are probably the last bastion for traditional advertising because no one wants to TiVo the Super Bowl or a big game.

One thing is certain: right now someone is looking out ahead of the curve and sees a potential solution.

FALK'S FUNDAMENTALS

Conventional wisdom is just an element of the status quo.

Successful people continually challenge the status quo: Some people see things as they are and ask *why?* Others dream things that never were and ask *why not?* Dare to be great.

You must know the difference between talent and value.

Talent is a constant; value is a variable. Being cognizant of market forces and trends enables us to differentiate our product. The textbook case is Starbucks selling a 20¢ cup of coffee for $3.

Artificial constraints don't work.

In a free-market economy, external regulation distorts the natural equilibrium of the market. The distortion creates opportunity. Look for the pressure points in the system.

**Preparation, instinct, and confidence
are the keys to success.**

The most instinctive hitter in baseball still studies the pitcher. His intense preparation enhances his confidence in his own abilities and bolsters his performance.

Afterword

Another Fifteen Minutes of FAME

In 1998, the direction of the NBA agent business was changing. Our sale of FAME signaled an acknowledgment of the fact that meeting players such as Patrick Ewing, Michael Jordan, James Worthy, and Juwan Howard at the invitation of their college coaches was going to be the exception rather than the rule going forward. In fact, after signing Elton Brand in the spring of 1999, I did not sign another rookie selected in the first round until the spring of 2007, when I met Georgetown University's Jeff Green, who became the No. 5 pick in that summer's NBA draft. I only met two other rookies during the eight-year period from 1998 to 2007, Jason Williams and Shane Battier, at the request of Duke coach Mike Krzyzewski. Although I felt I had a lot of game left in me and often felt my best performances were still ahead based on my extensive experience, rules changes and the increasingly unethical way agents began to operate told me I would not be able to maintain my presence in the business at the same level I had enjoyed for the previous fifteen years.

When the 1998–99 NBA lockout ended, Michael Jordan decided to retire from the NBA—for the second time. Shortly thereafter, we had a series of meetings with Ted Leonsis, vice chairman emeritus of AOL, who owned approximately 44 percent of the Washington Wizards and Capitals as well as what was then known as the MCI Center. Ted was anxious to have Michael join his investment group, Lincoln Holdings, and become president of operations for the Washington Wizards. I had a very strong emotional desire to join Michael and to continue our professional relationship on the other side of the table. But in 1999, Michael was thirty-six years old and his desire to leave his own personal imprint as president of a team meant that any significant involvement by me would create too many cooks in the kitchen.

NBPA rules do not allow agents who represent players to also represent management personnel, although some fringe agents continue to violate the rule and the union has yet to enforce its own rules. However, if I were the perpetrator and the management executive were Michael Jordan, you could bet that the union's laissez-faire attitude would change.

In the meantime, as a result of the sale of FAME to SFX and the subsequent sale of SFX to Clear Channel, I found myself chairman of the SFX Sports Group, which represented approximately nine hundred athletes in basketball, baseball, football, soccer, golf, hockey, and tennis, as well as corporate involvement in NASCAR, broadcast personalities, and a variety of other sports and entertainment related marketing business. At its height, SFX Sports had hundreds of employees. At first blush it appeared to be a very prestigious position.

At the conclusion of almost every agency acquisition that SFX Sports made, the senior executive of that agency would invariably tell me how much he was looking forward to working together to create a paradigm-altering business. However, once the acquisition closed, I felt like an NBA coach with fifteen players, all of whom wanted to be starters. Like that coach, I knew I couldn't keep all the employees happy. For example, some of the smaller agencies we acquired had two or three principals and these individuals were either the president or chairman of their own company. Once they were acquired, I wanted to tap in to their experience and expertise by making them vice presidents or senior vice presidents. Many viewed this as a demotion and couldn't understand why they couldn't maintain their previous title. You can imagine the position I found myself in after fourteen or fifteen acquisitions. It was a frustrating experience. I suggested to one or two of these individuals that I would happily give them their companies back if they would return the acquisition fee. That way they could go back to being president of a $1 million company. Or they could remain a senior vice president and help us grow the SFX Sports Group into a $1 billion enterprise.

The very fragmentation of the sports industry that allowed entrepreneur Bob Sillerman to roll up SFX Sports into a large integrated company also created a culture dominated by entrepreneurs who were unwilling to give up their independence, even after receiving a healthy multiple on their earnings. As a result, in the spring of 2001, barely one year after SFX sold to Clear Channel, I decided to step down as chairman and concentrate my efforts on the individual players I had committed myself to represent. I was trying to follow my own advice: A man's got to know his limitations. I truly believe I could have been a strong leader and that eventually I could have imposed my will on some of the recalcitrant executives at SFX Sports. I don't believe, however, that I could have done this and maintained the strong personal relationships with my own clients, which is what put me in the position of chairman in the first place. In crunch time, my decision was easy. I truly enjoyed the family-like environment of a small group of elite players that I experienced at FAME. While I enjoyed the challenge of managing a large group of agents and executives to build a twenty-first-century trendsetting superagency, I was not willing to sacrifice my client relationships to do so.

As a result of my decision, I experienced a cliché: When it rains it pours. Starting in 1998 with the sale of FAME, I began to receive overtures from a variety of businesses, many of which were totally unrelated to sports. Two young, bright, creative entrepreneurs who had worked with me at SFX Sports, Jesse Itzler and Kenny Dichter, formed a private aviation company, Marquis Jet. Their small company, Alphabet City, had been a part of Bob Sillerman's first roll-up. I loved spending time with Jesse and Kenny because they had tremendous creativity and energy. Beyond that they were just plain fun guys to be around. Alphabet City produced jingles for many of the professional teams in the NBA and NHL. Among his many talents, Jesse is a rapper in the mold of Vanilla Ice. As "Jesse James," the famous jingle at Madison Square Garden, "Go New York Go," is among his many successes.

When Jesse and Kenny approached Rich Santulli, president of NetJets, the largest fractional private aviation company in the world, Jesse wrote a hip-hop presentation that floored Santulli. The performance, coupled with their unique talents, enabled Jesse and Kenny to partner with NetJets and create an entirely new method of private jet travel utilizing twenty-five-hour debit cards. I was pleased and proud that they asked me to be a founding investor in the company. After several years, Jesse and Kenny returned my initial investment with an approximate return of 400 percent, and I rolled over a portion of my profits into the next venture, Tour GCX Partners, which took the debit card concept and applied it to golf course memberships.

At this point, a very dear friend of mine and former client, Michael Jackson, a star player at Georgetown and later a reserve point guard for the Sacramento Kings, introduced me to a young executive from Chicago, Jeffrey Hopmayer. Jeffrey and his family owned Original American Scones, which produced the baked goods sold at Starbucks. After the family sold the company, Jeff decided to start a spirits company selling flavored vodka, gin, and rum. I invested in Extreme Beverage and took a seat on the board. In the ultracompetitive spirits industry, Jeff's creativity and sheer determination allowed him to carve out a niche for Extreme that led to an international merger with Blavod, a European manufacturer of black vodka. Over time, Jeff acquired a number of important wineries to broaden the product line. The merged company became known as Blavod Extreme Spirits. In 2007, Jeff bought back the U.S. operations of BES and took the company private as Sapphire Brands. As a wine aficionado, I found the experience in the spirits industry to be a breath of fresh air—literally—compared to my locker room experiences.

I also joined an extremely talented young woman, Maryse Robinson Thomas, to develop an Internet advertising company called

Pokeware. As a baby boomer, I am part of the generation that has very reluctantly joined the Internet age. Although I am the proud owner of a BlackBerry and an iPhone, as well as an iPod, a Mac Air, and an iMac, I must profess that I still prefer the human voice to e-mails. My younger clients such as Elton Brand and Jeff Green have definitely gotten me hooked on text messaging, but I prefer old-fashioned telephone calls.

Around the same time, in 2005, my oldest daughter, Daina, graduated from Duke, and she aspired to join me in the sports management industry. Daina was born on February 20, 1983. Three days after my wife returned home from the hospital with her on Sunday, February 27, a decision was made at a seminal partners meeting to split ProServ into two companies. Over the next nine years the founder, Donald Dell, would witness twelve more spin-offs from ProServ in the Washington, D.C., area alone. The ultimate spin-off was FAME in January 1992. Daina literally grew up with my clients, Michael Jordan in 1984, Patrick Ewing in 1985, Johnny Dawkins in 1986, Rex Chapman in 1988, Danny Ferry in 1989, Dennis Scott in 1990, Dikembe Mutombo in 1991, Alonzo Mourning in 1992, Shawn Bradley in 1993, Juwan Howard in 1994, and so on. Her perspective of the sports industry was steeped in my relationships with these basketball superstars who also happened to be tremendous human beings. Unfortunately, by the time of her graduation, these individuals were not nearly as representative of the NBA population as they had been in the mid-1980s. Nor was my ability to meet them on an invitational basis the norm. I strongly dissuaded her from entering the business and she ultimately settled on a position with United Talent

Agency (UTA), a major Hollywood talent agency of which my good friend, Peter Benedek, is a principal. After a brief stint at UTA, Daina joined Maryse and me at Pokeware. Having two very bright, ambitious, and driven women as partners in the company often makes me question why I thought sports owners were tough to deal with. But it gives me a tremendous amount of pride and satisfaction to watch my daughter operate in a boardroom.

To that end, perhaps no experience was more enjoyable to me than our presentation to the NBA in the spring of 2006. Deputy Commissioner Adam Silver hosted Daina, Maryse, and me for a presentation at the NBA offices in Olympic Tower in New York. When David Stern learned I had brought my daughter, he was curious to find out what kind of person my offspring would be. He joined us midway through the meeting and asked for a brief synopsis of the Pokeware business. I began to respond, but he interrupted me and said, "No, David. I want a synopsis from Daina."

Midway through her summary, Daina paused to collect her thoughts, at which point I exhibited my typical level of patience and jumped in. David admonished me: "Please don't interrupt your daughter." Daina smiled and said, "You are my new best friend." Daina and David really hit it off, and I truly swelled with pride watching my daughter interact with a man for whom I have unbridled admiration.

In 2006, Clear Channel made a decision to spin off the entire SFX Entertainment division as a separate publicly traded company that came to be known as Live Nation. The young chairman of Live Nation, Michael Rapino, made an executive decision that their involvement in professional sports sent a confusing message to Wall Street about the company's commitment to the music industry, which is its primary business. Accordingly, Rapino sold off many of the smaller, unprofitable portions of the business such as tennis and golf events. Meanwhile, my consulting contract expired in December 2006. At that point the remaining portion of my business reverted to me.

On January 1, 2007, FAME was reborn after a nearly decade-long hiatus. It was not the company I had sold in June 1998. It was now an ultra boutique consisting of me; my executive assistant, Mary Ellen Nunes; and my marketing director, Danielle Cantor. We have eight NBA clients and two Hall of Fame coaches, John Thompson, Jr., Coach K, and a future Hall of Fame coach, John Thompson III. In the ten years since I sold FAME, virtually every agent in the business has tried to replicate our blueprint by selling their businesses to an entertainment company. Casey Wasserman, the grandson of legendary Hollywood agent and studio boss Lew Wasserman, began to acquire sports properties under the banner of Wasserman Media Group. My good friend Richard Lovett, president of Creative Artists Agency (CAA), also began to acquire major sports agencies.

After SFX was sold to Clear Channel, I had a series of meetings with Lovett, who was Jack Rapke's successor at CAA. I felt a tremendous affinity for Richard, who, despite his extreme position of power in Hollywood, was a very modest and understated gentleman. He was also a sports fanatic who had a strong desire to continue the discussions I had years earlier with Jack Rapke about merging the worlds of Hollywood and sports. True to his passion,

Richard introduced CAA Sports, his version of the integration of Hollywood and sports talent agencies. A number of former SFX executives, including Michael Levine, one of the three managing operators of CAA Sports, and others joined Tom Condon, a former Kansas City Chiefs lineman and president of the NFLPA, and a man I regard as among the most talented and successful football agents in the business, at CAA Sports.

As a friend and a fan, I am rooting for Richard Lovett to be successful in his sports enterprise. However, based upon my own experiences over the past thirty-five years, I have a healthy degree of skepticism about whether enough synergies exist to make these deals a good investment. Wasserman Media Group is slugging it out head-to-head with CAA across a number of sports platforms.

In 1998, we started a trend of selling a sports agency at a multiple of earnings to a large entertainment conglomerate. Nearly a decade later, Arn Tellem sold his agency to Casey Wasserman, others are selling to CAA, and now William Morris is becoming involved in the business. As I said, on the surface these appear to be very interesting mergers. Because sports agencies are so small and inherently entrepreneurial, it's exciting to consider the possibilities. But the entertainment agencies are much larger and much more corporate. I believe there are inherent cultural difficulties in merging the two, and I'm not convinced that the economics make sense when an agency is purchased for a multiple on its earnings.

Perhaps I didn't have the ability to exploit the synergies to the extent they exist, but I am skeptical that there are that many available. At the end of the day you walk down the hall to the marketing department and ask someone to sell rookie deals for $25,000 to $40,000. The player is paying the company a fee of $5,000 to $8,000. The person in the marketing department is getting a commission off that fee. Is that marketing person going to be motivated to do all the necessary work to sell those kinds of deals, or is he going to spend his time trying to sell a corporate sponsorship that earns him much more money?

At FAME, all Danielle Cantor does is sell our clients. She doesn't have the synergies that might come with a big organization, but she knows the people and she knows the relationships. At a time when everyone is trying to go big with these mergers, I want to set a new direction by going ultraboutique. It sort of reminds me of when Michael was a rookie. The very first Air Jordan shoes were black with a red swoosh. Many people thought they were ugly, but Nike sold $130 million worth of product in the first year. In 1986, virtually every competing company came out with a black shoe. To keep them on their toes, we made Air Jordan II all white. We said, "Sorry, black and red aren't cool anymore. What's cool is white." It would take the competition another year to catch up.

I think there are people and companies that set the trends and there are people and companies that follow the trends. I guess I have a certain amount of nonconformity in me. I like to set the trends. What people are doing now is a function of what they saw as our success ten years ago. In an environment where everyone believes bigger is better, I am going to be extremely small. I tell my players, "I don't want to be the average car dealership. The average Chevy dealer probably sells three hundred cars a month. That's how many he needs to sell to support the economics of the dealership. Go to a Ferrari or Aston Martin dealership and they might sell three cars a month. The guy who greets you in those dealerships isn't offering you introductory pricing or special financing. All they are offering you is a chance for you to buy the car. I want to be a Ferrari dealership."

We do contract negotiation, marketing, and career management. I believe the career management portion is very important. If you are small, then you can move players around to different teams when it's necessary, or advise a Shawn Kemp not to commit himself to a deal that is going to pay him nothing in the current term and put him behind the eight ball down the road.

I want to take all the things I've learned from representing some of the greatest players ever and interacting with some of the most successful businessmen in the world, and share that knowledge with my players. I guess I want to be a teacher. I think the role of agent probably takes up 5 percent of my time now in an average week. I'm a public relations advisor, I'm a marketing director, I'm a career counselor, and I'm a professional problem solver. The process of doing NBA contracts has become so mechanical that I can do that part of the business in a very short period of time. I want to be an ultraboutique to the stars. Really, it's what I was born to do and thankfully, I love it.

That's *The Bald Truth*!